More Eric Meyer on CSS

Contents at a Glance

MORE ERIC MEYER ON CSS

Eric A. Meyer

New Riders

www.newriders.com

1249 Eighth Street, Berkeley, California 94710

More Eric Meyer on CSS

Trademarks

Warning and Disclaimer

ASSOCIATE PUBLISHER
Stephanie Wall

PRODUCTION MANAGER
Gina Kanouse

SENIOR ACQUISITIONS EDITOR
Linda Bump Harrison

SENIOR PROJECT EDITOR
Lori Lyons

COPY EDITOR
Amy Lepore

INDEXER
Lisa Stumpf

MANUFACTURING COORDINATOR
Dan Uhrig

BOOK DESIGNER
Barb Kordesh

COVER DESIGNER
Aren Howell

COMPOSITION
Kim Scott

MARKETING
Scott Cowlin
Tammy Detrich

PUBLICITY MANAGER
Susan Nixon

In memory of my mother

Carol Suzanne Meyer

A true teacher and a joy to all who knew her

TABLE OF CONTENTS

PROJECT 3   STYLING A FINANCIAL REPORT   57

About the Author

Eric A. Meyer has been working with the Web since late 1993 and is an internationally recognized expert on the subjects of HTML, CSS, and Web standards. A widely read author, he is also the founder of Complex Spiral Consulting (www.complexspiral.com), which focuses on helping clients save money and increase efficiency through the use of standards-oriented Web design techniques and counts Macromedia and Wells Fargo Bank among its clients.

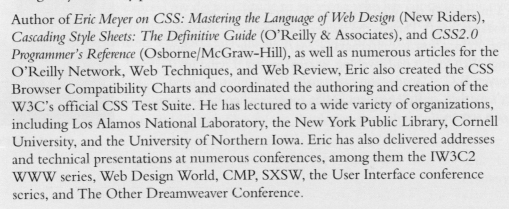

Beginning in early 1994, Eric was the visual designer and campus Web coordinator for Case Western Reserve University Web site, where he also authored a widely acclaimed series of three HTML tutorials and was project coordinator for the online version of the Encyclopedia of Cleveland History combined with the Dictionary of Cleveland Biography (ech.cwru.edu), the first example of an encyclopedia of urban history being fully and freely published on the Web.

Author of *Eric Meyer on CSS: Mastering the Language of Web Design* (New Riders), *Cascading Style Sheets: The Definitive Guide* (O'Reilly & Associates), and *CSS2.0 Programmer's Reference* (Osborne/McGraw-Hill), as well as numerous articles for the O'Reilly Network, Web Techniques, and Web Review, Eric also created the CSS Browser Compatibility Charts and coordinated the authoring and creation of the W3C's official CSS Test Suite. He has lectured to a wide variety of organizations, including Los Alamos National Laboratory, the New York Public Library, Cornell University, and the University of Northern Iowa. Eric has also delivered addresses and technical presentations at numerous conferences, among them the IW3C2 WWW series, Web Design World, CMP, SXSW, the User Interface conference series, and The Other Dreamweaver Conference.

In his personal time, Eric acts as List Chaperone of the highly active css-discuss mailing list (www.css-discuss.org), which he co-founded with John Allsopp of Western Civilisation and is now supported by evolt.org. Eric lives in Cleveland, Ohio, which is a much nicer city than you've been led to believe, and is the host of "Your Father's Oldsmobile," a Big Band-era radio show heard weekly on WRUW 91.1-FM in Cleveland (www.wruw.org). When not otherwise busy, he is usually bothering his wife Kat in some fashion.

Tell Us What You Think

As the reader of this book, you are the most important critic and commentator. We value your opinion and want to know what we're doing right, what we could do better, what areas you'd like to see us publish in, and any other words of wisdom you're willing to pass our way.

Email: `errata@peachpit.com`

Foreword

"Eric Meyer." Say that name, and you'll immediately grab my attention, and possibly engage me in a conversation, even if you're a complete stranger. I was browsing through the tech section of a bookstore last year when I heard a stranger announce to her companion the title of a book she had been thumbing through, "It's called *Eric Meyer on CSS*. I think I've heard of this guy."

I stepped a little closer, pardoned myself, and offered my unsolicited advice.

"Don't even hesitate if you're thinking about buying that book."

I qualified my statement, making sure she had at least been introduced to the basics of CSS. "It's good, and Eric Meyer is good. You'll be more enlightened after working through just one chapter of that book."

We talked a little more about the book, and my knowledge of Eric Meyer. She thanked me, and then tucked it confidently under her arm to head for the cashier.

If you knew just how pivotal Eric Meyer has been in turning around my understanding of CSS, and in how I use it to push the limits of Web design, you'd also know why I have no qualms recommending his books to complete strangers.

You see, I ignored CSS for years.

While I was working at HotWired, my colleagues thought I would love CSS, and took every opportunity they could to encourage me to dive into the world of style-sheet-driven Web design. Although I am first and foremost a designer, my colleagues knew I have a fairly strong technical mind that can wrap itself around confined logical concepts. However, I'm no good at tolerating inconsistency and unpredictability when it comes to code and its behavior.

When I finally gave in to pressure and started dabbling with CSS, I immediately hit a brick wall. With 4.0 versions of Netscape Navigator and Internet Explorer, I faced nothing but frustration every time I tried using CSS beyond color and basic type treatment. I wanted to see consistent margins, type size, and positioning across common browsers and platforms. In 1998, support for even these basic features was horrendous, causing big headaches for any designer who tried to produce the same look in multiple browsers.

Thus, I wrote off CSS as a failed pipedream that certainly wasn't for me. I wanted to continue reproducing beautiful, usable design, and I wasn't about to trust CSS and its buggy browser support as the means to implement and control my design.

During those trials with CSS, one of my good fortunes was coming across one of the only books at the time dedicated entirely to Cascading Style Sheets. Luckily for me, it was written by Eric Meyer.

Eric's book sat unused on my shelf for a few years while I avoided CSS. Eventually, circumstances began to change. I started seeing news of much-improved browser support for CSS. Small sites were using CSS more abundantly, and it looked like they were producing fairly consistent results. The changes piqued my interest enough to turn my head toward CSS and make me crave more information.

Almost everywhere I looked, I saw Eric Meyer's name—the author of the book I owned—attached to helpful resources. Articles on CSS, CSS test suites, a CSS mailing list, and his CSS master grid that I started using religiously to check possible properties and value combinations.

His book I had purchased several years prior no longer resided on the bookshelf, but on a corner of my desk where I could easily reach it, and make use of it as a constant reference. "How does positioning work again?" "What's that CSS equivalent of tracking called?" "In what order do those font values need to be?" I couldn't get enough of Eric Meyer's writings. Each new Meyer article I discovered helped me fit another piece into the puzzle.

Fast-forward to a year or so later. Eric's first book was still on the corner of my desk, becoming increasingly worn around the edges. I was neck-deep into the 2002 all-CSS Wired News redesign when *Eric Meyer on CSS*—his first invaluable project-based look at CSS—was released. The first night I had the new book in my hands, I dove straight into the chapter on Multicolumn Layout. I was instantly hooked. The epiphanies I had while going through that book made me wish it had been written (and that I had read it) long before I began creating Wired's complex style sheets.

So you can imagine my excitement when I learned that Eric and New Riders were publishing this sequel to *Eric Meyer on CSS*. We get to have more of what was already a great thing! More practical examples that hit home for every Web designer and developer. More real-world projects that mimic challenges we face every day. More of Eric's in-depth revelations and insights into basic and advanced uses of CSS. More wisdom bequeathed from the master. *More Eric Meyer on CSS.*

Eric's knowledge and mastery of CSS enables him to write authoritatively on the subject. Yet he writes with this personal, familiar tone that's easy to read and understand. This combination in a teacher makes for the best of both worlds—whether you're trying to learn something new or expand on your own accumulated knowledge. In addition to walking you through the concepts behind the "how" of what he's doing, Eric effortlessly explains the "why." I advocate that understanding the why's of CSS are just as important as the how's. With the project-based approach of this book and its predecessor, Eric strikes just the right balance between the two.

Following along with Eric's example files, or reading through notes and warnings in the sidebars, light bulbs constantly flick on: "Ah, that's how I solve this!" or "Oh, that's why my background disappeared under the float? I get it now."

Facing a pesky problem with the layout on a client project? Trying to figure out how to make your gallery pages more flexible? No idea why those background images aren't lining up? Spend a little time with this book, and Eric will walk you through a similar situation that will open your eyes to the possibilities. You'll wonder where you would have been without Eric Meyer's guidance to make sense of it all.

As with the first version of *Eric Meyer on CSS*, the organization of this follow-up book makes it easy to dive into any chapter to begin expanding your understanding of CSS in a way that's immediately relevant to you. The real-world challenges that Eric presents and solves in this book will spawn more ideas, providing the confidence you'll need to tackle other related challenges head on.

I've turned 180 degrees from total rejection of CSS to eager adoption of any new method or technique I can dream up or get my hands on. Eric Meyer has certainly played—and continues to play—a significant role in this turnaround, and in my appreciation of the power and flexibility of CSS. He can do the same thing for you.

If you're a Web designer or developer who has at least dabbled with a little CSS and are past the casual introduction, from my perspective, the real question is not whether this book—or the original *Eric Meyer on CSS*—should be in your possession. But rather, with which project will you start once you have the book all to yourself?

Douglas Bowman
Founder and Principal, Stopdesign
San Francisco

INTRODUCTION

What you're holding in your hands right now, assuming you aren't viewing a preview online, is more or less a sequel to *Eric Meyer on CSS*, which was published in 2002 to fairly resounding acclaim. The project-based approach drew high marks, and it seems that a lot of people liked the feeling of being able to watch over my shoulder as I worked through the projects. That was exactly the feeling I aimed to provide, and I've endeavored to create the same feeling with this book.

So, if you do buy this book and you like it, you can get more of the same in *Eric Meyer on CSS*. On the other hand, it's important to note that you don't have to own *Eric Meyer on CSS* to use and enjoy this book. Each stands on its own as a self-contained, independent work. So don't be afraid that you won't be able to understand what the characters in this book are doing because you never read the first one. I don't have any characters.

There is a plot, though (actually, two of them). The first plot describes a journey of learning and experimentation, wherein our hero (that's you) follows the path of an experienced guide and learns the ways of a new and wondrous land. The second plot (kind of a subplot) is an underhanded attempt to lure you into using more CSS by tempting you with design flexibility, improved accessibility, reduced page weight, and cool visual effects.

Should You Buy This Book?

This isn't a facetious question. As proud as I am of the work contained in these pages, I'm also keenly aware that this book is not for every reader. So let me take a moment to describe two kinds of readers: those for whom this book was written and those for whom it was not.

Those for Whom This Book Is Meant

You ought to find this book useful if you match one or more of the following criteria:

◆ You want a hands-on, practical guide to using CSS in real-world projects. That's exactly what this book is all about.

◆ You're a hands-on learner, someone who gets a lot more out of interactive experimenting than from just reading a book. Despite the fact that this is indeed a book, it's been intentionally designed to let the reader "play along at home," as it were.

◆ You've been meaning to increase your CSS skills for some time now, but you keep putting it off because CSS is a large, complex subject, and you don't have a roadmap for how to get to the next level.

- You've always wanted someone to show you how to convert a typical, old-school, pure-HTML design into a pure-CSS design and to explain why it's to your advantage to do so. If that's the case, go to Project 1, "Converting an Existing Page," without another moment's delay.

- If asked, you would describe your HTML skill level as "intermediate" or "expert" and your CSS skill level as "basic" or "intermediate." In other words, you understand HTML fairly well and have used enough CSS to have a basic grasp of how it's written.

Those for Whom This Book Is Not Meant

You might not find this book to be useful if one or more of the following describes you:

- You've never used or even seen CSS before. Although some basic terms are defined in the text, the assumption here is that the reader knows the basics of writing CSS and is fairly proficient with HTML authoring. Some readers of *Eric Meyer on CSS* said they were able to use it even though they'd hardly ever touched CSS before, but this book was not written with the beginner in mind.

- You want to understand all of the subtleties of the theory underlying CSS and grasp the nuances of the specification. There are now many books on the market that occupy that niche. The focus here is on demonstrating effects that work.

- You've only done Web design in a point-and-click editing environment. This book assumes that you can edit (or have edited) HTML and CSS by hand, and its narrative is based on that assumption. Its projects may be easily reproducible in a point-and-click editor, but the book was not written with such editors in mind. As it happens, *Eric Meyer on CSS* was a big hit with a lot of Dreamweaver and GoLive users, so that's a point to consider. Nevertheless, the text assumes you'll be dealing directly with the markup and styles.

- You want a book that will tell you how to write CSS that will look the same in all browsers on all platforms, including Netscape 4.x and Explorer 3.x. See the following section, "What You Can Expect from This Book," for details.

- You've read my other works and hate the personal, familiar tone I take in my writing. I promise you that my writing style has changed very little.

WHAT YOU CAN EXPECT FROM THIS BOOK

From the outset, my intent has been to write an engaging, interactive book that focuses on practical and interesting uses of CSS that can be deployed in today's browsers. To do this, each project evolves from having no styles to being fully styled and ready for deployment on the Web. If I've done my job well, you should get the feeling of watching over my shoulder as I work on a project, with me commenting on what I'm doing as I do it.

Although you can simply read the text and look at the figures to get a sense of how a project is evolving, I think the best way to work along with the book is to have a Web browser and a text editor open as you read. That way, you can follow along with the changes I make in the text by physically making the same changes in your project file and seeing the changes in your own Web browser.

There is one point on which I want to be very clear: The techniques shown in this book are generally meant for browsers whose version number is greater than or equal to 5 (well, and Safari 1.0+). If you have to design a site that looks the same in Explorer 4.x and Netscape 4.x as it does in IE6.x and NS7.x, this book is probably not for you.

Project Overview

In keeping with the practical, hands-on nature of the book, I've divided it up into a series of 10 projects—each one effectively a chapter. It is possible to skip around from project to project as the spirit moves you, as each project was written to stand on its own as much as possible. However, the book was still written with the "linear reader" in mind; if you read from front to back, you should find that the projects build on one another.

With a few exceptions, the projects are titled in as self-obvious a way as possible. For example, Project 1, "Converting an Existing Page," takes a page designed using only HTML markup and spacer GIFs, and converts it to a pure CSS design that uses positioning for layout instead of tables.

Projects 2 and 3 cover some fairly basic projects, from styling a photo gallery to making a financial report look better than it would by default. Project 4 increases the sophistication somewhat by showing how to use backgrounds in creative ways, and how to mix relative and absolute measures in order to set up translucency effects.

Then, in Projects 5 through 7, the topic of discussion is using lists in various ways. The first of these three projects uses a list of links to create a sidebar menu, complete with two different layouts for the same list. The second project in the trilogy takes a series of nested lists and turns them into a dynamic set of "drop-down" menus that work in most browsers (and that includes IE/Win). The last of the three projects explores using the Sliding Doors technique to turn a list of links into a set of "tabs."

Projects 8 and 9 consider the styling of a weblog and the styling of a home page around that weblog, respectively. Project 10 is the most ambitious and complex of the book: It takes a design for the CSS Zen Garden and works through the application from design to markup. This was done by soliciting a design from the Garden's creator and then working to translate the design into a styled document. For those of you who work in the print world, we take a comp and turn it into a finished product.

COMPANION WEB SITE

Each project in this book is based on the editing of a real project file. You can download the project files either for the entire book all at once or for each chapter individually. The project files are available on the book's companion Web site: `http://more.ericmeyeroncss.com/`. There you will find the files that were used to produce the figures throughout the book, any errata to the book, and supplemental materials like bonus text, commentary from the author, and links to useful online resources.

For each project, there will be an archive of all the files you need to work along with the text; this includes any graphic files needed as well as a version of the project file at its outset. These files follow a consistent naming scheme; for example, the figure that corresponds to Figure 7.3 will be named ch0703.html, the Project 1 working file will be `ch01proj.html`. This is the file you should open up with a text editor and make changes to as the project moves forward. You can also load it into a Web browser and hit Reload at each step to see what effect the new styles have.

You'll also find the files for the first book, *Eric Meyer on CSS*. You can download them whether or not you've read the book, but they probably won't make as much sense if you haven't.

CONVENTIONS

This book follows a few typographical conventions that you should be familiar with before proceeding.

A new term is set in *italics* the first time it is introduced. There will often be a short definition of the term nearby. Program text, functions, variables, and other "computer language" are set in a fixed-pitch font. In regular text, it will also be a dark blue color—for example, when mentioning the property `margin` or a value like `10px`.

Code blocks are set entirely in a fixed-pitch font. Any blue text within a code block indicates a change to the code from its previous state. Most code blocks show only a fragment of the overall document or style sheet, with the lines to be changed (or inserted) surrounded by unchanged text. This extra text provides a sense of context, making it easier to find the part you need to change if you're following along with the text. Here is an example:

```
<head>
<title>Cleveland Eats: Matsu</title>
<style type="text/css">
/* temporary styles */
table {border: 2px solid red; margin: 3px;}
td {border: 1px dotted purple; padding: 2px;}
</style>
</head>
```

Every computer book has its own style of presenting information. As you flip through this book, you'll notice that it has an interesting layout. Here are the layout conventions:

▶▶ ASIDES

These usually contain detailed explanations that are related to the main text but are not a part of the project itself. They might also offer alternative approaches or ideas to those demonstrated in a project. In every case, they can be skipped without disrupting the project's flow.

Note

These are meant to be helpful annotations to the main text, and there are a lot of them in this book. These are used to provide tips, comments, definitions of new terms, tangential points, or related bits of information.

Warning

These indicate a point that might cause problems in some browsers or a similarly grave note of caution.

Web site notes provide guidance as to which files to download or load into a Web browser, or things to check out on the Web.

Finally, at the end of each project you will find a section titled "Branching Out." This will present three short exercises that invite you to try modifying the finished project in certain ways. These "branches" are certainly not the end of what you can do, but they may help you start experimenting with the concepts presented in the project. Think of them as jumping-off points for your own design ideas and also as interesting challenges in their own right. If you can match the illustrations with your own styles, you'll be well on your way to writing creative CSS of your own.

1

CONVERTING AN EXISTING PAGE

Look inside a typical CSS [designer's] house. What do you see? Chairs, only chairs. No tables.

—JEAN-YVES STERVINOU

FOR YEARS UPON YEARS—about eight of them, as this is being written—we've been using tables and spacer images to lay out Web pages. For the first part of all those years, it was the only way to create compelling visual design. Tools grew up to support this desire, design firms embraced it wholeheartedly, and pages got more and more bloated as a result.

When CSS came along, there began to be some hope that the trend might reverse and that pages could get smaller and more meaningful. When CSS2 introduced positioning, the door was opened. It become theoretically possible to do almost everything that tables did and in a fraction of the page weight.

That was theory: The practice for at least a few years was very different, thanks to incomplete and incompatible browser implementations. That improved slowly until, by the dawn of the 21st century, positioned layouts were really held hostage only by the persistence of Netscape 4.x, and even there some simple positioning could be achieved.

A good way to get familiar with the basics of positioning layout is to take a table-driven layout and convert it to CSS positioning (CSS-P). This allows for comparisons between the document structures and serves as a primer in how basic positioning can make life a lot easier.

Project Goals

Our goal for this project is as straightforward as can be: to take an HTML-heavy design and convert it to use CSS-driven layout. In so doing, we'll explore how commonly used HTML structures and tricks can be replaced with vastly simpler markup and CSS, and how doing this makes the document markup a great deal easier to read. When we're done, we'll take some measurements to determine just how much of a savings our effort has yielded.

We'll assess each portion of the document as we reach it, so what approaches we'll take aren't known ahead of time. We can still articulate some general goals:

◆ The number of images on the page should be reduced to a minimum. This will have the dual benefit of making the document structure much cleaner and also reducing the potential number of server hits required to display the page.

◆ All tables intended solely for layout should be removed. When we're done, only tables that contain data appropriate for a table should remain.

◆ The markup that results from our conversion should have a strong structure; that is, headings should be enclosed in heading tags such as h2. Furthermore, the content should be in an order that makes sense if the page is presented with no style at all.

◆ The final product should look as much like the all-HTML design as possible. While there may not be a perfect pixel-for-pixel fidelity between the two, we should do our utmost to minimize any differences.

If we can fulfill all of these goals, we'll have done something fairly remarkable.

Preparation

See the Introduction for instructions on how to download files from the Web site.

Download the files for Project 1 from this book's Web site. If you're planning to play along at home, load the file ch01proj.html into the editing program of your choice. This is the file you'll be editing, saving, and reloading as the project progresses.

LAYING THE GROUNDWORK

The first thing we need to do is take a look at the existing all-HTML page in a Web browser and then look at its markup. Figure 1.1 shows what the page looks like.

FIGURE 1.1

The page as it exists in an all-HTML format.

Now it's time to look at the HTML itself. Unfortunately, we can't provide it here because a listing of the page's source code would be about seven pages long! So we'll have to consider another approach.

Instead of going through the HTML line by line, let's get a quick look at how the page has been put together. To do this, we're going to add some temporary styles to the simple style sheet that already appears at top of the document.

```
<head>
<title>Cleveland Eats: Matsu</title>
<style type="text/css">
body {font-family: Verdana, Arial, Helvetica, sans-serif;}
a.navlink {text-decoration: none;}
/* temporary styles */
table {border: 2px solid red; margin: 2px;}
td {border: 1px dotted purple; padding: 1px;}
/* end temporary styles */
</style>
</head>
```

The first of the new rules will put a two-pixel red border around the outside of any `table` elements and add two pixels of blank space (margin) around them. The second new rule gives `td` elements a one-pixel dotted purple border and one pixel of padding. The result of this addition is shown in Figure 1.2.

You can see the source code for Figure 1.1 by loading the file `ch0101.html` into your favorite text editor.

What's a Rule?

A *rule* in CSS is a complete style statement, which is composed of a selector and a declaration block. For example, `p {color: gray; font-weight: bold;}` is a rule.

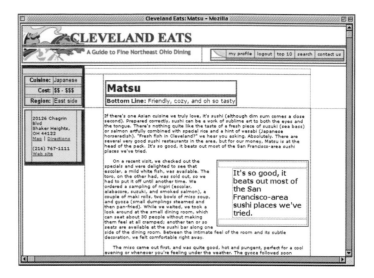

Since every thick red border represents the outer edge of a table, we can quickly determine the page's structure. The "banner" (or "masthead") across the top of the page is in its own table. The rest of the document is wrapped in a second table, with a few tables nested within it and a fairly complicated cell structure. One point of interest is that the left-hand sidebar is actually laid out using two separate tables in different cells, even though the visual effect is that of a single box.

Another layout trick revealed by these temporary styles is the use of "empty" table cells to hold open space. Look, for example, to either side of the main text column in the center of the page and also to either side of the large block of text set into the main content. (This is known as a "pullquote.") In both cases, you can see empty cells outlined by a dotted purple border.

These cells are not, in fact, empty—they contain image files called `spacer.gif`. This is a 1×1 image whose sole pixel has been set to be transparent. A quick search of the HTML reveals that there are 18 `img` elements that refer to this same image file. By the time we're done, they'll all be gone.

Converting the Document

You can see the fully stripped-down version of the page by loading the file `ch0104.html` into your favorite HTML or text editor.

Going from an all-HTML design to a CSS-driven layout requires two steps: shedding the HTML-based presentation and adding in CSS to replace it. In many cases, it's easier to do this in a gradual fashion by stripping down a small portion of the document and styling it before moving on to the next section. For this project, though, we're going to go the hardcore route and strip the file all the way down to its minimum state before we start styling. (It makes the figures look a lot better, too.)

Stripping Down to the Minimum

It's time to make a copy of the original all-HTML file and strip out nearly all of its HTML-based presentation. This is undeniably the toughest part of converting an all-HTML design to a CSS layout. A good deal of the work can be done using find-and-replace utilities, but there is still the need to go through and delete any leftover HTML-based presentation manually.

It should be mentioned that sometimes it's easier to just copy the text from a page and create a new structure around it, rather than trying to convert the old markup to newer, more efficient markup. We'll go through a conversion process in this project—that will help illustrate how certain kinds of table-oriented markup can be drastically simplified. Just keep in mind that it's sometimes easier to just bring across the content and build up new markup around that content.

No matter how you slim down the markup, things to eliminate include:

- ◆ `font` elements
- ◆ `<br>` elements
- ◆ ` ` entities
- ◆ Any attributes on the `body` element (for example, `text` and `link`)

We also want to cut out layout tables to the maximum extent possible. Because the original markup is kind of complicated, we'll take it a step at a time.

The Skeletal Structure

First assume that we've taken out all of the things mentioned in the preceding list. That leaves us with a document whose general structure is still fairly difficult to describe. For example, the masthead contains three different slices of an image, each in its own cell, and then another cell that contains a table holding the "navbar" links near the top right of the page. In the main page area, we have a left-hand sidebar that's been broken across two lines to achieve some alignment effects: The restaurant name and "Bottom Line" line up with the bottom of the table to their left. Managing this are a forest of interlocking table cells whose purpose is to make the sidebar look like a single continuous box, even though it isn't.

The list could go on for a while, but instead let's just rip out all the tables we can and see where it leaves us. After doing this, we end up with a document structured something like the skeleton shown in Listing 1.1.

Tidying Up Your Markup

It's possible to use one of a number of utilities to clean up markup and in the process strip out most or all of the presentational aspects of a document. HTML Tidy is one of the most popular such tools and is available for free download from `http://tidy.sourceforge.net/`.

Italic Stand-Ins

The italicized text in Listing 1.1 indicates stretches of text and HTML too long to include in the book.

Listing 1.1   The Table's Beginning

```
<table>
[...masthead...]
</table>
<div id="navbar">
[...navbar links...]
</div>
<div id="review">
[...title...]
[..."bottom line"...]
 <div id="info">[...sidebar info...]</div>
[...review...]
</div>
```

Wait a minute—a table? Yes, we're going to leave the masthead table in place for the moment. What we've done is simplify the table a bit and move the navbar outside of it. That makes the masthead's markup read like this:

```
<table cellspacing="0" id="masthead">
<tr>
<td><img src="mast1.gif" alt="Cleveland Eats"></td>
</tr>
<tr>
<td bgcolor="#666666"><img src="mast2.gif" alt=""></td>
</tr>
<tr>
<td><img src="mast3.gif" alt="A Guide to Fine Northeast
 Ohio Dining"></td>
</tr>
</table>
```

We're leaving this in place because it's simpler to do so right now. This is entirely due to the "stretchy" line in the middle of the masthead that extends from the bottom of the platter. In the table, this is done with a one-pixel slice out of the image and a background color on a cell. We could convert this to a nontable structure and actually will do so at the end of the project. Leaving this change until the end will help illustrate a point or two.

Meanwhile, let's look at the changes to the navbar. With the table cells all gone, we need to include something to separate the links from one another. In this case, we've chosen to insert a vertical-bar character wrapped in a b element.

```
<div id="navbar">
<a
 href="/myprofile">my profile</a><b>|</b><a
 href="/logout">logout</a><b>|</b><a
 href="/top10">top 10</a><b>|</b><a
 href="/search">search</a><b>|</b><a
 href="contact">contact us</a>
</div>
```

Tables? Boldface elements? Are we sure this is a CSS book? Yes! Have patience. All will be revealed in the fullness of time, but for now, remember that b is a part of the document type we're using (HTML 4.01 Transitional) and so is perfectly valid. We'll return to it in just a bit.

As for the rest of the document, it's just a div wrapping the whole review, which has been converted to a simple structure.

```
<div id="review">
 <h2>Matsu</h2>
 <p id="summary"><strong>Bottom line:</strong>
    Friendly, cozy, and oh so tasty</p>
  <div id="info">[...all sidebar info...]</div>
 [...review text...]
</div>
```

The last notable change is that the pullquote is now represented using a classed blockquote element.

```
<blockquote class="pull">
It's so good, it beats out most of the San Francisco-area
sushi places we've tried.
</blockquote>
```

That's it, and the result is shown in Figure 1.3. It may look like a train wreck right now, but just wait. It'll get better pretty quickly.

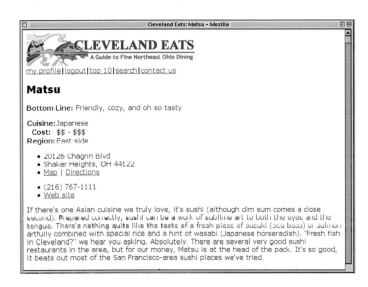

FIGURE 1.3

It's improved structurally, but the visuals could use some work.

Rebuilding the Design

Because our goal is to re-create the original design using CSS for both content styling and layout, we'll want to refer to the table-driven design throughout the rest of the project. Although we won't worry about exact to-the-pixel reproduction, we'll do our best to get as close as possible to the original, starting with some basic styles and working our way through the document, styling each piece as we come to it.

Basic Styles

Extra Small

Because the original HTML presentation called for the body text to be a font size of -2, we're using x-small, which is two steps below medium on the list of absolute keywords. Note that IE5 got this wrong and treated x-small the same as it would a font size of -1. IE6 fixed this bug.

Before we start reconstructing the overall layout, let's set some "global" styles (that is, styles that apply to the document as a whole). The first thing to do is bring the font size back in line with how it looked in the original HTML-driven design. The HTML approach used `<font size="-2">` to set most of the font sizes, and the closet CSS equivalent is the keyword x-small. Thus, we'll change the property font-family to font and drop in the size value.

```
<style type="text/css">
body {font: x-small Verdana, Arial, Helvetica, sans-serif;}
a.navlink {text-decoration: none;}
</style>
```

As part of our conversion process, we got rid of body element attributes like marginheight and topmargin. These were used to remove the "gutter" around the document content. To get the same effect in CSS, we'll need to zero out both the margin and padding of the body.

```
<style type="text/css">
body {font: x-small Verdana, Arial, Helvetica, sans-serif;
  margin: 0; padding: 0;}
a.navlink {text-decoration: none;}
</style>
```

We styled both margin and padding because some browsers enforce the gutter with one and some with the other. Setting both covers our bases, with the result shown in Figure 1.4.

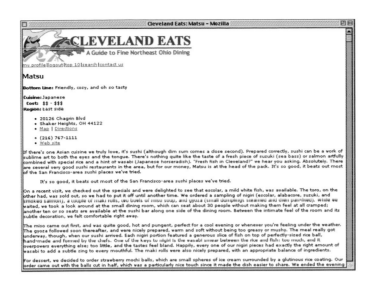

FIGURE 1.4

Starting out with a few global styles.

Tightening Up the Top

We are still using a table for the masthead, and since we took out the `cell-padding` and `width` attributes, we'll need to re-create them in the CSS. We'll just assume that all table cells should have no padding and that all tables should have a width of 100%. If we need to override either of those later, we'll do so.

```
body {font: x-small Verdana, Arial, Helvetica, sans-serif;
  margin: 0; padding: 0;}
table {width: 100%;}
th, td {padding: 0;}
a.navlink {text-decoration: none;}
```

Now we'll start on the navbar. It used to be that the links in the navbar were marked up like this:

```
<td nowrap><font size="-2"> <a href="/myprofile"
  class="navlink"><font color="#000000">my
 profile</font></a> </font></td>
```

This prevented line wrapping within the cell, reduced the font size for both the link and the whitespace around it, and set the text color of the link to black. In addition, each link had a `class` of `navlink`, which made it possible to remove the underlines with the rule `a.navlink {text-decoration: none;}`.

We stripped out those classes during the markup conversion because they aren't necessary. Now that the links are enclosed in a `div` with an `id` of `navbar`, we can just alter the rule's selector to target the links in their new location.

```
th, td {padding: 0;}
#navbar a {text-decoration: none;}
</style>
```

Now all we need is to set the color of the links and to prevent wrapping within the navbar. See Figure 1.5 for a summary of our progress to date.

```
th, td {padding: 0;}
#navbar {white-space: nowrap; background: #F0DFB4;}
#navbar a {text-decoration: none; color: #000;}
```

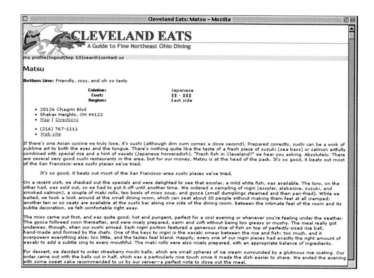

FIGURE 1.5

Fixing up the masthead and starting to style the navbar.

Filling Out the Navbar

Now it's time to actually place the navbar where it needs to go. To accomplish this particular task, we'll be positioning the div. Since none of the navbar's ancestor elements are positioned, the navbar will be positioned with respect to the initial containing block, which is generally regarded in HTML to be defined by the html element.

We know that the navbar will be up against the right edge of the document, so all we have to do is figure out how far down to place it. By counting pixels, we discover that the first pixel below the separator line is 44 down from the top of the document. So:

```
#navbar {position: absolute; top: 44px; right: 0;
    white-space: nowrap; background: #F0DFB4;}
```

Now we need to get the curve image back into place. In the original design, it was slotted into a table cell using an img element, but we stripped that out when converting the markup. We can reproduce the visual effect by placing the same image into the background of the navbar.

```
#navbar {position: absolute; top: 44px; right: 0;
    white-space: nowrap;
    background: #F0DFB4 url(tab-curve.gif) bottom left no-repeat;}
```

This sounds like a great idea until you realize that the image will be placed underneath the links, not to their left. To prevent that kind of overlap, we'll need some padding. The image is 32 pixels wide, so we'll set just that amount of padding for the moment (see Figure 1.6).

```
#navbar {position: absolute; top: 44px; right: 0;
   padding: 0 0 0 32px; white-space: nowrap;
   background: #F0DFB4 url(tab-curve.gif) bottom left no-repeat;}
```

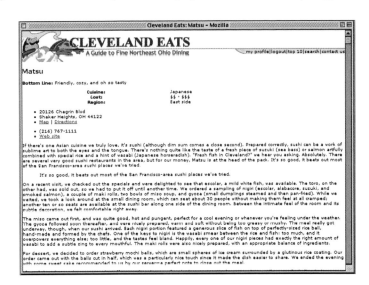

FIGURE 1.6

Positioning the navbar and adding an image to the background.

That's starting to look pretty darned good, although the text is still quite cramped. We'll add some extra top and bottom padding to spread things out vertically.

```
#navbar {position: absolute; top: 44px; right: 0;
   padding: 2px 0 2px 32px; white-space: nowrap;
   background: #F0DFB4 url(tab-curve.gif) bottom left no-repeat;}
```

Now we need to do something about the vertical-bar characters. Since we don't actually want them to appear, we can use the boldface elements to make them go away completely.

```
#navbar {position: absolute; top: 44px; right: 0;
   padding: 2px 0 2px 32px; white-space: nowrap;
   background: #F0DFB4 url(tab-curve.gif) bottom left no-repeat;}
#navbar b {display: none;}
#navbar a {text-decoration: none; color: #000;}
```

With this, the elements never appear in a styled document. If a browser doesn't get the CSS or the page is viewed using a CSS-incapable browser, the characters will be there to keep the links separated.

This means, of course, that in a CSS-aware browser, the links will be right up against each other. We can push them apart using margins or padding, so let's use padding. (We'll see why in a moment.)

```
#navbar a {text-decoration: none; color: #000;
   padding: 0 1em 0 0;}
```

Now all we really need to do is add in the border along the bottom of the navbar. Here's where things get a little tricky because we can't just add a bottom border to the `div`. If we did that, the border would stick out below the background image, and there's no way to make a background image overlap a border on the same element. So instead we'll add bottom borders to the links themselves.

```
#navbar a {text-decoration: none; color: #000;
   border-bottom: 1px solid gray;
   padding: 0 1em 0 0;}
```

Inline Padding

Adding bottom padding to the links doesn't actually change the height of the `div` in CSS-conformant browsers. That's because padding on non-replaced inline elements (which the links are) doesn't alter height calculations. With enough padding, we could actually push the link borders outside the `div`—at least in browsers other than Explorer.

That's why we used padding to push the links apart. If we'd used margins, the borders wouldn't have touched each other, destroying the illusion of a single border.

Now, because the `div` has two pixels of bottom padding, the borders we just added to the links will sit a pixel above the bottom of the tan background area. We'll need to push them down with some padding.

```
#navbar a {text-decoration: none; color: #000;
   border-bottom: 1px solid gray;
   padding: 0 1em 1px 0;}
```

This will actually bring the borders in line with the bottom of the background image, which is something the table layout didn't quite manage. If we wanted to push the borders down so that they precisely matched the effect seen in the original design, we would only have to increase that `1px` to `2px`, but we'll leave things as shown in Figure 1.7.

The big advantage in positioning the navbar is that it's easy to move around. Suppose we wanted to put it above that separator line instead of below it. Basically, we'd just have to adjust the value of `top` as needed and change the background image. For that matter, making the navbar straddle the separator line is a breeze with positioning. That kind of flexibility is what makes positioning so compelling as a layout tool.

FIGURE 1.7

Making the navbar complete.

►► PADDING AND INLINE ELEMENTS

It might not be immediately obvious that increasing the padding of the links would cause them to "stick out" of the div *that encloses them. Because of the way line layout is handled in CSS, that's exactly what should happen. As CSS says, top and bottom padding on inline non-replaced elements (like hyperlinks) has no affect on line height. Therefore, although the padding might be visible, it won't make a line of text taller, and thus won't affect the height of any containing elements, like a* div.

On the other hand, CSS also says that browsers don't have to render top and bottom padding on inline elements, and that's sort of what happens in IE/Win. In that browser, the borders and background get clipped by the edge of the div. *Thus, in order to get the same effect, you'd probably want to increase the padding on the* div. *The rest of the project will be written assuming that this isn't necessary, but it's something to keep in mind if you're having trouble.*

For those of you using IE/Win to work through the project, try adding a pixel or two of top and bottom padding to the navbar div *and see if that looks any better.*

Title and Summary Styles

With our masthead complete (at least until we go back and remove the table), let's take a look at the top of the review itself. Here we find some pretty simple markup.

```
<h2>Matsu</h2>
<p id="summary"><strong>Bottom Line:</strong>
Friendly, cozy, and oh so tasty</p>
```

Re-creating the look of the review title is simple enough; we just need to get the size and color to mimic the original design.

```
#navbar a {text-decoration: none; color: #000;
  border-bottom: 1px solid gray;
  padding: 0 1em 1px 0;}
#review h2 {color: #600; font-size: x-large;}
</style>
```

We'll also need to re-create the blank spaces, or lack thereof, above and below the title. In the original design, there were some spacer GIFs above the title, but below there was just a cell containing a dotted-line background. Rather than go with pixels, we'll take an initial stab at some em-based values and come back later to make any necessary adjustments.

```
#review h2 {color: #600; font-size: x-large;
  margin: 1em 0 0;}
```

And now for the summary line. This short line of text was a little bit larger than the main review text, so we'll need to change its font size. There was also a dotted line separating the summary from the title, so let's put that in as well. We can see the progress so far in Figure 1.8.

```
#review h2 {color: #600; font-size: x-large;
  margin: 1em 0 0;}
#review #summary {font-size: small; border-top: 1px dotted #600;}
</style>
```

FIGURE 1.8

The title and summary begin to come into focus.

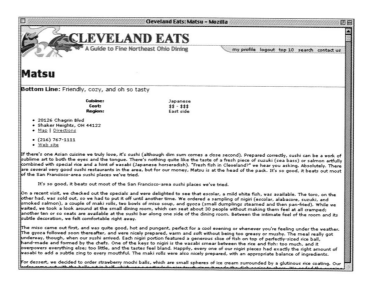

There are two problems here. The first is that there's space between the dotted line and the title; that's the top margin on the summary paragraph. The other problem is not necessarily a bad thing: The top border goes all the way across the page. In the original design, it was limited to the extent of the summary.

Now, we might decide, once the layout is completely done, that having a border that runs from one side of the main column to the other is not such a bad thing. To get as close to the original as possible, though, let's try an approach that will get rid of that top margin and limit the border to the summary text's width.

```
#review #summary {font-size: small; border-top: 1px dotted #600;
    display: inline;}
```

With this, we've changed the way the paragraph is laid out. Now it generates an inline box, the same as a hyperlink or a span element would. The paragraph itself is still a block-level element, but on the screen it generates an inline box. So the border will run along the top of the text, however long or short that might be.

There are potential drawbacks to having done this. If the summary text wraps to a second line, that second line will also have a top dotted border. There isn't a way to only apply a border to the first line of an inline element. Thus, if there's a chance that the summary could wrap to two lines, this is probably not a good approach.

The other possible drawback is a case in which the title is actually longer than the summary. In that case, the border will stop before the end of the title. A long restaurant name with a bottom line of "Yum!" would be an example. There isn't an easy way around this without using a table, which is unique in the HTML world in that it permits the width of one element to affect the width of several others.

With those caveats in mind, take a look at Figure 1.9, which shows that, in this particular case, the use of inline works out quite nicely. The separation between the title and summary has disappeared because top and bottom margins on inline elements have no effect on layout.

Line Expansion

It actually is possible to fake the effect of having a dividing border be as long as the length of two elements using negative margins, although it can get tricky. This technique is discussed in Project 8.

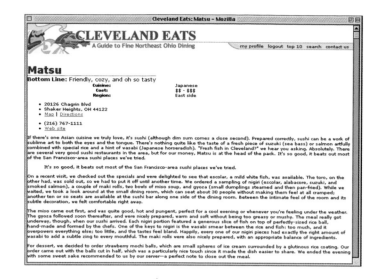

Information on the Side

As we work our way through the document, we come to the "info" `div`. This was laid out in the original design as a box over to the left, and we're going to do exactly the same thing here. The advantage is that, before, the sidebar was split across two rows and constructed out of a complex series of cells, whereas now we only have to style a single `div`.

To get the sidebar into place, we'll position it. Because none of the sidebar's ancestor elements is positioned, it will (like the navbar) be positioned with respect to the initial containing block. So we're working from the upper-left corner of the document this time. The masthead images total 72 pixels tall, so all we need to do is place the sidebar just below that point.

```
#navbar a {text-decoration: none; color: #000;
  border-bottom: 1px solid gray;
  padding: 0 1em 1px 0;}
#info {position: absolute; top: 73px; left: 0;}
#review h2 {color: #600; font-size: x-large;
  margin: 1em 0 0;}
```

Now, just that change means that the "info" `div` will be taken completely out of the document flow and placed as requested, 73 pixels from the top of the initial containing block and up against its left edge. That means the sidebar will now be completely overlapping the main text of the review. In fact, the sidebar is defaulting to a width of 100%, which means that if we gave it a background, it would stretch from one side of the document to the other.

Measuring Width

We've used a pixel width because the original design used pixel widths for the sidebar, but of course any measure could be employed instead. Percentages and ems are both popular choices in positioning-based layout.

This is, of course, not a permanent state of affairs, but it's what you'll discover if you preview the page right now. Let's add in a background for the sidebar and also set an explicit width, as shown in Figure 1.10.

```
#info {position: absolute; top: 73px; left: 0; width: 140px;
   background: #F0DFB4;}
```

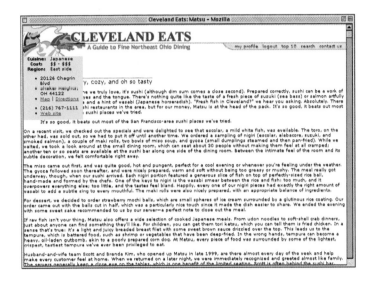

FIGURE 1.10

We've placed and sized the sidebar, but there is still work to be done.

Yes, the content is overlapping! We'll fix that after a bit, but first let's fill out the sidebar a bit more. We need to add in a border and also re-create the separation between the edge of the box and the content within.

```
#info {position: absolute; top: 73px; left: 0; width: 140px;
   background: #F0DFB4; padding: 0.75em 0;
   border: 1px solid #600; border-width: 2px 1px 2px 0;}
```

Just like that, we re-create the border effect that took so many cells to set up using the table layout. As for the padding, we're using ems to let the padding scale with any changes in text size and also to help ensure that we can get the same kind of vertical alignment seen in the original design.

The lists definitely need to be made more like the original design, which had no bullets in it. We can strip off the bullets and balance the indentation in one quick rule.

```
#info {position: absolute; top: 73px; left: 0; width: 140px;
   background: #F0DFB4; padding: 0.75em 0;
   border: 1px solid #600; border-width: 2px 1px 2px 0;}
#info ul {list-style: none; margin: 1em; padding: 0;}
#review h2 {color: #600; font-size: x-large;
   margin: 1em 0 0;}
```

Side Padding Issues

We zeroed out the side padding because it would be added to the `width` value, as CSS requires. It's easier to set margins or padding on elements inside the sidebar than it is to try to set it for the `div` itself.

By giving the lists an em of margin all the way around, they separate from each other and push inward from the edges of the sidebar, which is exactly what we want. Now all we really have left to do is make sure the table at the top of the sidebar is laid out properly. We need to right-align the labels, which are now `th` elements, so that's easy.

```
#info {position: absolute; top: 73px; left: 0; width: 140px;
   background: #F0DFB4; padding: 0.75em 0;
   border: 1px solid #600; border-width: 2px 1px 2px 0;}
#info th {text-align: right;}
#info ul {list-style: none; margin: 1em; padding: 0;}
```

A Table!

The information contained in the table is well-suited to such a structure, so we're going to leave it as is. We could convert it to a nontable structure that makes heavy use of floats, but there would be little point.

A little padding on the table cells would also help keep the contents from crowding together too closely, so we'll add that in.

```
#info th {text-align: right;}
#info td {padding: 0.125em;}
#info ul {list-style: none; margin: 1em; padding: 0;}
```

There's just one more thing to do: adjust the font for the table. The original design had it a bit larger than everything else but also in a different font face. We'll just style the table directly, as illustrated in Figure 1.11.

```
#info {position: absolute; top: 73px; left: 0; width: 140px;
   background: #F0DFB4; padding: 0.75em 0;
   border: 1px solid #600; border-width: 2px 1px 2px 0;}
#info table {font: small Arial, Verdana, Helvetica, sans-serif;}
#info th {text-align: right;}
```

FIGURE 1.11

Now the sidebar looks as good as ever, even if it is overlapping the review.

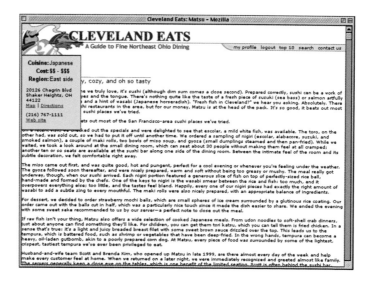

As with the navbar, the positioning of the sidebar gives us a great deal of flexibility. We could move it up or down a bit just by altering the `top` value, expand or contract its width, or even flip it to the other side of the page simply by changing the property `left` to `right`. In the same manner, changing the thickness and styles of the borders around the sidebar is a snap.

A Review with Style

The sidebar may be done with its style, but it's still sitting on top of the review itself, which is clearly not a good design choice for this project. We need to push the review text over a bit, but before we do that, let's take a look back at our original design. There we had a 40-pixel spacer GIF between the sidebar and the main content, and an 80-pixel spacer on the right side. We can roll both effects up into a single rule by styling the "review" `div`.

```
#info ul {list-style: none; margin: 1em; padding: 0;}
#review {margin: 0 80px 2em 180px;}
#review h2 {color: #600; font-size: x-large;
   margin: 1em 0 0;}
```

By adding 40 pixels to the sidebar's 140px width, we got `180px` for the left margin, and of course the right margin was a straightforward `80px`. The `2em` bottom margin was thrown in to create a little extra space underneath the end of the review.

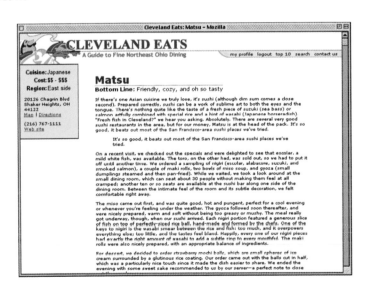

FIGURE 1.12

The columns emerge, and the review can be read.

With the overlap problems solved, we can concentrate on the text itself. If you look closely at Figure 1.12, you can see that the summary line doesn't quite line up with the "Region" line in the sidebar. This alignment is why the original design used such a complicated cell arrangement. Here, all that's required is an adjustment to the top margin of the title. Some experimentation reveals the following values make for a decent effect.

```
#review h2 {color: #600; font-size: x-large;
    margin: 1em 0 0; padding: 0 0 0.2em; line-height: 1em;}
```

Platform Jumps

Actually, the text is not fully accurate. The values used give the desired result in Windows browsers, but on Macintosh browsers, the alignment is off a bit. This seems to be due to differences in font handling in the two operating systems, and it's likely that other systems will have similar variances. This illustrates an excellent point about CSS-driven design: Alignments of this kind shouldn't be relied upon, if at all possible.

Why the line-height value? Because although that's close to the default for all browsers, there's no guarantee that it will actually be the default: One browser might use 1.2, another 1.25, and yet another 1.175. CSS doesn't require one specific value as the default, so browsers are allowed to do whatever they think is best. By explicitly declaring a line-height value, we overcome any potential problems from differing defaults.

Now it's time to look at the actual paragraphs in the review. The original design used a series of nonbreaking space entities to indent all paragraphs but the first one. We removed those entities, but they aren't needed; text-indent will do the job for us.

```
#review #summary {font-size: small; border-top: 1px dotted #600;
    display: inline;}
#review p {text-indent: 2em;}
</style>
```

This will indent the first line of all p elements in the review, including the first one and the summary. (Remember, it's contained in a p element.) Fortunately, we added a class to the first paragraph of the review:

```
<p class="lead">
If there's one Asian food we truly love, it's sushi (although
dim sum comes a close second).
```

We can use that and the rule we wrote earlier for the summary to turn off first-line indenting in those two elements, as can be seen in Figure 1.13.

```
#review #summary {font-size: small; border-top: 1px dotted #600;
    display: inline; text-indent: 0;}
#review p {text-indent: 2em;}
#review .lead {text-indent: 0;}
</style>
```

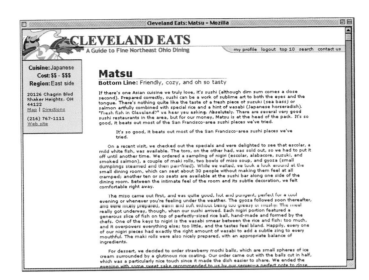

FIGURE 1.13

Indenting the first line of most, but not all, of the paragraphs in the review.

Pulling the Quote and Enhancing the Design

At this point, we're almost done. The only thing we really have to do is get the pullquote to actually look like a pullquote. Right now, it's just a `blockquote` sitting between a couple of paragraphs. Fortunately, it's easy to do. All we need is to float it to the right, bump up the font size and weight, and throw in some padding to make sure text doesn't get too close.

```
#review .lead {text-indent: 0;}
blockquote.pull {float: right; width: 40%;
  padding: 1em 0 1em 5%; margin: 0;
  font-size: medium; font-weight: bold;}
</style>
```

If you compare these styles to the original HTML design, you'll notice some differences. One is that we've converted the pixel-size spacer GIFs into `1em` padding. We could have used `10px` instead, but since we don't *have* to use pixels, why not try something more flexible?

As for the left padding of `5%`, this would seem to have almost nothing to do with the original spacer-cell width of `15%`. For that matter, the original table was `45%` wide, whereas the styles we just wrote call for a `40%` width.

The difference is the nature of tables versus CSS-styled elements. When we set up that `15%`-wide cell, it was 15% of the width of the table, which was itself 45% of the width of the cell in which it sat. Percentages in padding (as well as margins and `width` itself) refer to the width of the containing element—in this case, the "review" `div`. Furthermore, padding is added to width, so if we want the pullquote to add up to 45% of the width of the containing element, we have to take into account the addition. So 40% width plus 5% left padding equals 45% overall width. The result is shown in Figure 1.14.

FIGURE 1.14

Floating and styling the pullquote to mimic the original design.

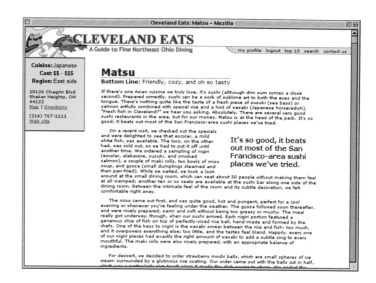

Having arrived back where we started, let's try enhancing the original design just a bit. The small text may pack a lot of information onto the screen, but it also makes the text a bit harder to read. In HTML design, there's not much you can do about that, but with CSS, spreading the lines apart is simple. All we have to do is alter the `line-height` of the paragraphs.

```
#review p {text-indent: 2em; line-height: 1.3;}
```

However, this has the potential to throw off the summary paragraph's layout a bit, so we'll reset it to the default.

```
#review #summary {font-size: small; border-top: 1px dotted #600;
   display: inline; text-indent: 0; line-height: normal;}
```

For an extra touch of interactivity, let's define a hover style for the navbar links. We'll generate a starting point for this effort by making any hovered navbar link appear as white text on a dark blue background (to match the text color in the masthead) and widen the bottom border.

```
#navbar a {text-decoration: none; color: #000;
   border-bottom: 1px solid gray;
   padding: 2px 1em 1px 0;}
#navbar a:hover {color: white; background: #336;
   border-bottom-width: 3px;}
#info {position: absolute; top: 73px; left: 0; width: 140px;
   background: #F0DFB4; padding: 0.75em 0;
   border: 1px solid #600; border-width: 2px 1px 2px 0;}
```

Missing Effects

Bugs in IE/Win often prevent elements from exceeding the boundaries of their parents, so the three-pixel border effect probably won't show up. The technique was shown anyway because it's a good example of design that still works in less-capable browsers, but looks better in more advanced browsers.

Doing this reveals a slight imbalance in our basic navlink styles. Notice in the preceding code that the padding on the links is 1em on the right and 0 on the left. This means that the hover effect will be offset with regard to the text. We need to balance those out so that the text will be centered within each link, as shown in Figure 1.15.

```
#navbar a {text-decoration: none; color: #000;
   border-bottom: 1px solid gray;
   padding: 2px 0.5em 1px;}
```

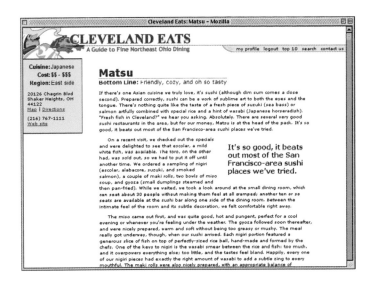

FIGURE 1.15

Spreading out the text and punching up the navigation links.

The Masthead Revisited

Okay, so we've re-created the layout and even improved a bit on the original, but what about that masthead? It's still sitting in a three-cell table, and the graphics are all sliced up. Let's see if we can improve on that.

We could bring all three slices back together into a single image, but it would be a lot more useful to merge the chef and page title into one image and put the subtitle ("A Guide to Fine Northeast Ohio Dining") in another. By having the subtitle separate, we can place it wherever we want through positioning. So we end up with the images shown in Figure 1.16.

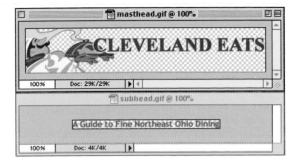

FIGURE 1.16

By combining the image and splitting out the subhead, we give ourselves a lot of layout options.

Now we just need to rework the HTML so that the images are still present but with much less markup. Just wrapping both in a div with some appropriate id attributes should suffice for the moment.

```
<body>
<div id="masthead">
<img src="masthead.gif" alt="Cleveland Eats">
<img src="subhead.gif" alt="A Guide to Fine Northeast Ohio
 Dining" id="subhead">
</div>
<div id="navbar">
```

The first order of business is to place the subtitle where it needs to be. Counting pixels in the original design works pretty well to determine the proper placement.

```
th, td {padding: 0;}
#subhead {position: absolute; top: 46px; left: 151px;}
#navbar {position: absolute; top: 44px; right: 0;
  padding: 2px 0 2px 32px; white-space: nowrap;
  background: #F0DFB4 url(tab-curve.gif) bottom left no-repeat;}
```

This places the top-left corner of the subhead graphic right where we want it. Of course, if we decide that it should be shifted around a bit—say, up a pixel or two to the left—we can move it just by fiddling with the values of top and left. For that matter, we could really move it, perhaps to the top-right corner of the page or right over the navbar. We won't do that here, although you can certainly experiment later on.

While we're here, we'll also set the images in the masthead to generate block-level boxes. Doing so eliminates the chance of some minor layout changes happening in Gecko-based browsers (like Mozilla), which treat image layout a little more strictly than most other browsers. Making their layout boxes block-level will eliminate the differences and give us the layout shown in Figure 1.17.

```
th, td {padding: 0;}
#masthead img {display: block;}
#subhead {position: absolute; top: 46px; left: 151px;}
```

Absolutely Blocked

The absolutely positioned subhead image actually already generates a block-level box. All absolutely positioned elements do so, no matter what kind of box they would have generated if they weren't positioned.

FIGURE 1.17

The subhead has been placed as before, although we could move it in a jiffy.

There's one thing missing: that dratted separator line. We know it should be 43 pixels from the top of the masthead, and that leads to a certain temptation. We could theoretically define an explicit height for the masthead of 43px, give it a bottom border, and let the image masthead.gif overflow the div. The CSS to accomplish this would be:

```
#masthead {height: 42px; border-bottom: 1px solid #666;}
```

If we did that, though, we'd have to adjust the "review" div's styles. Why? Because the masthead would now be 44 pixels tall (the height plus the bottom border) instead of the 73 pixels tall it is now. Thus, the review div would move upward by 29 pixels. Fixing it would be simple enough: A top padding of 29 pixels would counteract the effect.

Unfortunately, the obstacle to using that exact technique is Internet Explorer for Windows, which would ignore the 43px height and expand the masthead div to enclose the image. In effect, Explorer treats height as though it were min-height. So we have two options. One is to position masthead.gif, which would take it out of the normal flow and let Explorer do the right thing with regard to the height of the masthead div. The CSS to accomplish that would be:

```
#masthead {height: 43px; border-bottom: 1px solid #666;}
#masthead img {position: absolute; top: 0; left: 0;}
#masthead #subhead {top: 46px; left: 151px;}
#review {margin: 0 80px 2em 180px; padding-top: 30px;}
```

The other possibility is to leave things as they were in Figure 1.17 and just put a one-pixel image into the masthead's background, repeated horizontally, like this:

```
#masthead {background: white url(stripe.gif) 0 43px repeat-x;}
```

The benefit here is that it only requires one new rule to get the separator line to appear and any horizontally repeating pattern could be used, but the drawback is that it requires loading an extra image to make the effect work. Which you prefer is up to you; either way, you should get the result shown in Figure 1.18.

FIGURE 1.18

Fully re-creating the masthead without tables.

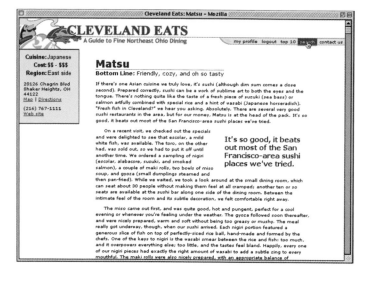

Telling the Difference

So which technique was used to create Figure 1.18? It shouldn't actually matter, but if you must know, check the file ch0118.html.

Since New Riders is already springing for a lot of money in nice heavy paper and color inks, we'll list the background-image version of the final style sheet—it's shorter than the other one.

Listing 1.2   The Background-Image Approach

```
body {font: x-small Verdana, Arial, Helvetica, sans-serif;
   margin: 0; padding: 0;}
table {width: 100%;}
th, td {padding: 0;}
#masthead {background: white url(stripe.gif) 0 43px repeat-x;}
#masthead img {display: block;}
#subhead {position: absolute; top: 46px; left: 151px;}
#navbar {position: absolute; top: 44px; right: 0;
   padding: 2px 0 2px 32px; white-space: nowrap;
   background: #F0DFB4 url(tab-curve.gif) bottom left no-repeat;}
#navbar b {display: none;}
#navbar a {text-decoration: none; color: #000;
   border-bottom: 1px solid gray;
   padding: 2px 0.5em 1px;}
#navbar a:hover {color: white; background: #336;
   border-bottom-width: 3px;}
#info {position: absolute; top: 73px; left: 0; width: 140px;
   background: #F0DFB4; padding: 0.75em 0;
   border: 1px solid #600; border-width: 2px 1px 2px 0;}
#info table {font: small Arial, Verdana, Helvetica, sans-serif;}
#info th {text-align: right;}
```

```
#info td {padding: 0.125em;}
#info ul {list-style: none; margin: 1em; padding: 0;}
#review {margin: 0 80px 2em 180px;}
#review h2 {color: #600; font-size: x-large;
margin: 1em 0 0; padding: 0 0 0.2em; line-height: 1em;}
#review #summary {font-size: small; border-top: 1px dotted #600;
  display: inline; text-indent: 0; line-height: normal;}
#review p {text-indent: 2em; line-height: 1.3;}
#review .lead {text-indent: 0;}
blockquote.pull {float: right; width: 40%;
  padding: 1em 0 1em 5%; margin: 0;
  font-size: medium; font-weight: bold;}
```

Assessing the Benefits

In describing a conversion process like the one we've undertaken in this project, you might meet with some bewilderment. "Why bother, when tables already work?" is the usual question. There are two good reasons.

First, the document structure is a lot cleaner and thus a lot easier to edit and generally maintain. Let's say you had an unclosed element somewhere in your markup, and it was completely messing up the layout. Would you rather sift through the HTML design, choked as it is with font tags and tables nested inside tables, or the relatively clean structure we had at the end of the conversion process? Probably the latter.

Second, there is a noticeable savings in terms of file size. Table 1.1 compares the file sizes, element counts, and server hits that are (or may be) necessary for each of three approaches: the all-HTML design, the converted document with embedded style sheet, and the converted document with the style sheet made external and linked in.

Table 1.1   A Qualitative Comparison of the Three Approaches

Method	Size*	Characters	Server Hits	Images	Tables	Font Tags
All HTML	100%	8,994	6–23	22 (18 repeat)	7	20 0
HTML + CSS	75.4%	6,785	5	4	1	0
HTML + linked CSS	59.8%	5,375 + 1,435	5–6	4	1	0

*Compared to all-HTML method; refers to size of HTML document only

A Range of Hits

The reason that some of the "Server Hits" values are given as a range is due to repeated images. In the all-HTML design, for example, there were 18 spacer.gif images. Most browsers will only download once and use a cached version of the image from then on, but a browser without a cache or with caching turned off has to load the image every time it's referenced in the HTML.

Even with the style sheet left inside the document, there's a nearly 25% reduction in the size of the file. If the style sheet is moved into an external file, the benefits are even more striking, down to just under 60% of its original size. Either way, the page will download faster, making users happier and reducing the amount of bandwidth for which we have to pay.

The 59.8% figure deserves a short explanation. It only counts the HTML, not the external style sheet. This is because browsers usually cache external style sheets after they're loaded the first time. Thus, the server won't be asked for the external style sheet after the user loads their first page (that uses this style sheet) from the server. For that first load, the bandwidth savings will be closely in line with the HTML + CSS version, which is still a one-quarter reduction.

In addition to those savings, the positioned version of the layout is much, much easier to alter whenever we want. Adjusting the width of the sidebar, moving the subtitle around, or even reworking the basic layout becomes a quick and simple editing operation. All in all, it seems like a worthwhile effort to have undertaken.

A Caveat

There is one word of caution about this layout. If there is ever a case in which the review column is shorter than the sidebar, strange things can happen. In tables, the cells in a row are all the same height; thus, if we put the sidebar in one cell and the review in another, both cells would be the height of the taller cell.

In positioning, there is no way to link two elements together like that. Once you've taken an element out of the document flow, its height is determined by its content and styles—period. It will not be influenced by other elements, nor will they be influenced by it. So, for a layout where the two columns have to be the same visual height or where some content needs to go after both columns and you don't know which column will be taller in the final layout, positioning may be a bad choice. This doesn't mean that positioning is useless. More and more high-profile sites, including Wired News, Sprint PCS, and Quark use CSS-P for layout. You just need to know where positioning excels and where it doesn't so that you can make the best decision regarding how to set up a given layout.

BRANCHING OUT

Starting with the styles we created in this project, try to accomplish the following modifications without changing the document's structure. Notice how easy it is to do it this way instead of trying to rewrite the tables.

1. Move the navbar into the upper-right corner of the page and put the subtitle below it so that the baselines of the subtitle and main title line up. Since that frees up some space under the masthead, move the review text upward so that you don't waste too much screen real estate.

2. Flip the layout around so that the sidebar is on the right and the review on the left. Remember that the chef gets cut off right where the sidebar sits now, so a visual finish of some kind will be needed. For extra credit, extend the summary's top border to touch the info box without allowing any of the text in the review to get within 40 pixels of the sidebar.

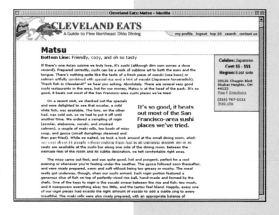

2

STYLING A PHOTO COLLECTION

All photographs are there to remind us of what we forget. In this—as in other ways—they are the opposite of paintings. Paintings record what the painter remembers. Because each one of us forgets different things, a photo more than a painting may change its meaning according to who is looking at it.

—JOHN BERGER

ALTHOUGH NOT EVERYONE PUTS his or her photographs online, such collections are an interesting layout challenge. Each photo and its associated information forms a small, self-contained unit that nevertheless has to be laid out with respect to the other photographs on the page. In a way, they're like portals, except with each "box" in this portal leading to more information about a photo instead of to the latest headlines or sports scores.

Photo collections are also reminiscent of another, far more common layout challenge: that of a catalog of products for sale via an e-commerce site. In fact, sometimes the photos themselves can be products for sale, which is the assumption we'll be making in this project.

PROJECT GOALS

In this project, we're looking for ways to present a collection of photographs for sale. Our client has given us the following requirements:

◆ We need to have three different possible presentations: a Contact Sheet view for the artist to check what's available and to show off to his peers, a Gallery view for users to be able to see all the offerings, and a more detailed Catalog view to allow for ordering.

◆ In the Gallery and Contact Sheet views, as many photographs as possible should appear "above the fold" and without requiring a horizontal scroll, no matter the browser window size. It is acceptable to show only the photo and its title in this view. However, the pictures should arrange themselves into a regular grid.

◆ In the Catalog view, every photograph should be presented along with its title, catalog number, and price. Scrolling is not a problem in this view.

◆ The same markup should drive all three views because our client doesn't want to pay for a dynamic site and therefore wants the page markup to be produced only once.

For this project, we're only working on the photo collection piece of the layout, so we don't have to worry about anything but that piece. We will assume that the layout will go into a main central column in a larger layout, but that doesn't really change anything for this project.

Due to the constraints of the project, particularly those of the Gallery and Contact Sheet views, we won't be able to use tables to lay out these photos. Why not? Because of the request to get as many pictures as possible "above the fold" (that is, into the browser window at page load).

So, instead of tables, we'll need to float the pictures and their information for those two "compact" views. Floating them will allow us to get as many pictures in each "row" as will fit in the browser window. In other words, a user with an 800×600 browser window might get four images per row, while a 1280×1024 user will get six or seven. Using floats allows for this kind of "flow" behavior, whereas using tables does not. As an added bonus, we can set up the floats so that each one is the same width. This will ensure that they lay themselves out in a grid-like fashion.

Preparation

Download the files for Project 2 from this book's Web site. If you're planning to play along at home, load the file `ch02proj.html` into the editing program of your choice. This is the file you'll be editing, saving, and reloading as the chapter progresses.

Laying the Groundwork

The first thing we ought to do is take a look at the markup with which we'll be working. Here are the first two sets of images and information in the document:

```
<div class="pic ls"><a href="orig/img01.jpg" class="tn"><img
  src="tn/thumb01.jpg" alt=""></a><ul>
<li class="title">The Ferrett's Daffodil</li>
<li class="catno">03F01</li>
<li class="price">$79.95</li>
</ul></div>
<div class="pic pt"><a href="orig/img02.jpg" class="tn"><img
  src="tn/thumb02.jpg" alt=""></a><ul>
<li class="title">At Lunch</li>
<li class="catno">03F02</li>
<li class="price">$59.95</li>
</ul></div>
```

That's a lot of classes, and we ought to find out what they all mean. Fortunately, we have a style guide.

- ◆ `pic` marks any `div` that contains a picture and its associated information. This helps keep these `divs` separate from any others that might be used.

- ◆ `ls` means the picture has landscape orientation (it's wider than it is tall), whereas `pt` refers to a portrait orientation (taller than wide).

- ◆ `tn` marks a link as being the hyperlink that's wrapped around the thumbnail image.

- ◆ `title` marks the picture's title, `catno` its catalog number, and `price`... okay, that one is fairly obvious.

The really important classes are `ls` and `pt`, as we'll see soon enough, but all of them will come in handy. For example, we'll use those classes to set the height and width of the images. These aren't expressed in the HTML, as you can see. We know that our landscape thumbnails are 128 pixels wide by 96 pixels tall (with the portraits being 96×128), but we'll have to say so in the CSS before the project is done.

See the Introduction for instructions on how to download files from the Web site.

Whitespace Blues

Take a close look at the markup: Notice how the ul element has been moved right up against the link before it, and the div's closing tag is after it. This was done to avoid certain whitespace-triggered bugs in older versions of Explorer. It's unfortunate, but whitespace is still significant to some older browsers, and sometimes adding or subtracting whitespace can fix mysterious layout problems.

To get started, let's add some basic body and footer styles. For the `body` element, we'll just add a light tan background and some margins. We know we'll be using `float` a lot, and we want the footer to show up after the images, so we'll `clear` it. These actions are illustrated in Figure 2.1.

```
<style type="text/css">
body {background: #EED; margin: 1em;}
div#footer {clear: both; padding-top: 3em;
  font: 85% Verdana, sans-serif;}
</style>
```

FIGURE 2.1

Taking the first steps.

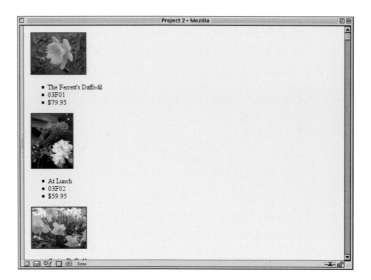

These styles won't change throughout the rest of the project, so we won't have to worry about them again. With that out of the way, let's get down to business!

CREATING THE CONTACT SHEET VIEW

At this stage, we can see the document structure itself: images followed by unordered lists. What we're after at this point is the creation of a "contact sheet" layout, in which the images are all laid out in a grid. This will let us see as many images as possible at once.

Floating Away

Since we aren't using a table, the obvious solution is to float the images. We know the images are no more than 128 pixels wide or tall, so we'll make our `divs` 128×128 and give them a white background and black border. Speaking of borders, we want to get rid of the blue link-border around the images as well.

Border Incidents

Not all browsers will put a border around a linked image, but some will, so it's a good idea to explicitly get rid of the border. It won't hurt in browsers that didn't have a border in the first place.

```
div#footer {clear: both; padding-top: 3em;
  font: 85% Verdana, sans-serif;}
div.pic {float: left; height: 128px; width: 128px;
  background: white;
  border: 1px solid black;}
div.pic img {border: none;}
</style>
```

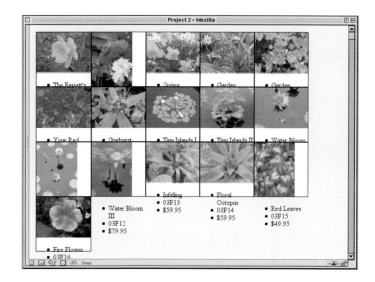

FIGURE 2.2

Floating the picture divs.

We've already taken a huge step toward our contact sheet, but there's an obvious problem—the lists! Because we forced the divs to be a specific height, there isn't enough room for the lists, so they're spilling out of the divs and generally messing up our layout. We need to get rid of them for now, so we'll remove them from the display routines.

```
div.pic img {border: none;}
div.pic ul {display: none;}
</style>
```

This will keep the information from being displayed at all. We'll bring back the lists in future changes to the styles, but for now we'll just get rid of them.

Spacing and Centering

Thanks to the floating, we now have our images forming a grid, but it feels a little too confined. Let's spread out the pictures a bit by adding margins to the floats.

```
div.pic {float: left; height: 128px; width: 128px;
  margin: 5px 3px; background: white;
  border: 1px solid black;}
```

Explorer Watch

In Explorer for Windows, the lists will expand the divs instead of sticking out of them, leading to a very different but equally bad layout. This is a bug in Explorer 5+ that treats height as if it were min-height (which, ironically, Explorer doesn't support).

Because margin floats don't collapse together, the actual spacing between two floats sitting next to each other will be 6 pixels (3px + 3px), and there will be 10 pixels between a float and the one below or above it. This can be adjusted to whatever spacing one prefers, of course. What we have so far is shown in Figure 2.3.

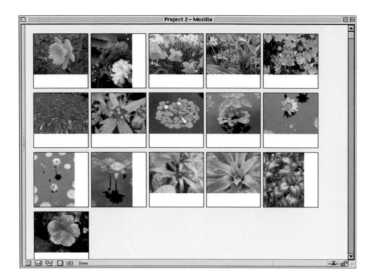

It's getting better and better, but the images look kind of weird as they are now, either up against the top of the box or against the left edge. They'd look much better centered within each box.

To do this, we should first define the size of the images. We can do this with two simple (and very similar) rules.

```
div.pic img {border: none;}
div.ls img {height: 96px; width: 128px;}
div.pt img {height: 128px; width: 96px;}
div.pic ul {display: none;}
```

All we've done here is express what we already knew to be true but the browser didn't: that landscape (ls) images are 96 pixels tall by 128 pixels wide and portrait (pt) images are the other way round.

Recall that our divs have been defined as 128×128 pixels. Now all we need to center the images are some margins on the images themselves. The difference between 128 and 96 is 32, and half of that is 16. Therefore, landscape images will need 16px of top and bottom margin, and portraits will need 16px of left and right margin. The result is shown in Figure 2.4.

```
div.ls img {height: 96px; width: 128px; margin: 16px 0;}
div.pt img {height: 128px; width: 96px; margin: 0 16px;}
```

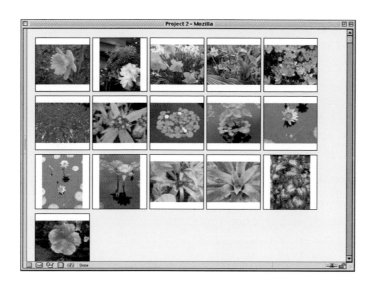

FIGURE 2.4

Centering the thumbnails.

Sliding into Style

That's already a decent layout, but let's take it a little further. Let's add some extra padding to the divs so that the thumbnails have white all the way around. We'll stick with our powers-of-two motif and add 16 pixels of padding.

```
div.pic {float: left; height: 128px; width: 128px;
  padding: 16px; margin: 5px 3px; background: white;
  border: 1px solid black;}
```

At this point, the contact sheet is beginning to resemble a collection of 35mm slides, so let's run with that idea. First we'll add a border back onto the images, one that makes them look like they've been inset into a slide frame.

```
div.pic img {border: 1px solid;
  border-color: #444 #AAA #AAA #444;}
```

These changes give all the images a dark gray top and left border, with a light gray right and bottom border. That's a decent enough inset effect.

However, there's a subtle imbalance that's been introduced by this rule. The images plus the borders are now longer than 128×96 pixels and vice versa; now they're 130×98 pixels because the borders are added to the height and width of the images. To address this, we'll need to alter the height and width declarations for the divs as well as the padding.

```
div.pic {float: left; height: 130px; width: 130px;
  padding: 15px; margin: 5px 3px; background: white;
  border: 1px solid black;}
```

Another Approach

Instead of the technique shown, we could have used a single color and the border style inset, but there's a drawback to this approach: Browsers are allowed to modify the colors for inset (as well as outset, groove, and ridge) however they like. Predictably, they all do it differently. Thus, in cases in which the shading of a border is important, it's better to make the border solid and set the colors the way *you* want them.

With these small changes, we've restored the balance we had before. To finish the effect, let's create an outset effect for the border of the divs. All we need there is the same colors we used for the inset effect, except reversed.

```
div.pic {float: left; height: 130px; width: 130px;
  padding: 15px; margin: 5px 3px; background: white;
  border: 1px solid; border-color: #AAA #444 #444 #AAA;}
```

Note that we removed the keyword `black` from the `border` declaration. It isn't needed any longer thanks to the `border-color` declaration, so to save on file size, it was taken out. We can see the result in Figure 2.5.

FIGURE 2.5

A sheet of slides, or something very much like it.

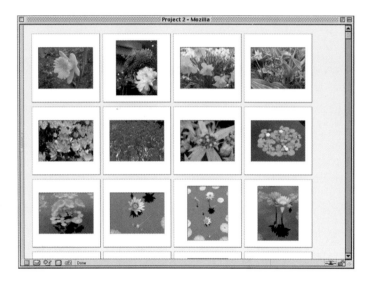

That's pretty close to looking like 35mm slides, but we can take the effect even further. Instead of relying on background color and borders, we can remove those and use a background image instead.

How? We already know the dimensions of the divs once all is said and done: They're 162×162 pixels. For example, landscape slides have the following dimensions along the horizontal axis:

128px `img` width + 2px `img` border + 30px `div` padding + 2px `div` border = 162 pixels total

Since we're going to be removing the borders on the divs, we can knock those off, leaving us with 160×160 pixels. Therefore, we'll make the background images for the divs that size. Because we have two kinds of images (portrait and landscape), we'll need two different backgrounds. We'll call them `frame-pt.gif` and `frame-ls.gif`. Whether they're created by scanning actual 35mm slide frames or by creating facsimiles in Photoshop is irrelevant. All we need is something that looks the part.

You can find images named `frame-ls.gif` and `frame-pt.gif` in the project files available on the book's companion site.

Once we've created the background images we need, all that remains is to add them to the styles. We'll start by applying the same image to all the divs, as well as removing our border styles.

```
div.pic {float: left; height: 130px; width: 130px;
  padding: 15px; margin: 5px 3px;
  background: url(frame-ls.gif) center no-repeat;}
```

This is great for the landscape thumbnails, but it will look weird when applied to the portrait images. So we just substitute the image we want used for portrait thumbnails with a short rule.

```
div.pic {float: left; height: 130px; width: 130px;
  padding: 15px; margin: 5px 3px;
  background: url(frame-ls.gif) center no-repeat;}
div.pt {background-image: url(frame-pt.gif);}}
div.pic img {border: 1px solid; border-color: #444 #AAA #AAA #444;}
```

This will override the background image value while leaving the other keywords (center no-repeat) alone, making the declaration background-image: url(frame-pt.gif) functionally equivalent to declaring background: url(frame-pt.gif) center no-repeat. Figure 2.6 illustrates the result.

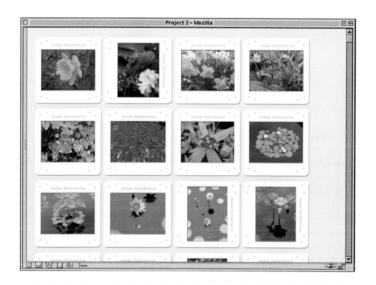

FIGURE 2.6

Now it really looks like a bunch of slides!

That's a pretty nifty effect, eh? The great thing is that you can substitute the "frame" background with a better one later on just by updating the image files.

Listing 2.1 shows the slide-collection style sheet we've created in its entirety.

This might be a good time to save the work you've done in a separate file because the next section will remove many of these styles even as it adds new ones.

Listing 2.1   The Complete "Slides" Style Sheet

```
body {background: #EED; margin: 1em;}
div#footer {clear: both; padding-top: 3em;
  font: 85% Verdana, sans-serif;}
div.pic {float: left; height: 130px; width: 130px;
  padding: 15px; margin: 5px 3px;}
  background: url(frame-ls.gif) center no-repeat;}
div.pt {background-image: url(frame-pt.gif);}
div.pic img {border: 1px solid; border-color: #444 #AAA #AAA #444;}
div.ls img {height: 96px; width: 128px; margin: 16px 0;}
div.pt img {height: 128px; width: 96px; margin: 0 16px;}
div.pic ul {display: none;}
```

CREATING THE GALLERY VIEW

As interesting as the preceding style sheet may be, the drawback is that it doesn't show us what photos are called. This might be a perfect presentation for the artist himself, who probably knows what they're all called and just wants to see everything in a compact form. For visitors, though, it won't be nearly as useful. Therefore, let's turn our slides into a gallery of photos, each one captioned with its title.

Removing the Slide Styles

To clear the field, so to speak, we'll want to drop the styles that place the background images into place (see Figure 2.7). This leaves us with the style sheet in Listing 2.2.

Listing 2.2   The Reduced Style Sheet

```
body {background: #EED; margin: 1em;}
div#footer {clear: both; padding-top: 3em;
  font: 85% Verdana, sans-serif;}
div.pic {float: left; height: 130px; width: 130px;
  padding: 15px; margin: 5px 3px;}
div.pic img {border: 1px solid; border-color: #444 #AAA #AAA #444;}
div.ls img {height: 96px; width: 128px; margin: 16px 0;}
div.pt img {height: 128px; width: 96px; margin: 0 16px;}
div.pic ul {display: none;}
```

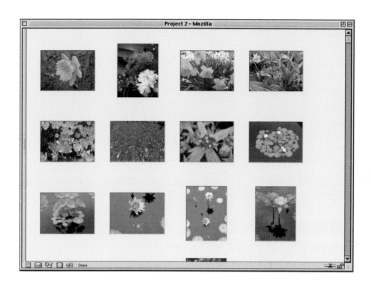

FIGURE 2.7

Stripping out the slide frames.

With this style sheet, we're actually most of the way to where we want to be. The next step is to reveal the titles.

Titular Revelations

To make this happen, we'll need to unhide the `ul` elements and hide the parts we don't want to see at this point. The unhiding part is simple enough: We remove `display: none;` from the `div.pic ul` rule. Of course, that leaves us with an empty declaration block:

```
div.pic ul {}
```

This is legal, even if it's kind of useless: The elements will be selected, but no styles will be applied. So let's fill in the blank. We'll set the padding and margins for the `ul` as well as its font styles.

```
div.pic ul {margin: 0.25em 0 0; padding: 0;
  font: bold small Arial, Verdana, sans-serif;}
```

Now the list will be visible again—all of it. Since we only want the titles to appear, we'll hide the other list items, as shown in Figure 2.8.

```
div.pic ul {margin: 0.25em 0 0; padding: 0;
  font: bold small Arial, Verdana, sans-serif;}
li.catno, li.price {display: none;}
</style>
```

FIGURE 2.8

*Revealing the title while
hiding the rest.*

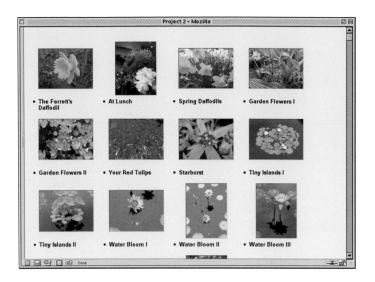

Not bad, but there's obviously still some work to do. We'll want to get rid of the bullets since they only serve to distract and look ugly. We could remove them using the property `list-style`, but on the other hand we could just change the `li` element so that it's no longer a list item. This would work great, except that IE/Win preserves the bullets, so we'll actually want to do both. While we're at it, we'll center the text.

```
div.pic ul {margin: 0.25em 0 0; padding: 0;
  font: bold small Arial, Verdana, sans-serif;}
li.title {display: block; list-style: none; text-align: center;}
li.catno, li.price {display: none;}
```

Now we'll move the titles up close to the images. If you remember, we added margins to the images while creating the "slides" style sheet in the preceding section. That margin is what is pushing the titles away from the landscape images.

Note that I say the *landscape* images. The portrait images have no top or bottom margins. Thus, we really only need to alter the margins on landscape images. Also note something interesting in Figure 2.8: The first lines of the captions in each row all line up. That's an effect worth preserving, so rather than just removing the bottom margin on landscape images, we're going to shift the entire margin to the top.

```
div.ls img {height: 96px; width: 128px; margin: 32px 0 0;}
```

So far so good, but there's something we haven't considered yet: the height of the divs. They're still locked at 130px tall plus some padding. All of that together means the captions are in danger of spilling out of the divs. If we add a subtle border to the divs, we can see what's happening without detracting too much from the overall progress we've made, as shown in Figure 2.9.

```
div.pic {float: left; height: 130px; width: 130px;
  padding: 15px; margin: 5px 3px; border: 1px dotted silver;}
```

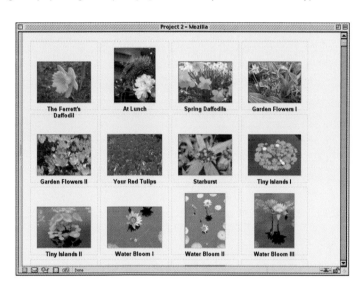

Explorer Watch

As before, the height bugs in Explorer for Windows will lead to a different result than that shown in Figure 2.9.

FIGURE 2.9

We're almost there, but there are some excesses.

Cleaning Up

At this stage, all we really need to do is increase the height of the divs so that the text has room to fit. Why bother? One reason is that, if we don't, the layout will be broken in Internet Explorer for Windows. Another reason is that, if a long title appears above a portrait image, the chance of overlap is fairly high. A third reason is that it just seems untidy to have elements intentionally sticking out of their parent elements (for the moment, anyway; we'll actually take advantage of that behavior in a later phase of the project).

So what we'll do is remove the top and bottom padding of the divs and increase their height. Oh, and remove that dotted border while we're at it.

```
div.pic {float: left; height: 190px; width: 130px;
  padding: 0 15px; margin: 5px 3px;}
```

With this change, we've arrived at our gallery style sheet, provided in Listing 2.3 and displayed in Figure 2.10.

This might be a good time to save the work you've done in a separate file because the next section will effectively start over, tossing out most of what we've done so far.

Listing 2.3 The Gallery Style Sheet

```
body {background: #EED; margin: 1em;}
div#footer {clear: both; padding-top: 3em;
  font: 85% Verdana, sans-serif;}
div.pic {float: left; height: 190px; width: 130px;
  padding: 0 15px; margin: 5px 3px;}
div.pic img {border: 1px solid; border-color: #444 #AAA #AAA #444;}
div.ls img {height: 96px; width: 128px; margin: 32px 0 0;}
div.pt img {height: 128px; width: 96px; margin: 0 16px;}
div.pic ul {margin: 0.25em 0 0; padding: 0;
  font: bold small Arial, Verdana, sans-serif;}
li.title {display: block; text-align: center;}
li.catno, li.price {display: none;}
```

FIGURE 2.10

A gallery of garden delights.

Height and Tables

A value of 190px was chosen to give enough room for the captions to be placed even if they go to three lines, but there's a potential flaw lurking there. Suppose the user resizes the text or a caption goes to five or six lines. If either happens, the layout will effectively be broken, with no real way to fix it.

This is an inescapable limitation of floated elements. In effect, every element is an island unto itself: Its dimensions are completely free of association with any other element. Put another way, the only elements in all of Web design that will size themselves to match their neighbors are table cells.

This means that there are times when a table is the best layout for a photo gallery. If you have a situation in which your captions are of unpredictable length, or if you just want each picture to occupy a box as tall as the tallest one in the row, you'll need to use a table. You can, of course, style the contents of that table using CSS and many of the techniques we've explored here.

Another situation in which using a table makes sense is if you want a certain number of images per row, no more or less. It's possible to hack the document structure to do this using CSS, of course. For example, consider this skeleton:

```
<div class="row">
  <div class="pic ls">...</div>
  <div class="pic pt">...</div>
  <div class="pic ls">...</div>
  <div class="pic ls">...</div>
</div>
```

By grouping every four pictures together, we can make sure there are ever only four pictures per row. But why would we bother, when we could just as easily use a table? The markup we just proposed is practically a table as it is. Consider this:

```
<tr>
  <td class="pic ls">...</td>
  <td class="pic pt">...</td>
  <td class="pic ls">...</td>
  <td class="pic ls">...</td>
</tr>
```

The table markup, in this case, is easier, requires fewer characters, and will easily limit the number of pictures per row. That's one of the things tables do.

Remember, though, that our original purpose was to allow the pictures to "flow," with each row containing as many images as possible, no matter how wide or narrow the window becomes. Tables can't do that, but floats can. So, as always, choose the tool most appropriate for the job and use it well.

CREATING THE CATALOG VIEW

Now that we've seen how to create flowing grids of pictures, let's consider a different approach. This time, we'll set up a vertical listing of images, next to each of which will be placed the title, catalog number, and price of the image. To do this, we'll toss out nearly all of the styles we had before and start over. The only things we'll keep are the body and footer styles, as shown in Listing 2.4. We're basically back to where we were at the beginning of the project (see Figure 2.1 for an illustration).

Tableless Table Layout!

There actually is an alternative to both floats and tables: Use the markup shown here and assign table display values to the divs. We could, for example, declare `div.row {display: table-row;}` and `div.row div {display: table-cell;}`. That would create a table-like structure out of non-table elements, and it would even work in current browsers—except, of course, in Explorer.

Listing 2.4   *Starting Nearly from Scratch*

```
body {background: #EED; margin: 1em;}
div#footer {clear: both; padding-top: 3em;
  font: 85% Verdana, sans-serif;}
```

Floating Again

To keep the layout from getting too outrageously long, we want to put the title and other information next to each image instead of beneath each one. Getting text next to an image is easy: You float the image. Except in this case, we're going to float the link that contains the image.

```
div#footer {clear: both; padding-top: 3em;
  font: 85% Verdana, sans-serif;}
div.pic a.tn {float: left;}
</style>
```

Because the link is floated, the image will come along with it, just as text will come along with a floated div. In both cases, the content gets placed into the float.

We'll also add a little styling to the divs, just a small margin and a border to help us see how the layout is progressing. The result is shown in Figure 2.11.

```
div#footer {clear: both; padding-top: 3em;
  font: 85% Verdana, sans-serif;}
div.pic {margin: 10px; padding: 0; border: 1px dotted gray;}
div.pic a.tn {float: left;}
```

FIGURE 2.11

Floating can be dangerous if you aren't careful.

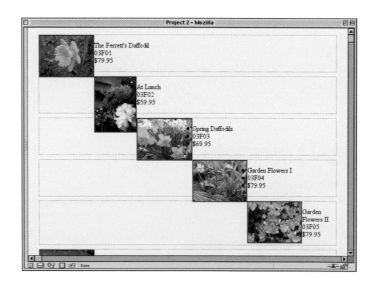

Yikes! If we'd meant to do that, then great, no problem; but that's not at *all* what we want for this layout.

What happened? Exactly what we asked to have happen. When you float something, it's removed from the normal flow, which means it doesn't participate in the height of any of its ancestors. Therefore, every div is as tall as its normal-flow content (in this case, the information list).

Furthermore, floats start from where they would fall if they were in the normal flow, and then they float to the side. In this case, we're floating left. So the second linked thumbnail started floating from the top of its div and headed to the left. Before reaching the left edge of the layout, it encountered another float (the first link), so it stopped and placed itself to the right of that other float. The same thing happened to the third, the fourth, and so on, each one floating over and stopping to the right of the link that came before it.

There are a number of ways we could fix this. If we wanted each picture's div to "stretch around" the floated links, we could also float the divs. In current browsers (and CSS2.1), a floated element will stretch to enclose any floated descendants. However, we don't actually want that here because the dotted borders are going to be removed later. They're really only for diagnostic purposes.

So, instead, we clear each div. Since the floats are all to the left, we can simply clear to the left. We'll also set the width of the divs because we'll want it to be restrained later on.

```
div.pic {margin: 10px; padding: 0; border: 1px dotted gray;
   clear: left; width: 350px;}
```

This will push each div below any leftward float that comes before it in the layout—like floated links, for example—as shown in Figure 2.12.

How's That Again?

That explanation might seem confusing; if so, try reading it slowly a few times. While you do, think about what happens if you float a bunch of images with no text near them. The same basic thing is happening here, except the text is making things more complicated.

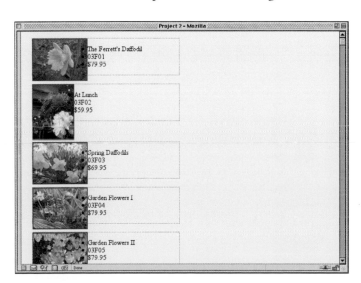

FIGURE 2.12

Clearing away the float problems.

Alignment and Placement

In looking at Figure 2.12, we can see one thing that needs to be fixed: The portrait image doesn't line up with the others. In a table, the image would probably be in its own cell, and we could just right align it, but we aren't afforded the same luxury here. Fortunately, we can just fiddle with the floated link's margin to get the effect we want. We'll just set its width to match the image it contains and set the left margin to make up the difference between its width and the width of landscape links.

```
div.pic a.tn {float: left;}
div.pt a.tn {width: 96px; margin-left: 32px;}
</style>
```

Since we've explicitly set the width of portrait links, we may as well go ahead and do it for landscape links. It won't hurt anything, and it might come in handy in the future.

```
div.pt a.tn {width: 96px; margin-left: 32px;}
div.ls a.tn {width: 128px;}
</style>
```

Since we're working on the images, let's replace those ugly blue borders with something a little less garish.

```
div.ls a.tn {width: 128px;}
a.tn img {border: 1px solid #333; border-width: 1px 2px 2px 1px;}
</style>
```

The setting of a thicker right and bottom border will lend a barely noticeable "drop shadow" effect to each image. This can be seen on some of the images in Figure 2.13.

FIGURE 2.13

Lining up and shadowing the images with borders.

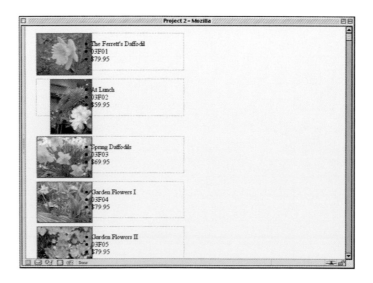

If you look closely at Figure 2.13, you'll notice two things. The first is that the text and the image borders are overlapping just a bit. That's because, thanks to the borders we just added, the images are now wider than the floating links that contain them. We should increase their widths to compensate. Actually, let's bump them up to be slightly wider than the images, just for the heck of it.

```
div.pt a.tn {width: 100px; margin-left: 32px;}
div.ls a.tn {width: 132px;}
```

The second thing you'll notice is that the list bullets are overlapping the images. This happens due to the way floats work and the way bullets are placed—and it doesn't happen in all browsers. If we wanted to keep these as a bulleted list, we might have problem, but we're going to take them away, so it's kind of irrelevant. In fact, let's do that now.

```
a.tn img {border: 1px solid #333; border-width: 1px 2px 2px 1px;}
div.pic li {list-style: none;}
</style>
```

That's good for preventing overlaps, but it still leaves the text right up against the floated links. Let's move the text over a little bit by using a combination of margins and padding. We'll add in a left border just so we can see where the list's border ends up. This will have the result shown in Figure 2.14.

```
a.tn img {border: 1px solid #333; border-width: 1px 2px 2px 1px;}
div.pic ul {margin: 0 0 0 140px; padding: 0 0 0 0.5em;
  border-left: 1px solid;}
div.pic li {list-style: none;}
```

Bullet Placement

Bullets are placed in relation to the left content edge of the list item; no matter where that edge lands, the bullet ends up a short distance away. Because the left edges of the list items are right up against the floated images, the bullets end up placed on top of the images.

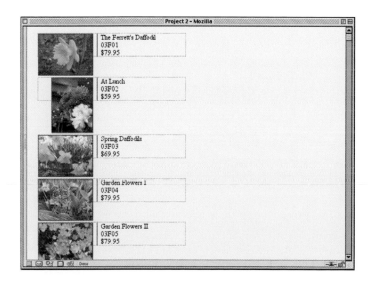

FIGURE 2.14

Margins and padding help separate the text from the linked images.

How did that work? The 140-pixel left margin is actually "sliding beneath" the floated link, extended all the way to the left edge of the `div`. If you look at the second `div` in Figure 2.14, you can see the `div` continuing on to the right of the link. In fact, that happens in all the `div`s, but only with the portrait links is it really obvious.

Improving the Listings

Now that the images and links are all lined up and the lists have been placed so that they're separated from the images a bit, let's turn our attention to the text inside those lists. The first thing we want to do is get rid of those borders since they're starting to get in the way. Thus, the `div.pic` rule should now look like this:

```
div.pic {margin: 10px; padding: 0;
  clear: left; width: 350px;}
```

Similarly, the `div.pic ul` rule should be altered to read as follows:

```
div.pic ul {margin: 0 0 0 140px; padding: 0 0 0 0.5em;}
```

With that done, let's make the titles stand out. Setting them in a bold, sans-serif font would be nice, as would a bottom border. Also, they ought to be shifted downward a bit from the top of the floated links (say, half an em).

```
div.pic li {list-style: none;}
div.pic li.title {font: bold small Arial, Verdana, sans-serif;
  padding-top: 0.5em; border-bottom: 1px solid;}
</style>
```

We've made the font size `small` here because sans-serif fonts look better when they're a little smaller than normal. Just to keep a sense of parallelism, let's make all of the list items' fonts small.

```
div.pic li {list-style: none; font-size: small;}
```

Now for the catalog number and price. These aren't as important as the title, so let's fade them into the background by using a darker shade of tan. We'll also right-align them and italicize the price to give it a little extra emphasis (see Figure 2.15).

```
div.pic li.title {font: bold small Arial, Verdana, sans-serif;
  padding-top: 0.5em; border-bottom: 1px solid;}
div.pic li.catno {color: #776; text-align: right;}
div.pic li.price {color: #776; text-align: right;
  font-style: italic;}
</style>
```

FIGURE 2.15

The text looks a lot better thanks to some alignment and color.

We could just stop here, but let's keep going. It would be kind of cool if the catalog number and price could sit side by side, wouldn't it? Well, maybe not cool, but more elegant perhaps. At any rate, let's do it. And let's do it without adding any floats to the layout.

To make this work, we're going to have to pull the price upward by the height of one line. To make *that* work, we need to make sure the line heights are equal across browsers and that the catalog number won't be in the way. First we'll regularize the list item heights by explicitly defining a `line-height` and zeroing out the margin and padding.

```
div.pic li {list-style: none; font-size: small;
  line-height: 1.2em; margin: 0; padding: 0;}
```

Now we'll move the catalog number aside. We'll do this by giving it a right margin of 4.5em.

```
div.pic li.catno {color: #776; text-align: right;
  margin-right: 4.5em;}
```

Now all we need to do is slide the price up into the space we just created for it. Remember the `line-height` value? We'll just set a negative top margin equal to that value, and the text will drop into place, as shown in Figure 2.16.

```
div.pic li.price {color: #776; text-align: right;
  font-style: italic; margin: -1.2em 0 0 0;}
```

FIGURE 2.16

Placing text next to text through the magic of margins.

⚠

Explorer Watch

Almost none of the rest of this project will work in Explorer 5.x for Windows, which doesn't understand auto margins. The first part of this section does work quite nicely in IE6, however, as long as you're in standards mode.

Boxing the Information

Let's take another step toward advanced layout by putting a vertical border to the left of the catalog number, another one between the number and price, and then enclosing the whole set of text information in a box.

To get the borders where we want them, we'll apply very similar styles to the catalog and price list items. The basic idea is to set a width for each one and then push them over as far to the right as needed. We'll do this by setting the left margin to be auto and the rest to be zero. So, for the price, we'll declare:

```
div.pic li.price {color: #776; text-align: right;
  font-style: italic; margin: -1.2em 0 0 auto;
  width: 4em; border-left: 1px solid;}
```

Then we'll replace the catalog number's `margin-right` with a `margin` declaration and give it the same width and border as we gave the price. You can see this in Figure 2.17.

```
div.pic li.catno {color: #776; text-align: right;
  margin: 0 4.5em 0 auto;
  width: 4em; border-left: 1px solid;}
```

Now to add the box around all the text information—here's where things get a little tricky. If we just add a border and background to the ul element, IE6 for Windows will get hopelessly muddled and start making elements disappear for no good reason. So, rather than confuse the poor dear, we'll just hide the offending styles from its sight. Here's how:

FIGURE 2.17

Placing borders using more margin magic.

```
div.pic ul {margin: 0 0 0 140px; padding: 0 0 0 0.5em;}
html>body div.pic ul {background: #CCB; border: 3px double #552;}
div.pic li {list-style: none; font-size: small;
  line-height: 1.2em; margin: 0; padding: 0;}
```

The first part of the selector, the `html>body` part, is what hides the rule from IE/Win. It's a child selector, which is perfectly valid CSS2 that IE/Win just doesn't understand. More capable browsers do, so they can see and apply those styles.

With the addition of the borders, we need to move the price over to the left just a bit so that it isn't right up against the double border. We'll do that with a quick change of its right margin.

```
div.pic li.price {color: #776; text-align: right;
  font-style: italic; margin: -1.2em 3px 0 auto;
  width: 4em; border-left: 1px solid;}
```

Finally, let's add some separation between each listing in our Catalog view. We have two choices: We can add a bottom margin to the floated links or to the images inside those links. Adding a top margin to the `div`s won't work because of the way `clear` is defined. To avoid a few obscure bugs in Explorer, we'll place the margin on the image.

```
a.tn img {border: 1px solid #333; border-width: 1px 2px 2px 1px;
  margin: 0 0 1em;}
```

With that, we've arrived at the style sheet shown in Listing 2.5 and illustrated in Figure 2.18.

Clear Rules

`clear` works by increasing the top margin of the cleared element until its outer top border edge is just below the bottom edge of previous floating elements. Thus, if we tried to set the top margin on the `div`s, our setting would be overridden by the clearing.

Listing 2.5 The Complete "Catalog" Style Sheet

```
body {background: #EED; margin: 1em;}
div#footer {clear: both; padding-top: 3em;
  font: 85% Verdana, sans-serif;}
div.pic {margin: 10px; padding: 0;
  clear: left; width: 350px;}
div.pic a.tn {float: left;}
div.pt a.tn {width: 100px; margin-left: 32px;}
div.ls a.tn {width: 132px;}
a.tn img {border: 1px solid #333; border-width: 1px 2px 2px 1px;
  margin: 0 0 1em;}
div.pic ul {margin: 0 0 0 140px; padding: 0 0 0 0.5em;}
html>body div.pic ul {background: #CCB; border: 3px double #552;}
div.pic li {list-style: none; font-size: small;
  line-height: 1.2em; margin: 0; padding: 0;}
div.pic li.title {font: bold small Arial, Verdana, sans-serif;
  padding-top: 0.5em; border-bottom: 1px solid;}
div.pic li.catno {color: #776; text-align: right;
  margin: 0 4.5em 0 auto;
  width: 4em; border-left: 1px solid;}
div.pic li.price {color: #776; text-align: right;
  font-style: italic; margin: -1.2em 3px 0 auto;
  width: 4em; border-left: 1px solid;}
```

FIGURE 2.18

The information presented in catalog style.

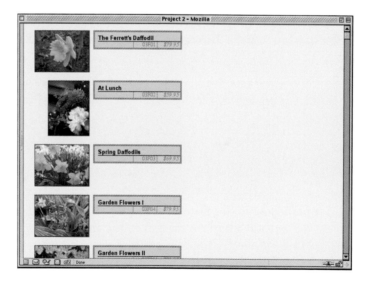

BRANCHING OUT

Try re-creating the following changes to the work in this project.

1. In the Contact Sheet view, try placing the title right below the picture, looking as if it were written onto the lower part of the slide frame. To do this, you'll need to remove the bottom margin from the images without throwing off the overall layout. Note that this will not be possible for portrait images since CSS is not able to rotate text, so you'll need to constrain your styles accordingly. Note also that long titles might flow off the slide, so a property like `overflow` might be useful.

2. In the Gallery view, add the catalog number and price back into the layout, but put them next to each other instead of one on top of the other. This will enhance the Gallery view without significantly changing the layout. Remember that a little extra height may be needed.

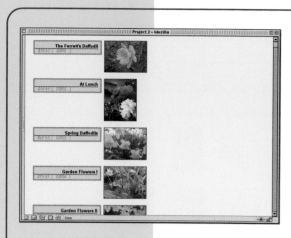

3. In the Catalog view, try flipping things around so that the picture is on the right and all of the textual information is on the left. This will mean more than changing the float's direction: You will also need to adjust the layout of the list items.

3

STYLING A FINANCIAL REPORT

The genius of capitalism consists precisely in its lack of morality. Unless he is rich enough to hire his own choir, a capitalist is a fellow who, by definition, can ill afford to believe in anything other than the doctrine of the bottom line.

—LEWIS H. LAPHAM

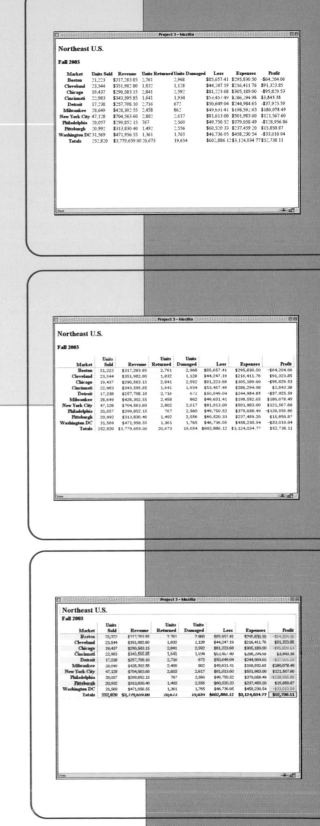

ALTHOUGH WE'RE USED TO THINKING of the Web as a collection of personal sites, e-commerce powerhouses, fringe groups, and nuggets of information, there's a lot more going on—albeit not all in the public eye. Corporate intranets, for example, are often awash in HTML-based information ranging from employee portals to Webmail interfaces and beyond.

Although an entire book could be devoted to exploring how just a sampling of this information could be styled, it will be sufficient here to examine one type of information that tends to be particular to corporate sites: a financial report showing profit and loss in a number of markets in a given quarter. We won't be seeking to replace the table markup with `div`s and CSS—that would be silly. Since we have a table of data, it will be contained in table markup. What we'll do is add useful hooks to the structure and use those to style the table and its contents.

Project Goals

Our goal for this project is to take a table of financial information and style it for both screen and print output while adding as little as possible to the markup. We'll accomplish this mainly by adding class and ID hooks to the elements already in place.

For this project, upper management has given us a detailed set of design goals:

◆ The Totals row at the bottom of the report should stand out visually, preferably by boldfacing the figures.

◆ The labels (both across the top of the report and down the side) should be right-justified and should be separated from the figures by gray lines. The top labels should be separated by gray vertical lines.

◆ In a browser, each line of the report should be separated from the others by a light gray line. In print, every other row should have a light gray background, and columns should be separated by light gray vertical lines.

◆ Any negative number should appear as red with a yellow background in a Web browser and as italicized in print.

◆ The profits (in the rightmost column) need to be visually highlighted in some fashion.

◆ All dollar amounts should line up at the decimal point, and all others should have their thousands-separator commas line up.

In addition, we've been given the vague (but useful) directive to "make things look good." So, with those goals in mind, let's get things underway.

Preparation

Download the files for Project 3 from this book's Web site. If you're planning to play along at home, load the file ch03proj.html into the editing program of your choice. This is the file you'll be editing, saving, and reloading as the project progresses.

See the Introduction for instructions on how to download files from the Web site.

Styling for the Screen

Since all of the users will be accessing the reports via a Web browser, we'll start by creating screen styles. During this phase, we'll leave aside the print-style design goals and just focus on what will be put onto the monitor.

Laying the Foundations

As the basis for our work, we'll be using a report table that's been created for us by the database guys. Its markup is, as we requested earlier, as simple and unadorned as possible. The first few rows of the table are shown in Listing 3.1, and the whole table in its default rendering is shown in Figure 3.1.

Listing 3.1 The Table's Beginning

```
<table cellspacing="0" summary="Q3 Financial Results">
<thead>
<tr>
<th>Market</th>
<th>Units Sold</th>
<th>Revenue</th>
<th>Units Returned</th>
<th>Units Damaged</th>
<th>Loss</th>
<th>Expenses</th>
<th>Profit</th>
</tr>
</thead>
<tr>
<th>Boston</th>
<td>21,223</td>
<td>$317,283.85</td>
<td>2,761</td>
<td>2,968</td>
<td>$85,657.41</td>
<td>$295,830.50</td>
<td>-$64,204.06</td>
</tr>
<tr>
<th>Cleveland</th>
<td>23,544</td>
<td>$351,902.80</td>
<td>1,832</td>
<td>1,128</td>
<td>$44,247.19</td>
<td>$216,411.76</td>
<td>$91,323.85</td>
</tr>
```

Cell Spacing

Note the presence of the HTML attribute `cellspacing`. The CSS2 way to enforce separation between table cells is to use the property `border-spacing` in conjunction with the proper value for the property `border-collapse`, but support for that approach is pretty bad, so we've left in `cellspacing`. It's still valid HTML (and even valid XHTML), so no worries.

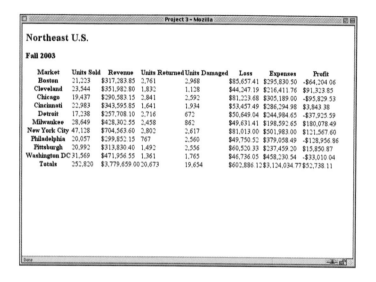

Northeast U.S.							
Fall 2003							
Market	Units Sold	Revenue	Units Returned	Units Damaged	Loss	Expenses	Profit
Boston	21,223	$317,283.85	2,761	2,968	$85,657.41	$295,830.50	-$64,204.06
Cleveland	23,544	$351,982.80	1,832	1,128	$44,247.19	$216,411.76	$91,323.85
Chicago	19,437	$290,583.15	2,841	2,592	$81,223.68	$305,189.00	-$95,829.53
Cincinnati	22,983	$343,595.85	1,641	1,934	$53,457.49	$286,294.98	$3,843.38
Detroit	17,238	$257,708.10	2,716	672	$50,649.04	$244,984.65	-$37,925.59
Milwaukee	28,649	$428,302.55	2,458	862	$49,631.41	$198,592.65	$180,078.49
New York City	47,128	$704,563.60	2,802	2,617	$81,013.00	$501,983.00	$121,567.60
Philadelphia	20,057	$299,852.15	767	2,560	$49,750.52	$379,058.49	-$128,956.86
Pittsburgh	20,992	$313,830.40	1,492	2,556	$60,520.33	$237,459.20	$15,850.87
Washington DC	31,569	$471,956.55	1,361	1,765	$46,736.05	$458,230.54	-$33,010.04
Totals	252,820	$3,779,659.00	20,673	19,654	$602,886.12	$3,124,034.77	$52,738.11

The first thing to note is that the th elements all have their contents boldfaced and centered. This is the browser's default rendering for th elements, and it can be represented like this:

```
th {font-weight: bold; text-align: center;}
```

In fact, many browsers on the market (such as those based on Mozilla) come with a default style sheet that probably contains a rule very much like this one. We'll have to override these default styles to meet our design goals.

The second thing to note is that we have th elements that are supposed to be styled differently but that don't appear to have anything that distinguishes them. So we'll have to take steps to make sure we can tell which th elements have which role and style them accordingly.

Finally, we have h2 and h3 elements that come before the table. We'll actually put off styling these until the table's done. That way, we can make sure whatever heading styles we end up writing will fit in with the table's layout.

Baseline Styles

Given our design goals, we can do a few things that will apply to all cells in the table, whether they're headers or data. For example, there's the directive that all labels (contained here in the th elements) should be right-justified. Then there's the requirement that the figures line up. These can both be covered, at least to some degree, by right-aligning everything.

```
<style type="text/css" media="screen">
th, td {text-align: right;}
</style>
```

This will get us most of the way there but not all the way. For the figures themselves, the periods and commas won't quite line up unless we use an appropriate font. That's because in a proportional font, like Times, each number can be a slightly different width than the others. Unless we convert them to a font that has the same width for every number, the dots and commas won't be in quite the same place. We could pick any monospace font for this, but we'll turn to the ever-popular Verdana instead, because its number glyphs are all the same width—something that isn't true of every sans-serif font. Just in case the user doesn't have Verdana available, we'll list some monospace alternatives.

```
<style type="text/css" media="screen">
th, td {text-align: right;}
td {font: smaller Verdana, "Andale Mono", Courier, "Courier New",
  monospace;}
</style>
```

We've made the font's size `small` because monospace and sans-serif fonts tend to look bigger to the human eye than serif fonts. By setting the size to be smaller, we've counteracted that effect.

The final step in our "global" styles is to add a little bit of padding to the sides of the cells. This will keep long numbers from crowding too close to their neighbors.

```
th, td {text-align: right; padding: 0 0.5em;}
```

Finally, let's set the row-separator lines at this stage. We'll actually apply a bottom border to all cells and override it where we need to later on.

```
th, td {text-align: right; padding: 0 0.5em;
  border-bottom: 1px solid #DDD;}
```

As we can see in Figure 3.2, the numbers are beginning to line up into columns rather nicely, and lines separate all the rows.

A few things will need to be fixed: Some of the rows are taller than others because of long city names, for example.

Character Alignment

Although CSS2 introduced the ability to align text to a character, this isn't yet supported by Web browsers, so we'll have to ignore it. This is a real shame because we could get the alignment we want with a declaration like `text-align: "."`, thus causing the numbers to align the decimals.

FIGURE 3.2

Laying the foundations.

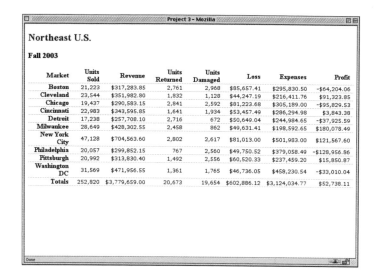

Northeast U.S.

Fall 2003

Market	Units Sold	Revenue	Units Returned	Units Damaged	Loss	Expenses	Profit
Boston	21,223	$317,283.85	2,761	2,968	$85,657.41	$295,830.50	-$64,204.06
Cleveland	23,544	$351,982.80	1,832	1,128	$44,247.19	$216,411.76	$91,323.85
Chicago	19,437	$290,583.15	2,841	2,592	$81,223.68	$305,189.00	-$95,829.53
Cincinnati	22,983	$343,595.85	1,641	1,934	$53,457.49	$286,294.98	$3,843.38
Detroit	17,238	$257,708.10	2,716	672	$50,649.04	$244,984.65	-$37,925.59
Milwaukee	28,649	$428,302.55	2,458	862	$49,631.41	$198,592.65	$180,078.49
New York City	47,128	$704,563.60	2,802	2,617	$81,013.00	$501,983.00	$121,567.60
Philadelphia	20,057	$299,852.15	767	2,560	$49,750.52	$379,058.49	-$128,956.86
Pittsburgh	20,992	$313,830.40	1,492	2,556	$60,520.33	$237,459.20	$15,850.87
Washington DC	31,569	$471,956.55	1,361	1,765	$46,736.05	$458,230.54	-$33,010.04
Totals	252,820	$3,779,659.00	20,673	19,654	$602,886.12	$3,124,034.77	$52,738.11

Tackling the Table Labels

Let's turn our attention to the column headings across the top of the table. We know that these will end up being styled differently than the row headings down the left side. To be able to distinguish the one set of `th` elements from the other set, we'll make use of the `thead` element that encloses the table's head row.

Doing this will allow us to target styles directly at these cells, and no others.

▶▶ **OTHER APPROACHES**

Actually, there are other things about the "top labels" that are structurally unique. For example, they are `th` elements that descend from a table row that is first `tr` child of the `thead` element. We could theoretically use the CSS2 `:first-child` pseudo-class to select them. It would look something like this:

```
tr:first-child th {...styles for "top labels" here...}
th {...styles for other 'th' elements here...}
```

The problem is that `:first-child` isn't supported by Internet Explorer 6, which sort of limits its usefulness. It really makes more sense to use `thead` anyway, since it's there. But in cases in which the intranet browser is Mozilla or a cousin, the `:first-child` pseudo-class could be used.

First let's vertically align the text of the column heads. These headings are usually bottom-aligned.

```
td {font: smaller Verdana, "Andale Mono", Courier, "Courier New",
  monospace;}
thead th {vertical-align: bottom;}
</style>
```

We also need to add vertical lines to separate the column heads and a gray border to separate these headings from the figures in the data cells.

```
thead th {vertical-align: bottom; border: 1px solid gray;
  border-width: 0 1px 1px 0;}
```

Because the selector thead th has a higher specificity than the selector th, the border styles from this rule will win out over those we created earlier using the following rule:

```
th, td {text-align: right; padding: 0 0.5em;
  border-bottom: 1px solid #DDD;}
```

Now we can take similar steps with the left-side labels. For these, we actually only want a gray line that separates the row headings from the data cells. That's simple enough, as Figure 3.3 illustrates.

```
thead th {vertical-align: bottom; border: 1px solid gray;
  border-width: 0 1px 1px 0;}
th {border-right: 1px solid gray;}
</style>
```

Vertical Variance

Note that vertical-align only acts this way when applied to table cells. For all other elements, it has very different effects because for non-table elements it's used to control how far an element is raised or lowered with respect to the normal baseline.

What's Specificity?

Specificity is the weight that CSS assigns to a given selector. A part of the cascade, specificity helps browsers figure out which styles should be used when two rules conflict. See section 6.4 of the CSS2.1 specification (http://www.w3.org/TR/CSS21) for details.

FIGURE 3.3

Visually separating the column and row headings.

Northeast U.S.

Fall 2003

Market	Units Sold	Revenue	Units Returned	Units Damaged	Loss	Expenses	Profit
Boston	21,223	$317,283.85	2,761	2,968	$85,657.41	$295,830.50	-$64,204.06
Cleveland	23,544	$351,982.80	1,832	1,128	$44,247.19	$216,411.76	$91,323.85
Chicago	19,437	$290,583.15	2,841	2,592	$81,223.68	$305,189.00	-$95,829.53
Cincinnati	22,983	$343,595.85	1,641	1,934	$53,457.49	$286,294.98	$3,843.38
Detroit	17,238	$257,708.10	2,716	672	$50,649.04	$244,984.65	-$37,925.59
Milwaukee	28,649	$428,302.55	2,458	862	$49,631.41	$198,592.65	$180,078.49
New York City	47,128	$704,563.60	2,802	2,617	$81,013.00	$501,983.00	$121,567.60
Philadelphia	20,057	$299,852.15	767	2,560	$49,750.52	$379,058.49	-$128,956.86
Pittsburgh	20,992	$313,830.40	1,492	2,556	$60,520.33	$237,459.20	$15,850.87
Washington DC	31,569	$471,956.55	1,361	1,765	$46,736.05	$458,230.54	-$33,010.04
Totals	252,820	$3,779,659.00	20,673	19,654	$602,886.12	$3,124,034.77	$52,738.11

There are just a couple more things we can do to clean up the layout. Note that two of the rows are taller than the others, thanks to the row headings wrapping to two lines. If we prevent this wrapping, it will make all of the rows the same height. While we're at it, let's de-emphasize the borders between the row headings by making the border less solid.

```
th {border-right: 1px solid gray; border-bottom-style: dotted;
   white-space: nowrap;}
```

Having done this, the th elements will not wrap, and that's a problem because it means that all the th elements won't wrap, including the column heads. If we do that, some of the columns will become much too wide, so we counteract the effect for the column heads by updating its styles.

```
thead th {vertical-align: bottom; border: 1px solid gray;
   border-width: 0 1px 1px 0;
   white-space: normal;}
```

This will override the nowrap value from the th rule and will thus allow the column head text to wrap, as we can see in Figure 3.4.

FIGURE 3.4

Getting consistent row height through wrap prevention.

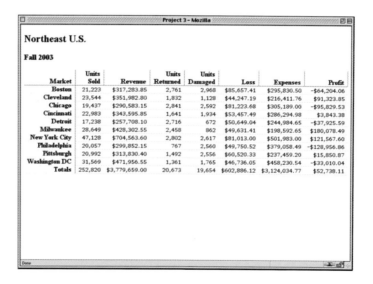

Profit Styles

Now that we've dealt with the leftmost column, let's work on the rightmost one. Remember that we have a design goal of visually highlighting the profit figures, even though there's no specific guidance as to what kind of highlighting we should use.

Here's the basic problem: We have no way, as the markup now stands, to style the profits differently than any of the other data cells. Let's look at a row of figures:

```
<tr>
<th>Cleveland</th>
<td>23,544</td>
<td>$351,982.80</td>
<td>1,832</td>
<td>1,128</td>
<td>$44,247.19</td>
<td>$216,411.76</td>
<td>$91,323.05</td>
</tr>
```

Each cell looks like every other from a markup point of view, so we have to arrange for a way to tell the profit cells apart from the others. This should do the trick:

```
<td class="profit">$91,323.85</td>
```

This has to be done for every profit-column cell, including the th element in the column-heads row. Once these cells all share a class, they can be styled together.

This is necessary because HTML tables don't actually contain columns; they only contain rows and cells. The columns are, at best, implied effects that arise from the way the cells in each row line up with each other. Thus, because all the rows in our report table have the same number of cells, the last cell in each row appears to share a column with all the other last cells. From a purely structural point of view, however, there is no column to style.

Since we've been given a blank check, so to speak, regarding how to highlight the profit figures, let's give them a green background and separate them with white lines. This will create an interesting "punch-out" effect with regard to the row separators, as we can see in Figure 3.5.

```
th {border-right: 1px solid gray; border-bottom-style: dotted;
  white-space: nowrap;}
td.profit {background: #CEC; border-bottom-color: white;}
</style>
```

HTML Columns

As some readers are no doubt aware, HTML and XHTML do contain column-related elements such as col and colgroup. We've chosen to ignore these because they're difficult to style consistently and because there is some disagreement as to how columns should be styled in any case. Although it's clumsier, it's generally easier to class cells as we've done here if you want to do column-oriented styling.

FIGURE 3.5

Highlighting our profit figures.

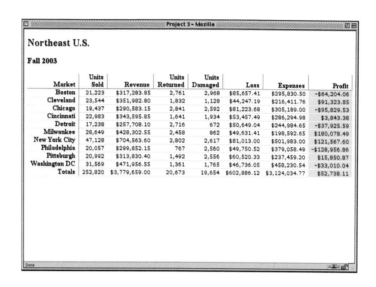

Northeast U.S.

Fall 2003

Market	Units Sold	Revenue	Units Returned	Units Damaged	Loss	Expenses	Profit
Boston	21,223	$317,283.85	2,761	2,968	$85,657.41	$295,830.50	-$64,204.06
Cleveland	23,544	$351,982.80	1,832	1,128	$44,247.19	$216,411.76	$91,323.85
Chicago	19,437	$290,583.15	2,841	2,592	$81,223.68	$305,189.00	-$95,829.53
Cincinnati	22,983	$343,595.85	1,641	1,934	$53,457.49	$286,294.98	$3,843.38
Detroit	17,238	$257,708.10	2,716	672	$50,649.04	$244,984.65	-$37,925.59
Milwaukee	28,649	$428,302.55	2,458	862	$49,631.41	$198,592.65	$180,078.49
New York City	47,128	$704,563.60	2,802	2,617	$81,013.00	$501,983.00	$121,567.60
Philadelphia	20,057	$299,852.15	767	2,560	$49,750.52	$379,058.49	-$128,956.86
Pittsburgh	20,992	$313,830.40	1,492	2,556	$60,520.33	$237,459.20	$15,850.87
Washington DC	31,569	$471,956.55	1,361	1,765	$46,736.05	$458,230.54	-$33,010.04
Totals	252,820	$3,779,659.00	20,673	19,654	$602,886.12	$3,124,034.77	$52,738.11

Accentuating the Negatives

Now we need to bring attention to the down side of business: the negative profit figures (otherwise known as deficits). We've been told that they have to be red on yellow, but once again, we're faced with the problem of distinguishing the cells containing negative figures from those that don't. Here's one such cell:

```
<td class="profit">-$64,204.06</td>
```

We don't have any way to tell, other than with our own eyes, whether the contents of the cell represent a positive or negative amount. CSS, by its nature, is concerned with styling content based on structure. It doesn't have the capability to style content based on the content itself. So we'll need to add information to the structure itself. Let's do that by adding a neg class to any negative number.

```
<td class="profit neg">-$64,204.06</td>
```

Here we're taking advantage of the nature of HTML class values, which are defined to be a space-separated list of one or more words. Even better, we can target each word separately from the others. Thus, we can add a rule that will style any cell with a neg class whether or not it has any other classes.

```
td.profit {background: #CEC; border-bottom-color: white;}
td.neg {background: #FF3; color: red;}
</style>
```

This will apply the foreground and background colors we want without overriding any other styles. Note in Figure 3.6 that the negative-figure cells still have a white bottom border. That's coming in from the td.profit rule.

FIGURE 3.6

Drawing attention to our deficits.

Northeast U.S.

Fall 2003

Market	Units Sold	Revenue	Units Returned	Units Damaged	Loss	Expenses	Profit
Boston	21,223	$317,283.85	2,761	2,968	$85,657.41	$295,830.50	-$64,204.06
Cleveland	23,544	$351,982.80	1,832	1,128	$44,247.19	$216,411.76	$91,323.85
Chicago	19,437	$290,503.15	2,841	2,592	$81,223.68	$305,189.00	-$95,829.53
Cincinnati	22,983	$343,595.85	1,641	1,934	$53,457.49	$286,294.98	$3,843.38
Detroit	17,238	$257,708.10	2,716	672	$50,649.04	$244,984.65	-$37,925.59
Milwaukee	28,649	$428,302.55	2,458	862	$49,631.41	$198,592.65	$180,078.49
New York City	47,128	$704,563.60	2,802	2,617	$81,013.00	$501,983.00	$121,567.60
Philadelphia	20,057	$299,852.15	767	2,560	$49,750.52	$379,058.49	-$128,956.86
Pittsburgh	20,992	$313,830.40	1,492	2,556	$60,520.33	$237,459.20	$15,850.87
Washington DC	31,569	$471,956.55	1,361	1,765	$46,736.05	$458,230.54	-$33,010.04
Totals	252,820	$3,779,659.00	20,673	19,654	$602,886.12	$3,124,034.77	$52,738.11

In theory, we could create rules that only apply to elements with two or more `class` words. For example, we might want to style any element that has class values of both `profit` and `neg` like this:

```
td.neg.profit {font-weight: bold;}
```

Internet Explorer doesn't handle this syntax very well, so it tends not to be used very often. The styles we used to create Figure 3.6, on the other hand, are supported by Explorer as well as every other modern browser.

Total Styles

Our last major screen-styling goal is to make the totals visually distinct through boldfacing. To do this, we'll class the row that contains the totals.

```
<tr class="totals">
```

Now boldfacing the cell contents is a trivially simple matter.

```
td.neg {background: #FF3; color: red;}
tr.totals td {font-weight: bold;}
</style>
```

To give the table an extra touch, let's set a solid gray bottom border on the cells and solidify the bottom border on the row heading.

```
tr.totals td {font-weight: bold; border-bottom: 1px solid gray;}
tr.totals th {border-bottom-style: solid;}
</style>
```

Table Footers

It's also the case that we could enclose the last row in a `tfoot` element, similar to the way the first row was enclosed in a `thead`. We're going with a `class` in this case to illustrate a way of using row and cell classes together.

Finally, we'll put a box around the total profit figure since it's probably the part about which people care the most.

```
tr.totals td {font-weight: bold; border-bottom: 1px solid gray;}
tr.totals td.profit {border: 1px solid black;}
tr.totals th {border-bottom-style: solid;}
```

The result of all these changes is shown in Figure 3.7.

FIGURE 3.7

Bringing style to our totals.

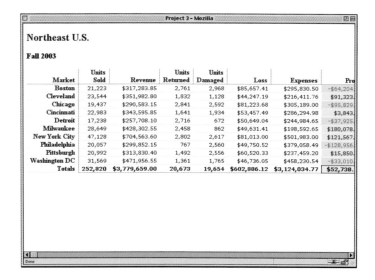

This does expose one potential problem with our layout: If the table gets too wide, it will force a horizontal scrollbar. Of course, that's been true of tables since the day they were introduced into the Netscape 1.x line, so it isn't exactly new. With CSS, we have ways to deal with this situation. Some ideas include:

◆ Try setting an explicit width for the td elements and hope that it will be enough to contain the data but not so much that it forces a scrollbar. This probably isn't any better than just letting the table lay itself out automatically.

◆ Reduce the font size of the entire table. This has the potential to shrink text to a point that makes it impossible to read, but if we're careful, it should be easy to keep things legible and still small.

◆ Reduce the amount of space between the numbers. They look kind of spread out anyway.

Let's try the last one. We'll introduce a new rule that applies to all the data cells.

```
th {border-right: 1px solid gray; border-bottom-style: dotted;
  white-space: nowrap;}
td {letter-spacing: -1px;}
td.profit {background: #CEC; border-bottom-color: white;}
```

We could take similar steps for the column and row headings, but we'll hold off for now.

Finishing Touches

There are a few more things we can do to make the report look better. First, we can put a gray border along the right side of the Profit column.

```
td.profit {background: #CEC; border-bottom-color: white;
  border-right: 1px solid gray;}
```

Now let's turn our attention to the h2 and h3 elements that come before the table itself. It would be interesting to have a line extend up from the right side of the table and wend its way between the report title and its date, so we'll do that. We can start by giving both headings a border and stripping off their margins. The result is shown in Figure 3.8.

```
<style type="text/css">
h2, h3 {margin: 0; border: 1px solid gray;}
th, td {text-align: right; padding: 0 0.5em;
  border-bottom: 1px solid #DDD;}
```

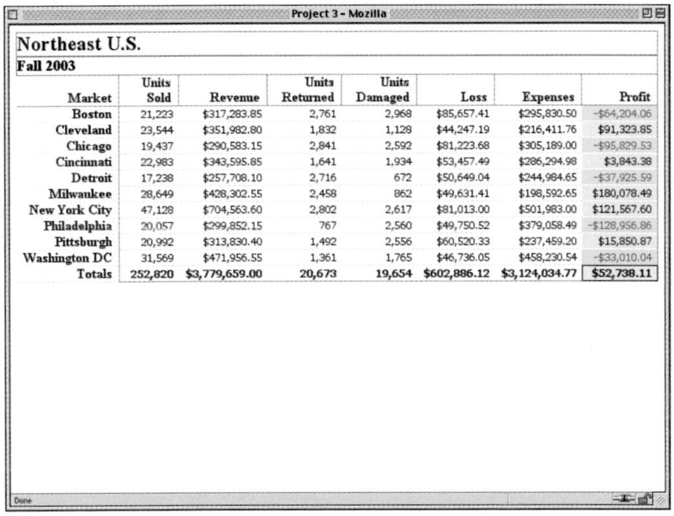

FIGURE 3.8

The beginning of style for the table headings.

Obviously, we don't want to leave things this way, so we'll add another rule to take away all of the h2 borders except for the left one, and we'll throw in some left padding while we're at it.

```
h2, h3 {margin: 0; border: 1px solid gray;}
h2 {border-width: 0 0 0 1px; padding: 0 0 0 0.25em}
th, td {text-align: right; padding: 0 0.5em;
  border-bottom: 1px solid #DDD;}
```

Now all we have to do is put a top and right border on the h3 and give it a little padding.

```
h2 {border-width: 0 0 0 1px; padding: 0 0 0 0.25em}
h3 {border-width: 1px 1px 0 0; padding: 0.1em 0.33em;}
th, td {text-align: right; padding: 0 0.5em;
  border-bottom: 1px solid #DDD;}
```

Because there is no separation between the h3 and the table (because neither has a margin), the right-side border on the h3 will line up with the right-hand border on the last th element in the table's first row. Similarly, the top border of the h3 and the left border of the h2 will come together to create the illusion of a continual line, as we can see in Figure 3.9.

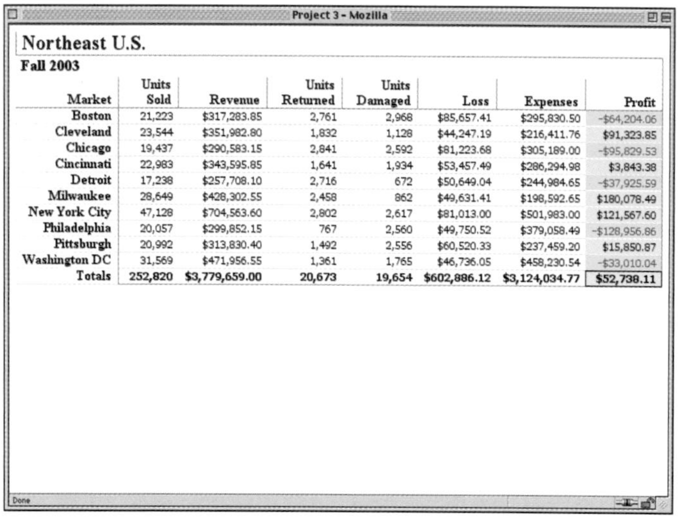

FIGURE 3.9

Visually integrating the headings with the table.

Northeast U.S.								
Fall 2003								
Market	Units Sold	Revenue	Units Returned	Units Damaged	Loss	Expenses	Profit	
Boston	21,223	$317,283.85	2,761	2,968	$85,657.41	$295,830.50	-$64,204.06	
Cleveland	23,544	$351,982.80	1,832	1,128	$44,247.19	$216,411.76	$91,323.85	
Chicago	19,437	$290,583.15	2,841	2,592	$81,223.68	$305,189.00	-$95,829.53	
Cincinnati	22,983	$343,595.85	1,641	1,934	$53,457.49	$286,294.98	$3,843.38	
Detroit	17,238	$257,708.10	2,716	672	$50,649.04	$244,984.65	-$37,925.59	
Milwaukee	28,649	$428,302.55	2,458	862	$49,631.41	$198,592.65	$180,078.49	
New York City	47,128	$704,563.60	2,802	2,617	$81,013.00	$501,983.00	$121,567.60	
Philadelphia	20,057	$299,852.15	767	2,560	$49,750.52	$379,058.49	-$128,956.86	
Pittsburgh	20,992	$313,830.40	1,492	2,556	$60,520.33	$237,459.20	$15,850.87	
Washington DC	31,569	$471,956.55	1,361	1,765	$46,736.05	$458,230.54	-$33,010.04	
Totals	252,820	$3,779,659.00	20,673	19,654	$602,886.12	$3,124,034.77	$52,738.11	

If the threading effect seems undesirable, we could simply remove the border from the h2 element and only put borders on the h3. Also, in order to keep the borders together at wider window widths, we need to add one little rule.

```
h3 {border-width: 1px 1px 0 0; padding: 0.1em 0.33em;}
table {width: 100%;}
th, td {text-align: right; padding: 0 0.5em;
```

With that last addition, the style sheet we've created is provided in Listing 3.2.

Listing 3.2   The Complete Style Sheet

```
h2, h3 {margin: 0; border: 1px solid gray;}
h2 {border-width: 0 0 0 1px; padding: 0 0 0 0.25em}
h3 {border-width: 1px 1px 0 0; padding: 0.1em 0.33em;}
table {width: 100%;}
th, td {text-align: right; padding: 0 0.5em;
  border-bottom: 1px solid #DDD;}
td {font: small Verdana, "Andale Mono", Courier, "Courier New",
  monospace;}
```

```
thead th {vertical-align: bottom; border: 1px solid gray;
  border-width: 0 1px 1px 0;
  white-space: normal;}
th {border-right: 1px solid gray; border-bottom-style: dotted;
  white-space: nowrap;}
td {letter-spacing: -1px;}
td.profit {background: #CEC; border-bottom-color: white;
  border-right: 1px solid gray;}
td.neg {background: #FF3; color: red;}
tr.totals td {font-weight: bold; border-bottom: 1px solid gray;}
tr.totals td.profit {border: 1px solid black;}
tr.totals th {border-bottom-style: solid;}
```

STYLING FOR PRINT

Now that we've created a style sheet for the screen, it's time to turn our attention to the print styles defined in the project goals. The goals specifically related to print are as follows:

◆ In print, every other row should have a light gray background, and light gray vertical lines should separate columns.

◆ Any negative number should be italicized in print.

These are in addition to the other project goals, but those have already been satisfied by the style sheet we've written. All we really need to do is override and adjust styles to optimize them for print.

Starting Out

The first thing to do is set up a second style sheet. Although it's eventually intended for print styling, this is what we'll add after the previous style sheet:

```
</style>
<style type="text/css" media="screen">

</style>
</head>
```

The attribute media="screen" is there because we'll be using a Web browser to preview our changes. When we're all done, screen will be changed to print and— hey presto!—a print style sheet.

The other thing we need to do is modify the markup a little bit more so that we can accomplish the alternate-row highlighting called for in the project goals. As of this writing, browsers didn't make it possible to accomplish such things with CSS alone, so we'll need to add some classes to our markup. To be as flexible as possible, we'll use the classes even and odd. Thus, the table will generally have the basic structure shown in Listing 3.3. (The cells were removed from the rows for the sake of brevity.)

A Better Way

CSS3 does define an easy way to select alternate rows (or really any pattern in a series of elements) using the pseudo-class :nth-child(). As of this writing, it was almost completely unsupported, so classes are the best way to accomplish effects such as these.

Listing 3.3 Basic Table Structure

```
<table cellspacing="0">
<thead>
<tr>...</tr>
</thead>
<tbody>
<tr class="odd">...</tr>
<tr class="even">...</tr>
<tr class="odd">...</tr>
<tr class="even">...</tr>
<tr class="odd">...</tr>
<tr class="even">...</tr>
<tr class="odd">...</tr>
<tr class="even">...</tr>
<tr class="odd">...</tr>
<tr class="even">...</tr>
<tr class="totals">...</tr>
</tbody>
</table>
```

Row Highlighting

Now that we've appropriately classed all the rows (remember that the first row is row 1, and 1 is an odd number), we can go ahead and highlight every other row. We'll choose to highlight the odd rows, as shown in Figure 3.10.

```
<style type="text/css" media="screen">
tr.odd {background: #EEE;}
</style>
```

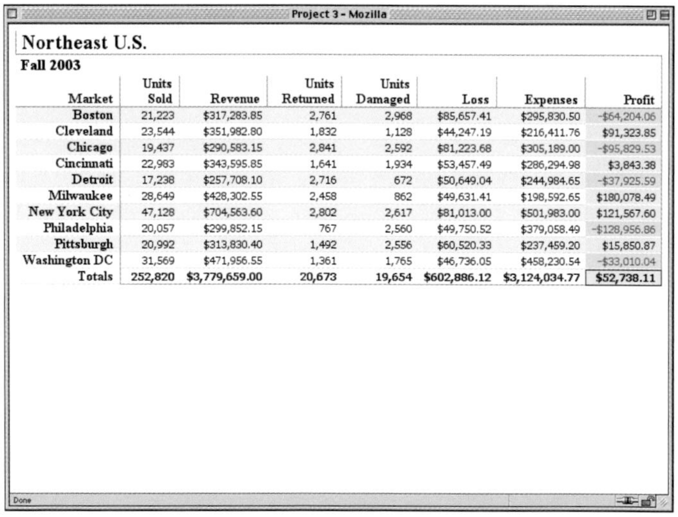
Project 3 - Mozilla
Northeast U.S.
Fall 2003
Done

Market	Units Sold	Revenue	Units Returned	Units Damaged	Loss	Expenses	Profit
Boston	21,223	$317,283.85	2,761	2,968	$85,657.41	$295,830.50	-$64,204.06
Cleveland	23,544	$351,982.80	1,832	1,128	$44,247.19	$216,411.76	$91,323.85
Chicago	19,437	$290,583.15	2,841	2,592	$81,223.68	$305,189.00	-$95,829.53
Cincinnati	22,983	$343,595.85	1,641	1,934	$53,457.49	$286,294.98	$3,843.38
Detroit	17,238	$257,708.10	2,716	672	$50,649.04	$244,984.65	-$37,925.59
Milwaukee	28,649	$428,302.55	2,458	862	$49,631.41	$198,592.65	$180,078.49
New York City	47,128	$704,563.60	2,802	2,617	$81,013.00	$501,983.00	$121,567.60
Philadelphia	20,057	$299,852.15	767	2,560	$49,750.52	$379,058.49	-$128,956.86
Pittsburgh	20,992	$313,830.40	1,492	2,556	$60,520.33	$237,459.20	$15,850.87
Washington DC	31,569	$471,956.55	1,361	1,765	$46,736.05	$458,230.54	-$33,010.04
Totals	252,820	$3,779,659.00	20,673	19,654	$602,886.12	$3,124,034.77	$52,738.11

FIGURE 3.10

Alternate-row highlighting via even and odd classes.

Pretty nifty, but there's a problem. The profit figures aren't taking on the high-lighting style, and we want them to do so. We could change the selector from `tr.odd` to `tr.odd td`, and that would get the profit cells to take on the highlight in odd rows. Since the city names are actually in `th` elements, though, they would lose the highlight effect. So we'll use a universal selector to select both.

```
table tr.odd * {background: #EEE;}
```

These simple little changes mean that *all* elements descended from a `tr` with a `class` containing the word `odd` that's descended from a `table` element will be selected and thus given a background color of #EEE. Both the `th` and `td` elements are descended from the `odd` rows, so both will be directly selected.

This means, however, that the profit cells in the even rows are still being given a green background (from the rule in our first style sheet). We need to override that, with the result shown in Figure 3.11.

```
table tr.odd * {background: #EEE;}
td.profit, td.neg {color: #000; background: #FFF;}
</style>
```

We've managed to remove the background and foreground colors from the profit and negative figures, but a close look at Figure 3.11 reveals another problem. The bottom border of each cell in the Profit column is white, whereas the bottom border of regular cells is still light gray. This made sense when the profit cells had background colors, but now it looks kind of ugly.

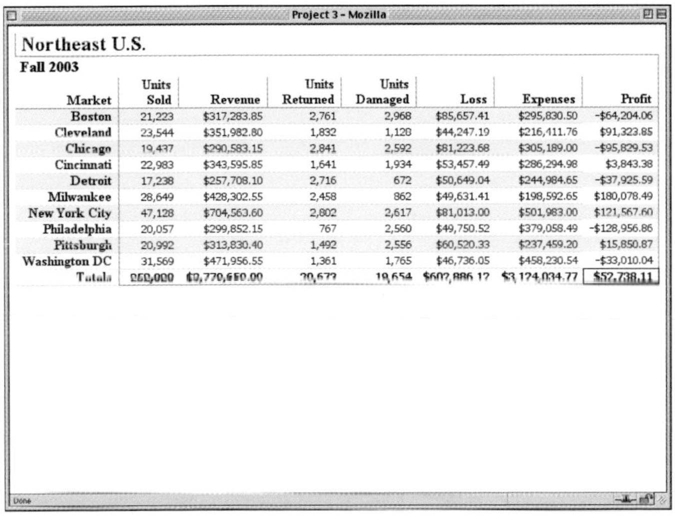

Northeast U.S.

Fall 2003

Market	Units Sold	Revenue	Units Returned	Units Damaged	Loss	Expenses	Profit
Boston	21,223	$317,283.85	2,761	2,968	$85,657.41	$295,830.50	-$64,204.06
Cleveland	23,544	$351,982.80	1,832	1,128	$44,247.19	$216,411.76	$91,323.85
Chicago	19,437	$290,583.15	2,841	2,592	$81,223.68	$305,189.00	-$95,829.53
Cincinnati	22,983	$343,595.85	1,641	1,934	$53,457.49	$286,294.98	$3,843.38
Detroit	17,238	$257,708.10	2,716	672	$50,649.04	$244,984.65	-$37,925.59
Milwaukee	28,649	$428,302.55	2,458	862	$49,631.41	$198,592.65	$180,078.49
New York City	47,128	$704,563.60	2,802	2,617	$81,013.00	$501,983.00	$121,567.60
Philadelphia	20,057	$299,852.15	767	2,560	$49,750.52	$379,058.49	-$128,956.86
Pittsburgh	20,992	$313,830.40	1,492	2,556	$60,520.33	$237,459.20	$15,850.87
Washington DC	31,569	$471,956.55	1,361	1,765	$46,736.05	$458,230.54	-$33,010.04
Totals	260,000	$9,770,650.00	20,672	19,654	$602,886.12	$3,124,034.77	$57,738.11

Being More Specific

We used the construction `table tr.odd *` because, by adding the `table`, we've ensured that this selector has more specificity than the selectors `td.profit` and `td.neg`, which appear in the all-media style sheet we wrote earlier in the project and which apply in print as well as onscreen. If we'd left off `table`, the selectors in the all-media style sheet would have the same specificity as the one we're writing now for print. When selectors have equal specificity, meaning that the last one declared wins, if the style sheet were ever reversed, the presentation would change. By making sure the print declaration is more specific, we make it sure it will always win and is therefore more robust.

FIGURE 3.11

Extending row highlighting and removing color highlights.

Background Printing

Even if you define a back-ground color to be printed, there is no guarantee that it actually will be. Most browsers come preconfig-ured to not print back-grounds, largely as a way to save on ink or toner. The user can change this configuration to enable printing of element back-grounds, but you as the author cannot.

Because we have the alternate rows highlighted, we have the option to remove the borders between rows altogether, but instead we'll make them consistent with the highlight color used for alternate rows.

```
table tr.odd * {background: #EEE;}
tr.odd *, tr.even * {border-bottom: 1px solid #EEE;}
td.profit, td.neg {background: #FFF;}
```

This will ensure that, even if backgrounds aren't printed, the rows will have some visual separation. We should also drop in the column separators called for in the design goals.

```
tr.odd *, tr.even * {border-bottom: 1px solid #EEE;}
td {border-right: 1px solid #CCC;}
td.profit, td.neg {color: #000; background: #FFF;}
```

By placing the border on the right side of every td element, we get column separators. In cases like the profit cells, there is already a right border defined by a rule with a more specific selector (td.profit), so this latest rule won't change them.

Speaking of the Profit column, we still need to make the profit figures stand out in a visual sense since that's one of the design goals. We've taken away the backgrounds, so let's boldface the numbers instead. We'll also italicize the negative numbers, as the goals require. This is illustrated in Figure 3.12.

```
td.profit, td.neg {color: #000; background: #FFF;}
td.profit {font-weight: bold;}
td.neg {font-style: italic;}
</style>
```

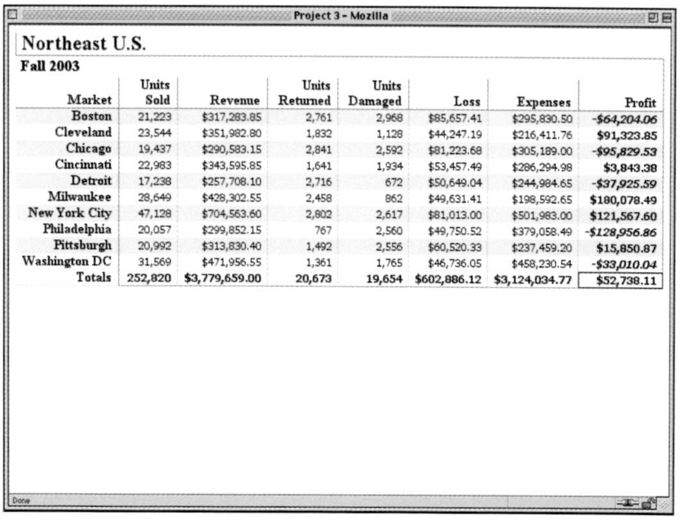

FIGURE 3.12

Drawing attention to both the profits and negative numbers.

| | Units | | Units | Units | | | |
Market	Sold	Revenue	Returned	Damaged	Loss	Expenses	Profit
Boston	21,223	$317,283.85	2,761	2,968	$85,657.41	$295,830.50	-$64,204.06
Cleveland	23,544	$351,982.80	1,832	1,128	$44,247.19	$216,411.76	$91,323.85
Chicago	19,437	$290,583.15	2,841	2,592	$81,223.68	$305,189.00	-$95,829.53
Cincinnati	22,983	$343,595.85	1,641	1,934	$53,457.49	$286,294.98	$3,843.38
Detroit	17,238	$257,708.10	2,716	672	$50,649.04	$244,984.65	-$37,925.59
Milwaukee	28,649	$428,302.55	2,458	862	$49,631.41	$198,592.65	$180,078.49
New York City	47,128	$704,563.60	2,802	2,617	$81,013.00	$501,983.00	$121,567.60
Philadelphia	20,057	$299,852.15	767	2,560	$49,750.52	$379,058.49	-$128,956.86
Pittsburgh	20,992	$313,830.40	1,492	2,556	$60,520.33	$237,459.20	$15,850.87
Washington DC	31,569	$471,956.55	1,361	1,765	$46,736.05	$458,230.54	-$33,010.04
Totals	252,820	$3,779,659.00	20,673	19,654	$602,886.12	$3,124,034.77	$52,738.11

Northeast U.S. — Fall 2003 — Project 3 - Mozilla

The Totals Row

The last thing we'll do is clean up the Totals row. We're doing this mostly to make the final result look better, not because it's part of the explicit design goals. In examining Figure 3.12, we can see that a quick way to make the Totals row stand out a little more would be to add a solid top border. We'll make sure this applies to both `td` and `th` elements in the row.

```
td.neg {font-style: italic;}
tr.totals * {border-top: 1px solid gray;}
</style>
```

It might also be a good touch to remove the bottom border from the "Totals" cell since it's left sort of hanging in midair. And, as a last little touch, let's use uppercase to the word "TOTALS."

```
tr.totals * {border-top: 1px solid gray;}
tr.totals th {border-bottom: none; text-transform: uppercase;}
</style>
```

Thanks to `text-transform`, we've changed the capitalization of the text without having to touch the HTML source. In this case, we can make use of it because the cell in question contains actual letters—uppercasing numbers generally doesn't have any useful effect. We can see the results in Figure 3.13.

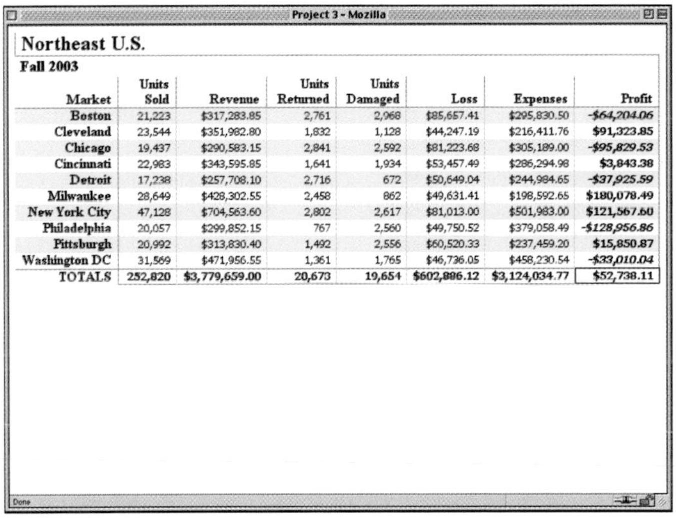

FIGURE 3.13

Putting on the finishing touches.

With that done, we're ready to have these styles apply only when printing. All we need to do is go back to the beginning of our second style sheet and change `screen` to `print`, as previously described. This last change is shown in Listing 3.4, which shows both style sheets we've created.

Styles in All Media

The first style sheet in Listing 3.4 applies in all media because the default value for the media attribute is all. Thus, the first style sheet is combined with the second when printing.

Listing 3.4 Both Style Sheets Together

```
<style type="text/css">
h2, h3 {margin: 0; border: 1px solid gray;}
h2 {border-width: 0 0 0 1px; padding: 0 0 0 0.25em}
h3 {border-width: 1px 1px 0 0; padding: 0.1em 0.33em;}
th, td {text-align: right; padding: 0 0.5em;
  border-bottom: 1px solid #DDD;}
td {font: small Verdana, "Andale Mono", Courier, "Courier New",
  monospace;}
thead th {vertical-align: bottom; border: 1px solid gray;
  border-width: 0 1px 1px 0;
  white-space: normal;}
th {border-right: 1px solid gray; border-bottom-style: dotted;
  white-space: nowrap;}
td {letter-spacing: -1px;}
td.profit {background: #CEC; border-bottom-color: white;
  border-right: 1px solid gray;}
td.neg {background: #FF3; color: red;}
tr.totals td {font-weight: bold; border-bottom: 1px solid gray;}
tr.totals td.profit {border: 1px solid black;}
tr.totals th {border-bottom-style: solid;}
</style>
<style type="text/css" media="print">
table tr.odd * {background: #EEE;}
tr.odd *, tr.even * {border-bottom: 1px solid #EEE;}
td {border-right: 1px solid #CCC;}
td.profit, td.neg {color: #000; background: #FFF;}
td.profit {font-weight: bold;}
td.neg {font-style: italic;}
tr.totals * {border-top: 1px solid gray;}
tr.totals th {border-bottom: none; text-transform: uppercase;}
</style>
```

BRANCHING OUT

Try creating styles to accomplish each of the variations described here. If the markup needs to be changed to make the variation easier or even possible, it will be noted in the text.

1. Come up with a visual highlight for the market names that is distinct from the profit figures. If you use the markup from the file shown in Figure 3.9, this will require a change to the markup in the form of adding some information. If you use the markup from the file in Figure 3.13, no markup has to be changed.

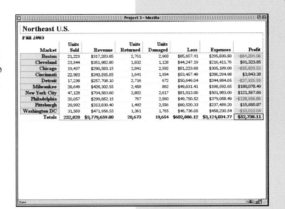

2. "Fill in" the top row and left column and create a box around the whole table of headings and figures. You should be able to do this in a number of ways, but for a challenge, try to find one that doesn't simply set a border on the table element itself.

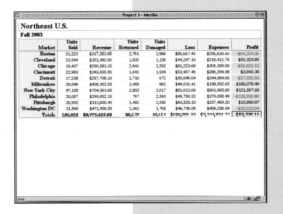

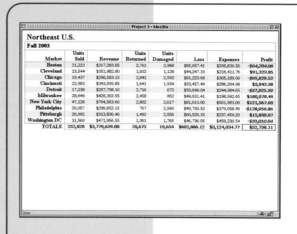

3. In the print styles, rework the borders so that the market rows from main table are bounded by a box and so is the h3, while the h2 does not have any borders to its sides. You may need to alter the markup to make this happen.

4

POSITIONING IN THE BACKGROUND

But I was told there would be no math!
Too bad.

—*MACINTOSH TECHNICAL NOTE #31*

IT'S A COMMON THING, at least in print design, to use shaded variations of a background to make portions of the design stand out. A good example is an ad in which there's a big picture of a mountain or beach or beautiful woman filling the entire ad, and in the middle is some compelling yet meaningless text, and surrounding that text is a region where the picture in the background has been washed out, as if the text were written on a half-opaque block of plastic.

Since opacity styles aren't part of CSS as of this writing, it's been generally thought that such effects are effectively impossible. There are fixed-attachment backgrounds (see Project 11 in *Eric Meyer on CSS* for more details), but they aren't supported by Explorer for Windows. One can use semi-opaque PNG graphics, but they aren't supported by Explorer for Windows. In fact, short of hacking the browser with proprietary behavior scripts, there's only one way to get a smooth translucency effect in Explorer for Windows, and that's by manipulating the position of background images.

Project Goals

We've taken on a project in which a local author is publishing some of his short essays and wants them to look artistic. He's a big fan of translucency effects, so he wants to see them used in his designs. Specifically:

◆ We are to use a sunrise picture for the first essay, "Mourning in Mansfield." This will include a dark shade over the background behind the title and a lightening effect over the background behind the essay's main text.

◆ For the essay "Gathering Stormclouds," we'll be using a picture of clouds at sunset. For this one, the title will have a lightening effect for the background, while the main text will have a darkened background and light text.

The author is supplying the images, so fortunately we don't have to worry about acquiring them. All we really have to do is pull a little sleight of style to get the translucency effects our client has requested.

Preparation

See the Introduction for instructions on how to download files from the Web site.

Download the files for Project 4 from this book's Web site. If you're planning to play along at home, load the file ch04proj.html into the editing program of your choice. This is the file you'll be editing, saving, and reloading as the project progresses.

Style at Dawn

For the first half of this project, we'll take the first of the two documents and add the styles necessary to create translucent effects using ordinary JPEG images. As we'll soon see, the images in question make it fairly easy to create an attractive design.

Getting Started

As usual, our first step should be to look at the structure of the document. As we can see from Listing 4.1, there isn't a whole lot to it really, just a masthead div with a heading and a "main" div containing the text of the entry. Without any styles, we get the very plain rendering shown in Figure 4.1.

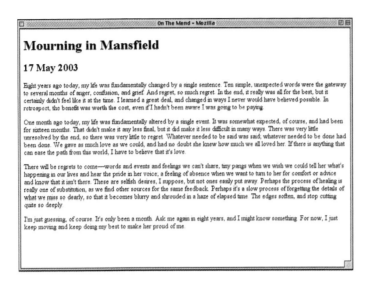

FIGURE 4.1

The journal entry in its
unstyled state.

Listing 4.1 The Basic Document Structure

```
<div id="masthead">
  <h1>Mourning in Mansfield</h1>
</div>
<div id="main">
  <h2>17 May 2003</h2>
  [...entry text...]
</div>
```

Now, with nothing more than what we already have in the document and some background images, we need to create a tasteful design that makes use of translucent effects. To aid us in this goal, we have the three images shown in Figure 4.2: a basic image (`morn-base.jpg`), a faded version of that same image (`morn-fade.jpg`), and a washed-out version (`morn-wash.jpg`).

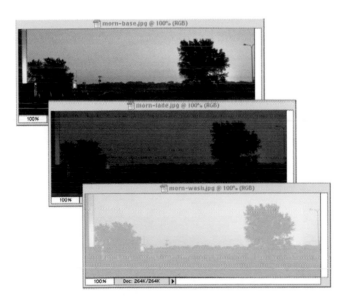

FIGURE 4.2

The three background
images we have at our
disposal.

To lay the groundwork, the first thing we want to do is strip the "gutter" from the body element itself. We'll do that with a familiar rule:

```
<style type="text/css">
body {margin: 0; padding: 0;}
</style>
```

The next thing to do is drop an image into the body's background. It's important to choose the right one since the background color will have to match the background image, and the body background is the one that will be seen throughout most of the design. For maximum readability, we'll pick the washed-out version of the image for the body. A quick check with a color-sampling tool reveals that the background value is a shade of gray that's 71% white, so we'll do the following:

```
body {margin: 0; padding: 0;
   background: rgb(71%,71%,71%) url(morn-wash.jpg);}
```

That's a start, but we'll need more. As this rule stands, the image will start out in the upper-left corner of the body's background and will tile infinitely both horizontally and vertically. For our design, we want the image to appear once and *not* repeat, and we want to place it in the top-right corner. We can do that by adding just a bit more to the background declaration, with the result shown in Figure 4.3.

```
body {margin: 0; padding: 0;
   background: rgb(71%,71%,71%) url(morn-wash.jpg) 100% 0 no-repeat;}
```

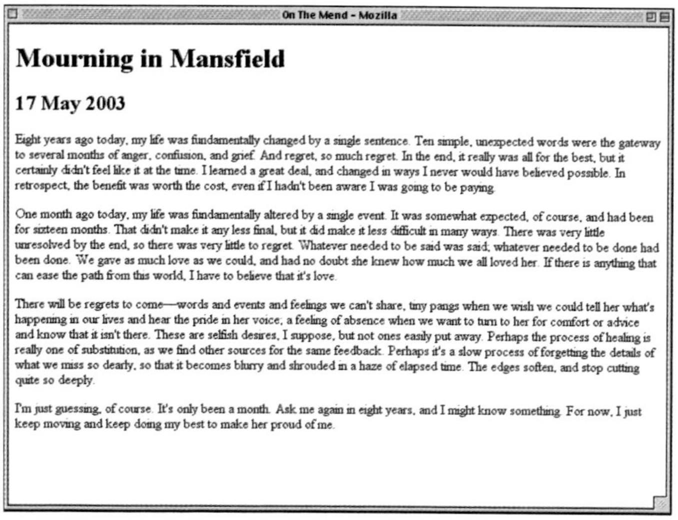

Words Instead of Numbers

We could have used the keywords `right top` instead of the values `100% 0` for the background position, but since later backgrounds will be positioned using offsets, we're going to avoid the use of keywords throughout this project.

FIGURE 4.3

Starting out with some basic styles for the body *element.*

Mourning in Mansfield

17 May 2003

Eight years ago today, my life was fundamentally changed by a single sentence. Ten simple, unexpected words were the gateway to several months of anger, confusion, and grief. And regret, so much regret. In the end, it really was all for the best, but it certainly didn't feel like it at the time. I learned a great deal, and changed in ways I never would have believed possible. In retrospect, the benefit was worth the cost, even if I hadn't been aware I was going to be paying.

One month ago today, my life was fundamentally altered by a single event. It was somewhat expected, of course, and had been for sixteen months. That didn't make it any less final, but it did make it less difficult in many ways. There was very little unresolved by the end, so there was very little to regret. Whatever needed to be said was said; whatever needed to be done had been done. We gave as much love as we could, and had no doubt she knew how much we all loved her. If there is anything that can ease the path from this world, I have to believe that it's love.

There will be regrets to come—words and events and feelings we can't share, tiny pangs when we wish we could tell her what's happening in our lives and hear the pride in her voice; a feeling of absence when we want to turn to her for comfort or advice and know that it isn't there. These are selfish desires, I suppose, but not ones easily put away. Perhaps the process of healing is really one of substitution, as we find other sources for the same feedback. Perhaps it's a slow process of forgetting the details of what we miss so dearly, so that it becomes blurry and shrouded in a haze of elapsed time. The edges soften, and stop cutting quite so deeply.

I'm just guessing, of course. It's only been a month. Ask me again in eight years, and I might know something. For now, I just keep moving and keep doing my best to make her proud of me.

Masthead Styles

The document's masthead is next to fall under our scrutiny. We'll apply the basic background image (`morn-base.jpg`) to the masthead itself, but let's consider for a moment exactly how.

Our aim is to have the background images line up with each other to create the illusion of translucency. To make that happen, we'll need to make sure the masthead's top edge is lined up with the body's top edge. We'll also need to get the background image to not repeat and to sit in exactly the same place as the body's. Thus, the values `100% 0` and `no-repeat` are going to make another appearance. A quick run through a color sampler gives us the background color we need to match the image.

```
body {margin: 0; padding: 0;
  background: rgb(71%,71%,71%) url(morn-wash.jpg) 100% 0 no-repeat;}
#masthead {background: rgb(2%,4%,4%) url(morn-base.jpg)
  100% 0 no-repeat;}
</style>
```

There is one more thing that needs to be done: We need to take the margins off the `h1` element inside the masthead `div`. If we don't, the margins will actually stick out of the `div` in CSS-conformant browsers, which will push the top edge of the `div` down from the top of the document. By removing the margins, we get the result shown in Figure 4.4.

```
#masthead {background: rgb(2%,4%,4%) url(morn-base.jpg)
  100% 0 no-repeat;}
#masthead h1 {margin: 0;}
</style>
```

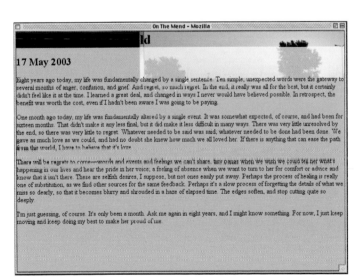

FIGURE 4.4

A different background image is added to the masthead.

Thanks to the masthead and body lining up along the top edge, their backgrounds do the same thing, which gives us exactly the kind of effect we wanted. Although the masthead's background is actually "on top" of the body's, it looks as if there is a grayish translucent layer between us and the "page background." It's an illusion, but a very useful one!

Of course, we can't leave things as they are. The heading text is now basically black on a black background, so it isn't very readable. Let's change its color to a light color that reflects the "sunrise" theme and update its font styling to look a little more professional.

```
#masthead h1 {margin: 0;
   color: #EED;
   font: small-caps bold 2em/1em Arial, sans-serif;}
</style>
```

Default Line Heights

Why bother with the explicit 1em value for line-height? Because that isn't the default—most browsers default to a line-height value somewhere around 1.2. That makes the height of each line a little taller than the font-size value. Our 1em value overrides that default behavior, which will come in handy later on.

The font-size and line-height values were actually chosen with some care. By setting the font-size of the h1 to 2em, we've made the text twice as big as its parent element, the #masthead div, which inherits its font-size value from its parent, the body. With the line-height value of 1em, we've defined the height of the h1's content to be exactly equal to its font-size.

Actually, now that we've cleaned up the masthead text, it might be nice to increase the height of the masthead by dropping some top padding on the masthead div.

```
#masthead {padding: 2.5em 0 0;
   background: rgb(2%,4%,4%) url(morn-base.jpg) 100% 0 no-repeat;}
```

By doing this, we're basically wedging a space between the top border of the masthead div and the top margin edge of the h1. By making the top padding value 2.5em, we allow the spacing to stay in proportion to any changes in text size, no matter how they happen.

With this done, we can see a lot of improvement in Figure 4.5, although we aren't home free just yet.

The light text is now on a background that's mixed light and dark, which will make the text very difficult to read no matter what color we assign. We could put the text over to the right side so that it's more over the light portion of the background, but the dark tree will still prevent us from changing the text to be dark.

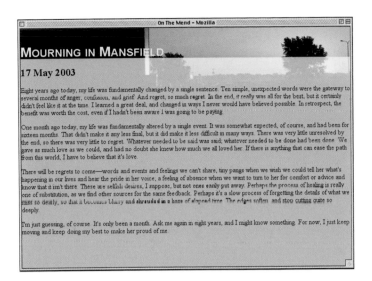

FIGURE 4.5

Padding the masthead and styling the heading bring drastic improvements.

What we need is a background for the heading itself that's more consistent, and fortunately, we already have one: `morn-fade.jpg`. We can add that to the background of the `h1` element.

```
#masthead h1 {margin: 0;
  background: rgb(4%,4%,4%) url(morn-fade.jpg) 100% 0 no-repeat;
  color: #EED;
  font: small-caps bold 2em/1em Arial, sans-serif;}
```

Since we now have a darker background for our light text, we can actually shift it over to the right side of the design. At the same time, we'll pad out the `h1` element a little bit so that the text doesn't get too close to the edge of the dark area.

```
#masthead h1 {margin: 0; padding: 0.25em 0.33em;
  background: rgb(4%,4%,4%) url(morn-fade.jpg) 100% 0 no-repeat;
  color: #EED;
  font: small-caps bold 2em/1em Arial, sans-serif;
  text-align: right;}
```

The quarter-em top and bottom padding will nicely center the text in the dark background, and the third-em padding on the right and left will keep the title text from getting too cozy with the edge of the browser window, as illustrated in Figure 4.6.

FIGURE 4.6

The third background is added, although it's out of alignment.

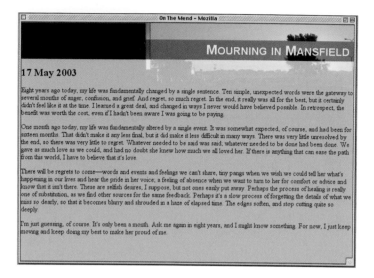

Measuring Ems

Remember that one em is always equal to the font-size of the element on which the em is being used. Thus, given our styles, 1em for the h1 is twice the size of 1em for a paragraph.

Whoops—there's a problem. The background image we just added isn't lining up with the other images, and this is creating a discontinuous tree. That's because the top edge of the h1's background area isn't lined up with the tops of the other two.

We could fix this by moving the h1 to the top of the page, but that wouldn't look very good. Instead, let's bring the h1's background into alignment with the others but leave the element where it is now. To pull this off, we'll have to do a little math.

We know that the h1's top edge is 2.5em from the top of the masthead, thanks to the top padding we gave the masthead div. However, the h1's font-size is twice that of the masthead div's, due to the 2em value in the font declaration, so we have to divide that number in half to get the right offset. Therefore, if we position the background image of the h1 so that its top edge is actually −1.25em above the top edge of the h1's background area, then all the backgrounds should line up.

```
#masthead h1 {margin: 0; padding: 0.25em 0.33em;
   background: rgb(4%,4%,4%) url(morn-fade.jpg) 100% -1.25em no-repeat;
   color: #EED;
   font: small-caps bold 2em/1em Arial, sans-serif;
   text-align: right;}
```

One more touch should make the masthead look more polished, and that's a solid black border along the top and bottom of the dark background. However, doing this means that the background area of the h1 will be effectively shifted downward by a pixel (thanks to the top border), which will cause the images to go out of alignment in CSS-conformant browsers. We can fix that with a negative one-pixel top margin.

```
#masthead h1 {margin: -1px 0 0; padding: 0.25em 0.33em;
   background: rgb(4%,4%,4%) url(morn-fade.jpg) 100% -1.25em no-repeat;
   color: #EED; border: 1px solid black; border-width: 1px 0;
   font: small-caps bold 2em/1em Arial, sans-serif;
   text-align: right;}
```

There's just one problem: IE/Win goes completely bonkers when the negative margin is introduced. So we'll actually need to change the margin back to what it was, and use another of IE's bugs against it to hide the negative margin.

```
#masthead h1 {margin: 0; padding: 0.25em 0.33em;
   background: rgb(4%,4%,4%) url(morn-fade.jpg) 100% -1.25em no-repeat;
   color: #EED; border: 1px solid black; border-width: 1px 0;
   font: small-caps bold 2em/1em Arial, sans-serif;
   text-align: right;}
html>body #masthead h1 {margin: -1px 0 0;}
</style>
```

Thanks to the html>body part of that rule, Explorer will just skip right over the new rule. Other browsers, such as Safari, Opera, and Gecko-based browsers like Mozilla, will understand and apply the rule. Thus, we get a good cross-browser layout.

Although these new styles may be off by a pixel in some browsers, it's an acceptable price to pay. The difference will hardly be noticeable one way or the other, as Figure 4.7 illustrates.

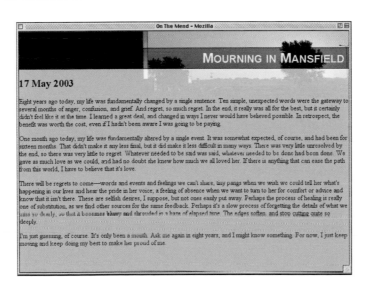

FIGURE 4.7

With a little negative positioning, the backgrounds are lined up nicely.

Cleaning Up

At this stage, the masthead is pretty well in hand; all that remains is to clean up the entry itself. Since the text doesn't have much to do with our background-alignment project, we'll just drop in all the styles at once. With some margins on the main div, no margins and a `font-size` for the h2, and some massaged margins for the paragraphs, we should be all set.

```
html>body #masthead h1 {margin: -1px 0 0;}
#main {margin: 1.25em 5em 0 5em;}
#main h2 {margin: 0; font-size: 1.25em;}
#main p {margin: 0.5em 0 1em;}
</style>
```

Thus, we arrive at the complete set of styles provided in Listing 4.2 and illustrated by Figure 4.8.

Listing 4.2   The Full Style Sheet

```
body {margin: 0; padding: 0;
  background: rgb(71%,71%,71%) url(morn-wash.jpg) 100% 0 no-repeat;}
#masthead {padding: 2.5em 0 0;
  background: rgb(2%,4%,4%) url(morn-base.jpg) 100% 0 no-repeat;}
#masthead h1 {margin: -1px 0 0; padding: 0.25em 0.33em;
  background: rgb(4%,4%,4%) url(morn-fade.jpg) 100% -1.25em no-repeat;
  color: #EED; border: 1px solid black; border-width: 1px 0;
  font: small-caps bold 2em/1em Arial, sans-serif;
  text-align: right;}
html>body #masthead h1 {margin: -1px 0 0;}
#main {margin: 1.25em 5em 0 5em;}
#main h2 {margin: 0; font-size: 1.25em;}
#main p {margin: 0.5em 0 1em;}
```

FIGURE 4.8

The completed journal styles.

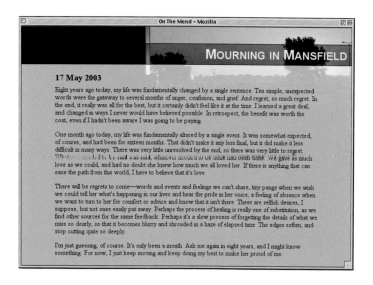

To a degree, our job in this part of the project was easy because two of the three elements with backgrounds lined up along the top edge. Because that was the case, we could give two of the background images exactly the same position values, and the third only required a vertical offset.

Suppose, however, that we want to set up a translucency effect similar to those we've explored, but none of the element tops line up with each other. Given such a situation, we'd need to do a little more math and be careful about the length units we use. Let's move to the second document in our project and see how to handle such issues.

Beached Styles

In this half of the project, we'll take a new document with a slightly different structure and give it a translucent-effect makeover. We'll use the principles explored in the first half of the project, but we'll use them in a more sophisticated way because in this document none of the elements will line up along the top edge.

Assessing Structure and Style

As always, our first order of business is to scout out the lay of the land, so to speak, by examining the document structure and any styles that may already exist. The basic structure looks like this:

```
<div id="main">
  <h1>Gathering Stormclouds</h1>
  <div id="content">
    [...content...]
  </div>
</div>
```

As it happens, there's already a basic style sheet embedded with the document, and this leads to the result shown in Figure 4.9.

```
<style type="text/css">
body {margin: 0; padding: 0;
  background: rgb(14%,26%,30%);}
#main {width: 600px; margin: 2em auto;
  border: 3px solid black;}
</style>
```

Auto-Margins

By giving the main div's left and right margins the value auto and the width an explicit value, we've centered the div within its parent. Note that this will not work in versions of IE/Win before IE6 that improperly centered elements using text-align: center.

FIGURE 4.9

Basic, if dark, beginnings for our new document.

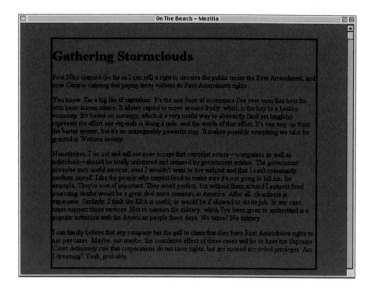

Of course, we'll be filling in other backgrounds, so the text will be more legible by the time we're done. We've just set up these styles to start so that we can dive into the background positioning.

Now we need to use each of the three images shown in Figure 4.10: a basic image (`storm-base.jpg`), a faded version of that same image (`storm-fade.jpg`), and a washed-out version (`storm-wash.jpg`).

FIGURE 4.10

The background images we have at our disposal.

For this design, we aren't going to apply any of these images to the `body` element. Instead, we'll use the main `div` and some of its descendants, but first let's style the text and place the elements.

Title Styles

The first thing we ought to do in setting up text and element styles is temporarily give the main `div` a background color. This will make it easier to see what we're doing.

```
#main {width: 600px; margin: 2em auto;
   border: 3px solid black;
   background: gray;}  /* temporary background */
```

Now we can get down to design. For the title of the page, we'll give it some size and height styles copied from the layout in the first half of the project.

```
#main {width: 600px; margin: 2em auto;
   border: 3px solid black;
   background: gray;}
#main h1 {font: 2em/1em "Times New Roman", serif;}
</style>
```

This will, as before, set the `h1`'s text in relation to its parent (in this case, `div#main`) and make sure its `line-height` is exactly equal to its `font-size`. We'll also center and lowercase the text and spread out the letters just a bit, as demonstrated by Figure 4.11.

```
#main h1 {font: 2em/1em "Times New Roman", serif; letter-spacing: 0.1em;
   text-transform: lowercase; text-align: center;}
```

Quoted Fonts

It's only necessary to quote font names if they contain spaces or non-alphabetic characters.

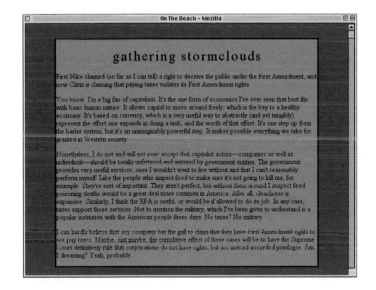

FIGURE 4.11

A temporary background helps us see the changes to the page title.

Having the title all jammed up against the edges of the box feels a little claustrophobic, so let's add some margins to the h1.

```
#main h1 {font: 2em/1em "Times New Roman", serif; letter-spacing: 0.1em;
    text-transform: lowercase; text-align: center;
    margin: 1.25em 1em 0;}
```

To give some definition to the area of the design that holds the text, it might look kind of cool to add some thin borders around the title and the content. We'll start with the title but have borders appear only on the top, right, and left sides.

```
#main h1 {font: 2em/1em "Times New Roman", serif; letter-spacing: 0.1em;
    text-transform: lowercase; text-align: center;
    margin: 1.25em 1em 0;
    border: 1px solid black; border-bottom: none;}
```

Of course, this means that the title text is up against a border again, so we'll add in some padding.

```
#main h1 {font: 2em/1em "Times New Roman", serif; letter-spacing: 0.1em;
    text-transform: lowercase; text-align: center;
    margin: 1.25em 1em 0; padding: 0.5em 0.25em;
    border: 1px solid black; border-bottom: none;}
```

You may have noticed that we're sticking to margin and padding values that are evenly divisible by 0.25. This will make it much easier to do the math that's looming near the end of the project. In the meantime, let's see where we are now (see Figure 4.12).

FIGURE 4.12

The addition of margins, padding, and a border makes the title stand out.

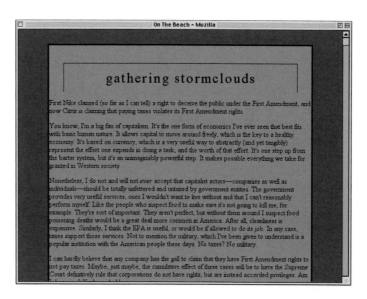

Content Styles

Bringing the main content of the page into line with the title shouldn't be too difficult. The first step is simple enough: We'll add a border to the content `div` that encloses all the text.

```
#main h1 {font: 2em/1em "Times New Roman", serif; letter-spacing: 0.1em;
  text-transform: lowercase; text-align: center;
  margin: 1.25em 1em 0; padding: 0.5em 0.25em;
  border: 1px solid black; border-bottom: none;}
#content {border: 1px solid black;}
</style>
```

That isn't sufficient, of course. If we left things there, the content `div` would be as wide as the main `div`, and the edges wouldn't line up with the edges of the title. Thus, we'll need to give the content `div` some margins. But how big?

Well, the `h1` was given a top margin 1.25em tall and side margins 1em wide. Recall, however, that the `font-size` value of the `h1` is `2em`. Since its em-based margins are calculated with respect to its calculated `font-size`, this means that we'll need to double the values for margins on our content `div`. That gives us 2cm right and left margins and a 2.5em bottom margin. Since we want the content border right up against the title, that means no top margin.

```
#content {margin: 0 2em 2.5em;
  border: 1px solid black;}
```

As with the title, we don't want the content text getting too close to the borders around it. We could double the padding used on the title, but instead, let's give the content `div` a generous padding of an em and a half.

```
#content {margin: 0 2em 3em; padding: 1.5em;
  border: 1px solid black;}
```

Finally, let's add some styling to the content text. The first thing is to take the top margin off of all the paragraphs; this will ensure that the first paragraph is as close to the top of the content `div` as the `div`'s padding will allow while still keeping all paragraphs separated by an em. We'll also fully justify the text, as seen in Figure 4.13.

```
#content {margin: 0 2em 3em; padding: 1.5em;
  border: 1px solid black;}
#content p {margin: 0 0 1em; text-align: justify;}
</style>
```

FIGURE 4.13

The main content integrates with the title.

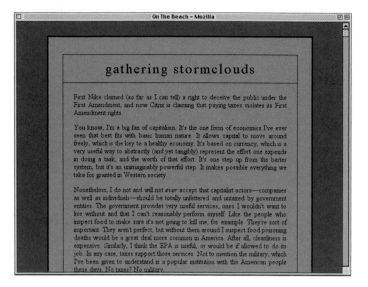

At this point, we've done enough that we can start adding in the background images. So let's get started!

Adding the Backgrounds

Looking at the design in Figure 4.13 and the images we have available, let's take this approach: The main div will get the basic image (storm-base.jpg), the title will get the washed-out image, and the content div will get the faded image. This will necessitate changing the text color to something light, but we'll get to that in a minute. First, here's the main div's background.

```
#main {width: 600px; margin: 2em auto;
  border: 3px solid black;
  background: rgb(7%,13%,15%) url(storm-base.jpg) 0 0 no-repeat;}
```

Next, we'll add a background to the title.

```
#main h1 {font: 2em/1em "Times New Roman", serif; letter-spacing: 0.1em;
  text-transform: lowercase; text-align: center;
  margin: 1.25em 1em 0; padding: 0.5em 0.25em;
  border: 1px solid black; border-bottom: none;
  background: url(storm-wash.jpg) 0 0 no-repeat;}
```

Finally, the content div gets its background.

```
#content {margin: 0 2em 2.5em; padding: 1.5em;
  border: 1px solid black;
  background: rgb(4%,8%,9%) url(storm-fade.jpg) 0 0 no-repeat;}
```

Alert readers will already have caught the problem: All of these elements set the background to start in their upper-left corner, but the elements don't line up. This means the backgrounds won't line up either, as we can see in Figure 4.14.

Top Left Zeroes

The background position value 0 0 is equivalent to top left. We're using numbers here because we're going to have to change some of them to negative values, and it isn't possible to combine keywords and numbers. Thus, something like left 50px is forbidden in CSS, but 0 50px is not. (This restriction was removed in CSS2.1, but some browsers still obey the restriction.)

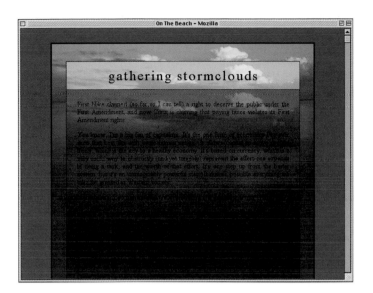

FIGURE 4.14

The backgrounds make their appearance, but they don't line up yet.

So now we have to figure out the offsets needed to get the background images to line up. The main `div` can be left alone, of course, so we'll work on the title first. It's actually pretty simple. We know that it has a top margin of 1.25em and a left margin of 1em, so those are the offsets we'll use because the em for margins is the same em that's used for background offsets.

```
#main h1 {font: 2em/1em "Times New Roman", serif; letter-spacing: 0.1em;
   text-transform: lowercase; text-align: center;
   margin: 1.25em 1em 0; padding: 0.5em 0.25em;
   border: 1px solid black; border-bottom: none;
   background: url(storm-wash.jpg) -1em -1.25em no-repeat;}
```

For the content `div`, the situation is a bit more complicated. The horizontal offset is easy: It's `2em`, the same as the left margin. For the vertical, though, we have to figure out how far it is from the top of the content `div` to the top of the main `div`.

Most of that distance is occupied by the `h1` element, so let's figure it out first. Within its own frame of reference, the content of the `h1` is effectively 1em tall, and it has top and bottom padding of 0.5em. It also has a top margin of 1.25em (and no bottom margin), and all that together adds up to 3.25em tall. We have to double that, remember, because of the doubled `font-size` of the `h1`. Therefore, in terms of the content `div`'s ems, the `h1` is 6.5em tall. With that information and a light red color in hand, we can update the rule appropriately.

```
#content {margin: 0 2em 2.5em; padding: 1.5em;
   border: 1px solid black;
   color: rgb(210,185,150);
   background: rgb(4%,8%,9%) url(storm-fade.jpg) -2em -6.5em no-repeat;}
```

Position and Order

We didn't get those backwards: `background-position` length and percentage values always put the horizontal offset before the vertical offset. Thus, `-1em -1.25em` offsets the image 1em to the left and 1.25em upwards. With keywords, the order is less important; `top left` and `left top` are equivalent, although the latter can trip bugs in the Netscape 6.x line.

That should do it—or should it? We've forgotten one thing: the top borders of the h1 element and the content div, which cause a 2-pixel push downward for the background area of the content div. In fact, the h1's background is also offset by a pixel, but we can let it slide since it isn't nearly as noticeable.

As it turns out, Explorer has forgotten those two pixels as well. Thanks to the way it places background images, the backgrounds already line up. So, if we were to change the offset to fix alignment in CSS-conforming browsers, the alignment would be thrown off in Explorer. So here's what we'll do: We'll leave the rule as it is and add in a new one that Explorer won't understand but more current browsers will.

```
#content {margin: 0 2em 2.5em; padding: 1.5em;
  border: 1px solid black;
  color: rgb(210,185,150);
  background: rgb(4%,8%,9%) url(storm-fade.jpg) -2em -6.5em no-repeat;}
html>body #content {margin-top: -2px;}
#content p {margin: 0 0 1em; text-align: justify;}
```

As in the previous half of the project, Explorer will just skip right over the rule we've just added. Other browsers, such as Safari, Opera, and Gecko-based browsers like Mozilla, will understand and apply the rule. Thus, we get a good cross-browser layout, as shown in Figure 4.15.

Pros and Cons

As powerful as this technique can be visually, it does make for pages that are weightier than they might otherwise be. In addition to the HTML and CSS, designs like this also require the loading of multiple backgrounds, most of which will only be seen in part. Thus, some of the bandwidth required for the page to download might be considered wasted since it contains image portions that the user will not see.

This is admittedly a drawback and one worth considering. In the examples used for this project, the background images were not too large, plus the faded and washed-out versions were highly compressed, which kept the weight down. A design that relied on five variations of a background image, with each one 800×600 or bigger, would create a monstrously weighty page!

Downloading full images and placing them as we did in this project carries a benefit: If the text in the document is resized, the translucency effects will still hold true (that is, unless text starts wrapping in unexpected ways). For example, in the "stormclouds" example, if the title text wrapped to two or more lines, the alignment of the content div would be thrown off quite a bit. We could in theory avoid the problem with fixed-attachment backgrounds, but Explorer for Windows doesn't support such techniques.

We could also get around the alignment problems caused by wrapping text with a simple change in structure. Instead of putting the content div after the h1, we could put the h1 inside the content div. This, along with a suitable rearrangement of the CSS, would prevent misalignment if the title text ends up wrapping to multiple lines.

A much simpler and less weighty approach, at least in cases in which you want to lighten or darken a background, is to use semi-opaque PNG graphics for the elements that need to be faded or lightened. The problem, again, is Explorer for Windows, which supports PNG images but not the alpha channel, which wrecks the translucency. Instead, Explorer just shows a fully opaque version of the PNG. It's also the case that you can really only achieve lightening or darkening effects with PNGs, which limit the range of visual effects. With the offset-alignment approach we've discussed, you could use a basic image, one with the image contours traced, and another with a rippled-glass effect.

At any rate, it's important to employ the techniques explored in this project with care. They are most often useful in situations such as mastheads, section titles, or other places where the content is short and the area to be decorated is both wide and short.

Fixed-Background Layout

For more information on fixed-attachment layout techniques, see Project 12 of *Eric Meyer on CSS*.

5

List-Based Menus

In America, even your menus have the gift of language....
Oh, those menus. In America, they are poetry.

—Laurie Lee

THERE HAS BEEN A MOVEMENT in the CSS design community toward an increased use of unordered lists to contain, well, just about everything. Although this has on occasion been taken a little too far, a very common technique nowadays is to take collections of links (sometimes called menus) and place them inside lists, with one link per list item.

Why is this such a popular approach? There are a few reasons. The most important is that, when you have a list of links, it makes a great deal of sense to enclose them in a list. From the semantic-markup point of view, it's a pretty close match.

From a styling point of view, there are some major benefits as well. Because each list item contains a link, two different elements (li and a) can be styled independently. Since the basis of styling is elements, the more elements you have to work with the better.

Project Goals

After doing a great deal of work on various client projects, it seems like a good time to take a breather and work on a personal project. To that end, we'll work on enhancing the presentation of the sidebar links in a personal journal. Let's define some basic design directions and see where they take us.

◆ We'll be starting with a page that already has some styles, so the menu's styles need to fit in with the presentation that already exists.

◆ The links in the menu should be visually separated from one another; that is, we don't want a list of links with no separators or other visual effects.

◆ We should come up with a design that makes the menu feel open and airy so that the links seem to be a part of the other content in the design.

◆ We should come up with another design that encloses the links in a box or some other visual device that obviously separates them from the main content.

With these goals in mind, it's time to get set up and start styling!

Preparation

See the Introduction for instructions on how to download files from the Web site.

Download the files for Project 5 from this book's Web site. If you're planning to play along at home, load the file `ch05proj.html` into the editing program of your choice. This is the file you'll be editing, saving, and reloading as the project progresses.

Laying the Groundwork

Second Time Around

Readers of *Eric Meyer on CSS* may recognize the design in this project because it's taken from that book's Project 9, "Multicolumn Layout." The difference here is that the links are now contained in an unordered list, and the entry text is from another date.

Since we're going to focus on ways to style an unordered list of links within an existing design, we'll start with some CSS already applied. The starting style sheet is provided in Listing 5.1 and illustrated by Figure 5.1.

Listing 5.1   The Starting Styles

```
<style type="text/css">
html {margin: 0; padding: 0;}
body {font: 80% Verdana, Arial, Helvetica, sans-serif;
   margin: 0; padding: 0;
   background: rgb(95%,95%,80%); color: black;}
h1 {font-size: 200%; text-transform: lowercase; letter-spacing: 3px;
   margin: 0; padding: 0.66em 0 0.33em 29%;
   background: rgb(85%,85%,70%);}
h3 {font-size: 1.33em; margin: 0; padding: 0;
   border-bottom: 1px solid black;}
```

```
h4 {font-size: 1em; margin: 0; padding: 0.33em 0 0;
    border-bottom: 1px solid rgb(50%,50%,35%);}
h1, h3, h4 {line-height: 1em;}
p {line-height: 1.5; margin: 0.5em 0 1em;}
div#entry {margin: 2em 10% 1em 30%; padding: 0;}
div#sidebar {float: left; width: 23%; margin: 2em 0 0 2%;}
</style>
```

FIGURE 5.1

The design as it now stands.

Basically, all we need to do is style the list of links so that it fits in better with the rest of the design. In the course of doing this, we'll actually look at a few different presentation options for the same list.

Examining the Markup

To properly plan our styling, we need to get a look at the markup that contains the links. It's shown in Listing 5.2.

Listing 5.2   The Markup for the Links

```
<div id="sidebar">
<h4>Other Mutters</h4>
<ul>
<li><a href="mutter01.html">13 September 2002</a></li>
<li><a href="mutter02.html">6 September 2002</a></li>
<li><a href="mutter03.html">25 October 2002</a></li>
<li><a href="mutter04.html">8 November 2002</a></li>
<li><a href="mutter05.html">14 November 2002</a></li>
<li><a href="mutter06.html">17 November 2002</a></li>
<li><a href="mutter07.html">3 December 2002</a></li>
<li><a href="mutter08.html">4 December 2002</a></li>
</ul>
</div>
```

Explorer Jog

If you're working on this project in IE/Win, you might notice a small "jog" in the text that flows past the floated sidebar. This is due to a bug in IE, but fortunately it's one that can be worked around. Space prevents us from exploring it here, but you can get all the details at http://www. positioniseverything. net/explorer/ threepxtest.html.

It's straightforward enough: a simple, unordered list with a link inside each list item. This probably comes as no surprise, given what we saw in Figure 5.1, but it was worth taking a look to see what we had available.

The first thing we'll want to do is get rid of the bullets and indentation of the list itself. Since this will be constant across all the design ideas we'll try out, we'll do it now to beat the rush.

```
div#sidebar {float: left; width: 23%; margin: 2em 0 0 2%;}
#sidebar ul {list-style: none; margin: 0; padding: 0;}
</style>
```

By removing all padding and margin, we've made sure to eliminate the usual "indent" effect that lists have. Since some browsers use margin to create that indentation and others use padding, zeroing out both covers our bases, as we can see in Figure 5.2.

FIGURE 5.2

The list bullets and indentation are removed.

Now we can try various design ideas for our list of links.

Open and Airy

For our first approach, we'll create a set of styles that place visible separators between some spread-out links. That is, we'll push the links apart vertically and then drop separators in between each link.

Separation

The first thing we'll do is spread apart the links by padding the list items that contain them. A little top and bottom padding should do the trick nicely.

```
#sidebar ul {list-style: none; margin: 0; padding: 0;}
#sidebar li {padding: 0.5em 0 0.25em;}
</style>
```

That's really all we need to do to spread the links apart. The nice thing about this approach is that, if we ever decide the links need to be further apart (or closer together), all we have to do is change the padding value.

And now for the separators. This is as simple as adding a bottom border to each of the list items.

```
#sidebar li {padding: 0.5em 0 0.25em;
  border-bottom: 1px solid rgb(84%,84%,69%);}
```

By creating a solid border with a color that's a blend of the shades used for the background and the bottom border on the "Other Mutters" heading, we can create a nicely subtle effect like that shown in Figure 5.3.

Uneven Padding?

We've made the padding uneven on purpose. Because of the way English text is formed, there generally tends to be more apparent space underneath text than above it. Thus, we've added more padding above than below. This is one design decision. Others are possible, and in cases where the text is all uppercase, top and bottom padding should probably be symmetric.

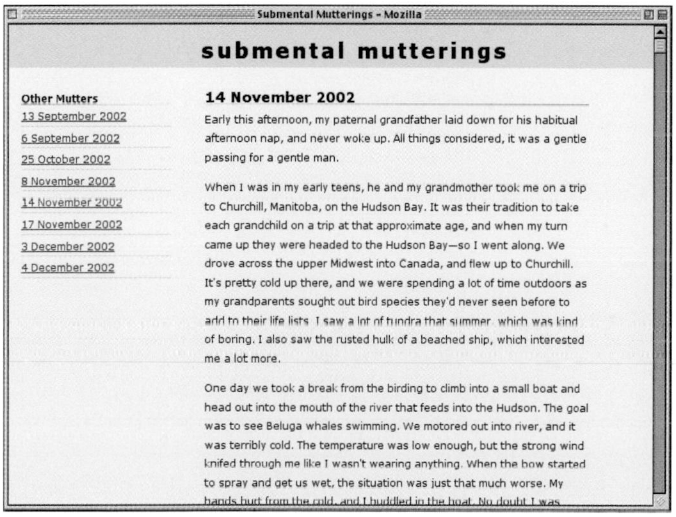

FIGURE 5.3

Separating the links with borders on the list items.

Color Blending

The color shades in this particular design were discovered using the Color Blender found at http://www.meyerweb.com /eric/tools/ color-blend/.

The links are nicely spaced out and separated, but the colors need some work; that blue just does not go with the lovely earth tones we're using for the rest of the design. And the underlines have to go, too. Let's do that first.

```
#sidebar li {padding: 0.5em 0 0.25em;
  border-bottom: 1px solid rgb(84%,84%,69%);}
#sidebar a {text-decoration: none;}
</style>
```

Now all we need are some good colors to complement the rest of the design. Green and tan often go well together, so let's try that combination.

```
#sidebar a {text-decoration: none;}
#sidebar a:link {color: rgb(20%,40%,0%);}
</style>
```

That's a pretty good choice, so we'll pick a variant color for visited links. Let's assign such links a color halfway between rgb(20%,40%,0%) and the body's back-ground color of rgb(95%,95%,80%). This is illustrated in Figure 5.4, where the link for the current entry takes on the visited color. (After all, it's the current page, so it's been visited.)

```
#sidebar a:link {color: rgb(20%,40%,0%);}
#sidebar a:visited {color: rgb(58%,68%,40%);}
</style>
```

FIGURE 5.4

Unvisited and visited links are given more complementary colors.

That's pretty much all we need to do to make these links fit in with the design. It's just a beginning, of course; there is an almost infinite number of ways we could alter the markup to meet design needs.

Arrow Style

To spice up the sidebar a little bit, let's add some arrow graphics. In doing this, we'll need to adjust the sidebar styles, but as we'll see, that's easy enough to do. Let's add an arrow image to the bottom-right corner of sidebar's background.

```
div#sidebar {float: left; width: 23%; margin: 2em 0 0 2%;
  background: url(arrow.gif) 100% 100% no-repeat;}
```

Having done this, we need to provide enough space for the arrow to stick out past the bottom of the last list item. Some bottom padding exactly equal to the height of the image should just do the trick, as shown in Figure 5.5.

```
div#sidebar {float: left; width: 23%; margin: 2em 0 0 2%; padding: 0 0 15px;
  background: url(arrow.gif) 100% 100% no-repeat;}
```

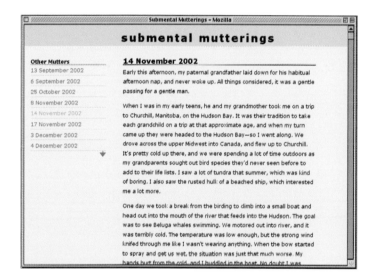

FIGURE 5.5

An arrow is added to the bottom-right corner of the sidebar.

The immediate problem that jumps out is that the link separators stick out past the arrow's centerline, which doesn't really work here. We'll need to push the right edge of the links back a bit, and a close scrutiny of the arrow reveals that there are six pixels from its right edge to its centerline. Therefore, we'll need to give the list itself a margin of that length. If we're going to do that, we'll also need to adjust the "Other Mutters" h4 so that its margin is the same as the list's.

```
#sidebar ul {list-style: none; margin: 0; padding: 0;}
#sidebar h4, #sidebar ul {margin: 0 6px 0 0;}
#sidebar li {padding: 0.5em 0 0.25em;
  border-bottom: 1px solid rgb(84%,84%,69%);}
```

The Case for Grouping

We've created a grouped-selector rule because it makes later adjustment easier. If we set the margins for the h4 and ul individually, we'd have to edit both rules any time we wanted to adjust their margins. This way, one rule handles both.

Now we'll tie the links and the arrow together. Thanks to the way the arrow graphic is constructed, with a three-pixel-wide centerline, this is as easy as adding a border that's the appropriate width, style, and color.

```
#sidebar ul {list-style: none; margin: 0; padding: 0;
   border-right: 3px double rgb(50%,50%,35%);}
```

A quick check reveals that the arrow seems a little too close to the links; the effect is a bit cramped. Thus, we'll extend the list border and push the arrow downward by adding some bottom padding to the list, as illustrated in Figure 5.6.

```
#sidebar ul {list-style: none; margin: 0; padding: 0 0 10px;
   border-right: 3px double rgb(50%,50%,35%);}
```

FIGURE 5.6

Merging the list's border with the sidebar's background image.

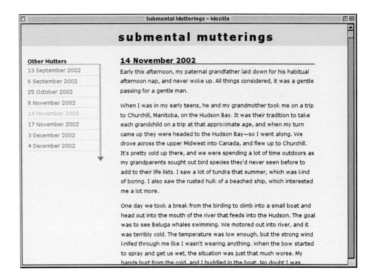

How does this work? Since the background image sits inside the sidebar's padding, and the list sits inside that same padding, any increase in the height of the list (such as through additional padding) will increase the height of the sidebar and thus push the arrow image downward. The bottom padding also extends the list's right border, so it remains visually merged with the background image.

Styling the Links

Our arrow styles are pretty nifty, but we aren't done yet. Let's move the link text over to the right and make modifications based on that change. First we'll align the text.

```
#sidebar ul {list-style: none; margin: 0; padding: 0 0 10px;
   border-right: 3px double rgb(50%,50%,35%);
   text-align: right;}
```

This will jam the text right up against the right border, which we don't really want. We could set a margin on the list items, but that would separate the bottom borders from the double border on the right, so that's out. We could also give the list items right padding, but let's set right padding on the links themselves instead.

```
#sidebar a {text-decoration: none; padding: 0 0.5em 0 0;}
```

Why set the padding? Because our next step will actually be to remove the borders from the list items. For the moment, we'll do this by simply commenting out the border-bottom declaration.

```
#sidebar li {padding: 0.5em 0 0.25em;
  /* border-bottom: 1px solid rgb(84%,84%,69%); */}
```

So you're probably wondering, why are we taking away the separators we already created? Because we're going to tackle the problem by another route. Instead of bordering the list items, we're going to border the links themselves. The result is shown in Figure 5.7.

```
#sidebar a {text-decoration: none; padding: 0 0.5em 0 0;
  border-bottom: 1px solid rgb(84%,84%,69%);}
```

FIGURE 5.7

Shifting the borders to the links results in an interesting variation.

Does that last change look familiar? It should: The border style we applied to the links is the same as what we just commented out of the list items' rule.

There are obvious differences between the two approaches. When the list items had the borders, they ran from one side of the sidebar to the other. That's because list items generate block-level boxes, much as paragraphs and divs do. The links, on the other hand, generate inline boxes, which means the borders will only run underneath the text itself. That's true even if the link wraps to multiple lines.

Arbitrary Hovering

The CSS specification actually allows hover styles to be applied to any element—not just links—and most modern browsers actually permit it. Explorer is not among them, sadly, restricting hover effects to links. Or at least it did until Peter Nederlof found a way to extend IE/Win's capabilities to allow arbitrary-element hover styling. You can you can read about it at `http://www.xs4all.nl/~peterned/csshover.html`.

The effect is still potentially very useful because, with this new approach, we can style the borders differently when the link is hovered. That's something we couldn't do in Explorer when the list items were bordered. So let's add in a rule that will change both the text and the border color when a link is in the hover state.

```
#sidebar a:visited {color: rgb(58%,68%,40%);}
#sidebar a:hover {color: rgb(10%,20%,0%);
  border-color: rgb(98%,48%,40%);}
</style>
```

This alone might suffice because it darkens the text and reddens the border on whatever link is being hovered. We can take it further, though, by adding a background image to the link when it's hovered. We can only put the image in the link background, so we'll use a half-arrow graphic called `arrow2.gif`. This will be placed in the lower-left corner of the link.

```
#sidebar a:hover {color: rgb(10%,20%,0%);
  border-color: rgb(98%,48%,40%);
  background: url(arrow2.gif) 0 100% no-repeat;}
```

As with the sidebar's arrow, we need to insert enough padding for the background to appear and not be overlapped by text. Since we only need that padding when the background image appears, we'll just increase the link padding during the hover. This has the effect shown in Figure 5.8.

```
#sidebar a:hover {color: rgb(10%,20%,0%);
  border-color: rgb(98%,48%,40%);
  background: url(arrow2.gif) 0 100% no-repeat;
  padding-left: 15px;}
```

FIGURE 5.8

Adding in hover effects makes the links more interactive.

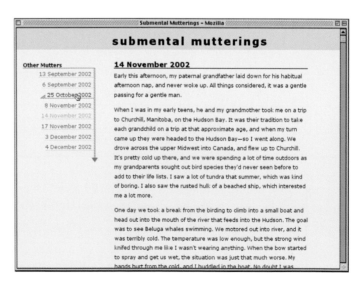

Remember that these effects work well because the links aren't wrapping to multiple lines. In settings in which wrapping is likely, another design approach would probably be better.

However, let's do our best to guard against potential wrapping problems. Suppose one of the links had content that was between 0 and 15 pixels more narrow than the list itself. In that case, the padding that is applied on hover would cause line wrapping, which means the link could radically change in appearance between the hovered and nonhovered states. We could prevent any wrapping with white-space: nowrap, but that might force links to stick out of the sidebar completely, which isn't acceptable.

Therefore, we'll replace the 15-pixel padding with an invisible equivalent: a 15-pixel margin on the sidebar links.

```
#sidebar a {text-decoration: none;
  padding: 0 0.5em 0 0; margin-left: 15px;
  border-bottom: 1px solid rgb(84%,84%,69%);}
```

We want that left margin to effectively be replaced by the padding when a sidebar link is hovered, so we need to remove the margin in the hover state.

```
#sidebar a:hover {color: rgb(10%,20%,0%);
  border-color: rgb(98%,48%,40%);
  background: url(arrow2.gif) 0 100% no-repeat;
  padding-left: 15px; margin-left: 0;}
```

This won't prevent links from wrapping, but it will prevent reflowing. If the link and its margin fit, so will the hovered link and its padding, as we can see in Figure 5.9, where the browser window has been narrowed.

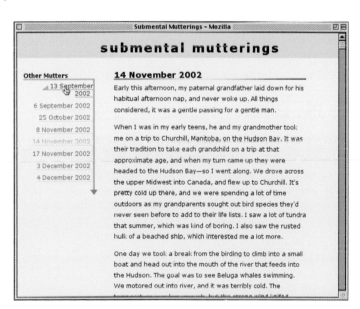

FIGURE 5.9

Trading off margin for padding keeps the links from unexpectedly reflowing.

With that change, we have the style sheet shown in Listing 5.3.

Listing 5.3   The "Open Links" Style Sheet

```
html {margin: 0; padding: 0;}
body {font: 80% Verdana, Arial, Helvetica, sans-serif;
   margin: 0; padding: 0;
   background: rgb(95%,95%,80%); color: black;}
h1 {font-size: 200%; text-transform: lowercase; letter-spacing: 3px;
   margin: 0; padding: 0.66em 0 0.33em 29%;
   background: rgb(85%,85%,70%);}
h3 {font-size: 1.33em; margin: 0; padding: 0;
   border-bottom: 1px solid black;}
h4 {font-size: 1em; margin: 0; padding: 0.33em 0 0;
   border-bottom: 1px solid rgb(50%,50%,35%);}
h1, h3, h4 {line-height: 1em;}
p {line-height: 1.5; margin: 0.5em 0 1em;}
div#entry {margin: 2em 10% 1em 30%; padding: 0;}
div#sidebar {float: left; width: 23%; margin: 2em 0 0 2%; padding: 0 0 15px;
   background: url(arrow.gif) 100% 100% no-repeat;}
#sidebar ul {list-style: none; margin: 0; padding: 0 0 10px;
   border-right: 3px double rgb(50%,50%,35%);
   text-align: right;}
#sidebar h4, #sidebar ul {margin: 0 6px 0 0;}
#sidebar li {padding: 0.5em 0 0.25em;
   /* border-bottom: 1px solid rgb(84%,84%,69%); */}
#sidebar a {text-decoration: none;
   padding: 0 0.5em 0 0; margin-left: 15px;
   border-bottom: 1px solid rgb(84%,84%,69%);}
#sidebar a:link {color: rgb(20%,40%,0%);}
#sidebar a:visited {color: rgb(58%,68%,40%);}
#sidebar a:hover {color: rgb(10%,20%,0%);
   border-color: rgb(98%,48%,40%);
   background: url(arrow2.gif) 0 100% no-repeat;
   padding-left: 15px; margin-left: 0;}
```

We still aren't done, though—that's only the first half of the project.

ENCLOSING THE LINKS

Since we've experimented with styles that give the sidebar links an open, airy appearance, let's try a different approach: enclosing the links in a box and making them into button-like objects. To do this, we'll return to an earlier version of the project and build from there.

Changes

We're going to replicate the file we had at the time Figure 5.3 was created and make five changes. First, we'll take the border off the h4 and change its text color so that the rule looks like this:

```
h4 {font-size: 1em; margin: 0; padding: 0.33em 0 0;
   color: rgb(50%,50%,35%);}
```

Second, we'll simplify the sidebar by removing its background image and padding.

```
div#sidebar {float: left; width: 23%; margin: 2em 0 0 2%;}
```

Third, we'll change the list's right-side double border to a one-pixel solid boxed border.

```
#sidebar ul {list-style: none; margin: 0; padding: 0 0 10px;
  border: 1px solid rgb(73%,73%,58%);
  text-align: right;}
```

Fourth, we'll remove the left margin from the links.

```
#sidebar a {text-decoration: none;
  padding: 0 0.5em 0 0;
  border-bottom: 1px solid rgb(84%,84%,69%);}
```

Finally, we'll reduce the hover styles on links to a simple change of the text and background colors; the declarations that changed the border color, added some padding, and inserted a background image are all removed.

```
#sidebar a:hover {color: rgb(10%,20%,0%);
  background: #FFF;}
```

The cumulative effect of these changes is shown in Figure 5.10.

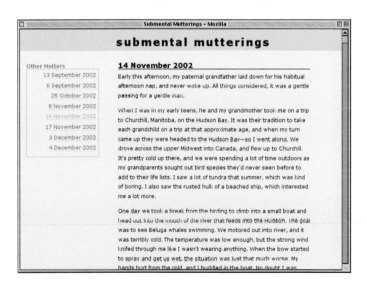

FIGURE 5.10

After a number of changes, the sidebar looks quite a bit different.

Boxed Links

We've created a box that surrounds the links entirely, but let's take the boxy look a bit further and actually box in each of the links. Doing this is as simple as changing the bottom border to a full border and adjusting the padding so that the link text doesn't get too close to the borders.

```
#sidebar a {text-decoration: none;
   padding: 0 0.25em;
   border: 1px solid rgb(84%,84%,69%);}
```

Aligning Blocks

Another reason to use the sidebar for text alignment is because the links them-selves are inline-level elements, and thus text-align cannot be applied to them directly. text-align applies only to block-level elements.

At this point, we probably don't want the links right-aligned because that would put the link borders adjacent to the border set for the list. Instead we'll center them, which will get the edges of the links away from the list's border. So that the h4's text will also center-align, we'll apply text-align to the sidebar div and remove it from the list.

```
div#sidebar {float: left; width: 23%; margin: 2em 0 0 2%;
   text-align: center;}
#sidebar ul {list-style: none; margin: 0; padding: 0 0 10px;
   border: 1px solid rgb(73%,73%,58%);}
```

Now we just need a way to separate the links from each other. To do that, the easiest thing would be to restore the bottom borders of the list items and adjust the padding so that it's a little more balanced, as we see in Figure 5.11.

```
#sidebar li {padding: 0.5em 0;
   border-bottom: 1px solid rgb(84%,84%,69%);}
```

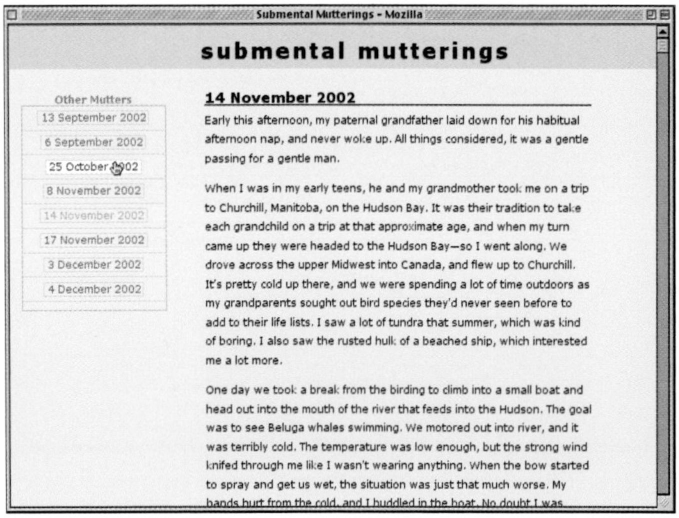

FIGURE 5.11

Boxing in the links with borders.

![Screenshot of a browser window titled "Submental Mutterings - Mozilla" showing the page "submental mutterings" with a sidebar of "Other Mutters" dates and a main entry "14 November 2002".]

Straddling the Lines

In examining Figure 5.11, an idea that suggests itself is to shift the links downward so that they sit "on top" of the list-item borders. By doing this, we can make it look like each link is a small placard strung with taut wire between the sides of the list.

We might choose to do this with a negative margin, except we can't: The lists are inline, and top and bottom margins don't have any effect on the layout of an inline element. Fortunately, relative positioning does affect inline layout, so we'll use that instead.

We know the list items contain only the links, and each has an em of padding (half on top, half on the bottom). Since we want to remove all of the potential variables from the situation, we'll set the `line-height` of the list items to be `1em` rather than leave it up to the browser default.

```
#sidebar li {padding: 0.5em 0; line-height: 1em;
  border-bottom: 1px solid rgb(84%,84%,69%);}
```

Now we can offset the links the appropriate amount. Thanks to our `line-height` and `padding` values, we know each list item is 2em tall. We want to shift the links downward by half that, so:

```
#sidebar a {text-decoration: none;
  padding: 0 0.25em;
  border: 1px solid rgb(84%,84%,69%);
  position: relative; top: 1em;}
```

Now each link will be offset downward by an em. This means that the list-item borders will cut right through them because the links (like any element) have a transparent background by default. Let's use the same background colors as the `body` itself. This will give us the result shown in Figure 5.12.

```
#sidebar a {text-decoration: none;
  padding: 0 0.25em;
  border: 1px solid rgb(84%,84%,69%);
  background: rgb(95%,95%,80%);
  position: relative; top: 1em;}
```

Top or Bottom?

We also could have used `bottom: -1em` to get the same effect, as that is exactly equivalent to `top: 1em` when relatively positioning an element. In such cases, you should feel free to use `top` or `bottom` as fits your mood.

FIGURE 5.12

Using relative positioning and backgrounds on the links.

Pretty cool, although there's a slight problem: The last link in the list is too close to the bottom of the box. In fact, the only reason it isn't jutting out of the list is that the list has 10 pixels of bottom padding. If we change this to equal the height of the list items, it will give us the space we need.

```
#sidebar ul {list-style: none; margin: 0; padding: 0 0 2em;
  border: 1px solid rgb(73%,73%,58%);}
```

At this stage, all we really need is a bit of finishing for the sidebar's title, "Other Mutters." We could leave it as is, but it looks a bit odd just sitting on top of the box. The solution: Put it into a box of its own, one that matches up with the border around the list.

```
div#sidebar {float: left; width: 23%; margin: 2em 0 0 2%;
  text-align: center;}
#sidebar h4 {border: 1px solid rgb(73%,73%,58%);}
#sidebar ul {list-style: none; margin: 0; padding: 0 0 2em;
  border: 1px solid rgb(73%,73%,58%);}
```

Since the h4 now has a bottom border (along with all the other sides) and the list has a top border—and the two are adjacent—it will create the illusion that there is a two-pixel border between the title and the links. To get rid of it, we can remove either the top border from the list or the bottom border from the heading. Since we're already here, let's do the latter.

```
#sidebar h4 {border: 1px solid rgb(73%,73%,58%);
  border-bottom: none;}
```

Now, for a last little touch, let's darken the background of the title just a bit. This will give it a subtle visual punch that doesn't overwhelm other pieces of the layout.

```
#sidebar h4 {border: 1px solid rgb(73%,73%,58%);
   border-bottom: none;
   background: rgb(90%,90%,75%);}
```

This change is enough to call the second half of the project done, so we'll call a halt to the styling. The end result is given in Listing 5.4 and illustrated by Figure 5.13.

Listing 5.4   The "Boxed Links" Style Sheet

```
html {margin: 0; padding: 0;}
body {font: 80% Verdana, Arial, Helvetica, sans-serif;
   margin: 0; padding: 0;
   background: rgb(95%,95%,80%); color: black;}
h1 {font-size: 200%; text-transform: lowercase; letter-spacing: 3px;
   margin: 0; padding: 0.66em 0 0.33em 29%;
   background: rgb(85%,85%,70%);}
h3 {font-size: 1.33em; margin: 0; padding: 0;
   border-bottom: 1px solid black;}
h4 {font-size: 1em; margin: 0; padding: 0.33em 0 0;
   color: rgb(50%,50%,35%);}
h1, h3, h4 {line-height: 1em;}
p {line-height: 1.5; margin: 0.5em 0 1em;}
div#entry {margin: 2em 10% 1em 30%; padding: 0;}
div#sidebar {float: left; width: 23%; margin: 2em 0 0 2%;
   text-align: center;}
#sidebar h4 {border: 1px solid rgb(73%,73%,58%);
   border-bottom: none;
   background: rgb(90%,90%,75%);}
#sidebar ul {list-style: none; margin: 0; padding: 0 0 2em;
   border: 1px solid rgb(73%,73%,58%);}
#sidebar h4, #sidebar ul {margin: 0 6px 0 0;}
#sidebar li {padding: 0.5em 0; line-height: 1em;
   border-bottom: 1px solid rgb(84%,84%,69%);}
#sidebar a {text-decoration: none;
   padding: 0 0.25em;
   border: 1px solid rgb(84%,84%,69%);
   background: rgb(95%,95%,80%);
   position: relative; top: 1em;}
#sidebar a:link {color: rgb(20%,40%,0%);}
#sidebar a:visited {color: rgb(58%,68%,40%);}
#sidebar a:hover {color: rgb(10%,20%,0%);
   background: #FFF;}
```

FIGURE 5.13

Finishing up the sidebar's appearance.

►► Caveat Styler

Remember the potential link-wrapping problems discussed in the first half of the project? They all apply to the styles we wrote in the second half. To see what can happen, try loading ch0513.html *into a browser and then making the browser window really narrow. When the lines wrap, the borders wrap with them, which is correct behavior. Annoying, perhaps, but correct.*

As is often the case in CSS, what suffices for one situation is a poor choice in another. In other words, although the techniques explored in this chapter are very useful, they aren't useful in all cases. A great deal of becoming proficient in CSS is learning what techniques work in which situations and applying that knowledge in creative ways.

Typically, the kinds of styling we did in this project are best used in situations in which you have short elements, preferably those with a single word since those can't word-wrap. Another obvious situation is one in which you're styling a list of graphical links (or indeed a list of any kind of images) because you know the images aren't about to start word-wrapping.

BRANCHING OUT

With the elements we have available, there are almost too many choices for ways to style our menu. Here are a few ideas to get you thinking:

1. Change the hover effect from the first half of the project so that it encloses the whole link in a border but without causing any offset to the left when hovering. The background image should also move to the right side of the link. While you're at it, tie the sidebar heading and the main entry heading together visually by using negative margins and add in some padding to get the sidebar title's text to right-align with the double border on the right side of the sidebar.

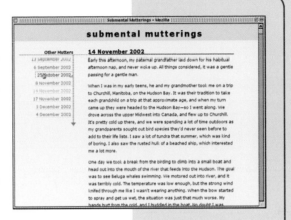

2. Rewrite the menu styles from the second half of the project so that the links appear to be written on the background but are surrounded by a dark shade similar to that used in the masthead. Thus, the links should have a background that matches the body and should be "connected" to it with lines of color that match both links and body.

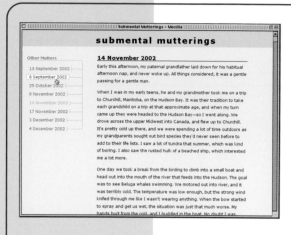

3. Take the styles from the second half of the project and combine them with principles from the first half of the project to create a hybrid style. For example, have an inverted "L" border that runs along the top and right sides of the menu and make each link sit to the left of a rotated "T" shape that extends from the "L" and ends just to the right of each link's text.

6

CSS-Driven Drop-Down Menus

Parents who want a fresh point of view on their furniture are advised to drop down on all fours and accompany the nine or ten month old on his rounds.

—Selma H. Fraiberg

As we saw in the preceding project, it's possible to take a simple, unordered list of links and make it look good. The missing component there was the capability to have submenus and even sub-submenus. Is there a way to use CSS and simple HTML to create drop-down menus, and menus within menus?

As you might have expected, the answer is "yes." It does require using a bit of proprietary technology to get one browser on board, but since that browser is Internet Explorer for Windows, the nonstandard bit is very likely more than worth it. As we'll see in this project, we can take simple nested lists of links and turn them into multi-level menu systems.

PROJECT GOALS

Our basic goal is simple: to create a multilevel menu system using nothing more than some unordered lists and CSS. Embedded within that overall goal are a number of more specific goals:

◆ The menu system we create needs to be able to handle multiple levels of drop-downs so that we can have menus spawn from menus.

◆ It should be easy to set up our menus as either sidebars or horizontal tool-bars. This should also be possible without changing the markup at all.

◆ If we can avoid using JavaScript, we will. In other words, we want to have the menus dynamically shown and hidden via CSS alone. Doing so will reduce page load since the browser will only have to load the page and the style sheet.

◆ The menus need to work in as many browsers as possible, and that includes IE/Win.

It might sound like we have our work cut out for us, but the whole process will be simpler than you might believe right now. Most of what we have to do is lay out the menus how we want. Once that's done, we'll just add in a few extra bits to make the menus appear and disappear dynamically, and we'll be good to go!

PREPARATION

See the Introduction for instructions on how to download files from the Web site.

Download the files for Project 6 from this book's Web site. If you're planning to play along at home, load the file ch06proj.html into the editing program of your choice. This is the file you'll be editing, saving, and reloading as the project progresses.

LAYING THE GROUNDWORK

The first thing to consider is the way the document is structured. In this case, there are three major components to the document:

◆ The page's title

◆ The navigation links

◆ The main content of the page

As the ordering of the bullet points suggests, the navigation links are contained in a div that comes after the h1 that contains the page title but before the main div that holds the text content of the page. The file already has some basic styles, which are shown in Listing 6.1 and illustrated by Figure 6.1.

Listing 6.1   The Basic Styles

```
<style type="text/css">
body {background: #EEE; color: #000;}
h1 {color: #AAA; border-bottom: 1px solid; margin-bottom: 0;}
#main {color: #CCC; margin-left: 7em; padding: 1px 0 1px 5%;
  border-left: 1px solid;}
div#nav {float: left; width: 7em;
  background: #FDD;}
</style>
```

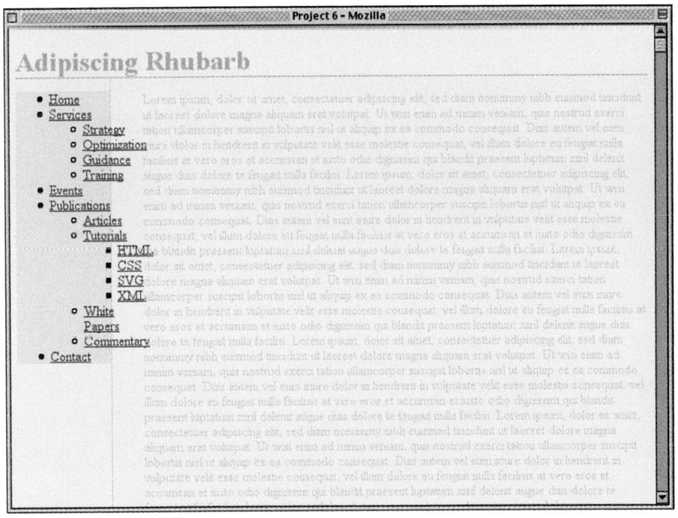

FIGURE 6.1

Our starting point, with the basic styles already applied.

The point of these basic styles is to get the page laid out properly and to visually de-emphasize the text so that it doesn't distract us while we work on the menu system. The light red background for the menu div is there solely to let us see where the navigation div is laid out. Speaking of menus, the markup that creates them is given in Listing 6.2.

Listing 6.2   The Navigation Menu Markup

```
<div id="nav">
<ul>
 <li><a href="/">Home</a></li>
 <li><a href="/services/">Services</a>
  <ul>
   <li><a href="/services/strategy/">Strategy</a></li>
   <li><a href="/services/optimize/">Optimization</a></li>
   <li><a href="/services/guidance/">Guidance</a></li>
   <li><a href="/services/training/">Training</a></li>
  </ul>
 </li>
 <li><a href="/events/">Events</a></li>
 <li><a href="/pubs/">Publications</a>
  <ul>
```

nav Naming

You may be wondering why we're referring to the navigation div as div#nav instead of just #nav. This is being done to avoid a bug in IE/Win: It won't dynamically show the submenus if the selectors just use #nav. We don't know why, exactly, adding the element name to the selector fixes this bug, but it does.

continues

Listing 6.2 Continued

```
  <li><a href="/pubs/articles/">Articles</a></li>
  <li><a href="/pubs/tuts/">Tutorials</a>
   <ul>
    <li><a href="/pubs/tuts/html/">HTML</a></li>
    <li><a href="/pubs/tuts/css/">CSS</a>
    <li><a href="/pubs/tuts/svg/">SVG</a>
    <li><a href="/pubs/tuts/xml/">XML</a>
   </ul>
  </li>
  <li><a href="/pubs/wpapers/">White Papers</a></li>
  <li><a href="/pubs/comment/">Commentary</a></li>
 </ul>
 </li>
 <li><a href="/contact/">Contact</a></li>
</ul>
</div>
```

Proper Nesting

Note that each nested list is inside a list item from its parent list; for example, the list item for Services contains a link, a nested list, and then the `</li>` appears. This is correct because lists cannot be children of lists, but they can be children of list items. A very common mistake is to place a nested list between list items instead of inside one of them.

That's right—it's some nested, unordered lists containing links and nothing more. This is almost all that we'll need. As we get further into the project, we'll add a few classes to the markup to make the menu system work, but that's all.

Laying Out the Menus

Before we get to the point of having the submenus appear and disappear, we're going to style them to look decent. In other words, we'll get the menus and submenus all styled and then take the steps necessary to make them appear and disappear in response to the user's actions.

Planning Ahead

Our first step will be to call a behavior file using the Windows Internet Explorer–only property `behavior`. This lets us bring in a separate file that will add capabilities to IE/Win that it doesn't ordinarily have.

```
body {background: #EEE; color: #000;
   behavior: url(csshover.htc);} /* WinIE behavior call */
```

For this to work, you'll need to get the `.htc` file from the book's Web site or get a copy from its original author, Peter Nederlof. His demonstration of this technique, which uses the same `.htc` file that we'll be using here, can be found at `http://www.xs4all.nl/~peterned/csshover.html`.

Before Peter's publication of `csshover.htc`, IE/Win could only support CSS-driven menu systems if the author added some JavaScript that added capabilities to IE/Win. In a sense, Peter did the same thing, except he put the additional capabilities into a Windows behavior file instead of a JavaScript file. This has one major advantage: Only IE/Win will try to download the behavior, which means that other browsers (which don't need it anyway) won't waste bandwidth getting the file. With the JavaScript solution, all browsers had to download the script.

There is one disadvantage to using the behavior approach: The `behavior` declaration will prevent the style sheet from validating. If this is a major concern for you, you could move the `behavior` declaration into a separate style sheet and then `@import` it. This would allow the main style sheet to validate and would quarantine the nonvalid `behavior` declaration in a separate file. What you do will probably depend on how you regard validation.

At the moment, the behavior file isn't changing anything about our page, mostly because we haven't gotten to the point where it would be useful. First we need to get our menus styled. The first step is to strip away all of the indentation and set the list widths to equal the width of the `div`. The result is shown in Figure 6.2.

```
div#nav {float: left; width: 7em;
   background: #FDD;}
div#nav ul {margin: 0; padding: 0; width: 7em;}
</style>
```

Margins and Padding

List indentation is handled with margins in some browsers and with padding in others. By zeroing out both, we make sure to cover all our bases.

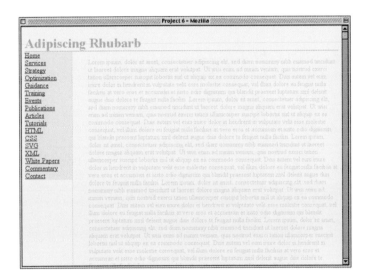

FIGURE 6.2

Having removed the indentation from the lists, they fit much better into the sidebar.

For the moment, it's become much harder to tell where the submenus start and end. We'll fix that in a big way in the next phase of the project.

Positioning the Submenus

The next step is to place the submenus where we'll want them to appear when the system is fully working. A very common technique is to have a submenu appear to the right of the item that triggered its appearance, lined up along the top. We can very easily do this by positioning the lists with respect to the list items that contain them.

To make this happen, we first need to make sure that every list item will act as a starting point for the position of its descendant submenu by establishing a *containing block*. That's as easy as relatively positioning the list items with no offsets.

```
div#nav ul {margin: 0; padding: 0; width: 7em;}
div#nav li {position: relative;}
</style>
```

By doing this, every list item sets up a containing block (think of it as a positioning context) for any descendant elements that are absolutely positioned. So, if we absolutely positioned the links inside the list items with `right: 0;`, each link would be positioned against the right edge of the list item that contained it.

Instead of positioning links, of course, we're going to position unordered lists. For any list that's inside another list, we want to place it so that the top of the submenu is aligned with the top of the list item that contains it.

```
div#nav li {position: relative; list-style: none; margin: 0;}
div#nav ul ul {position: absolute; top: 0;}
</style>
```

This will place the top edge of each submenu along the top of its containing block. Now all we need to do is put the submenu just to the right of its containing list item. We'll pull a fast one to make this happen. Thanks to our `div#nav ul` rule, we know that the lists are all `7em` wide. This means that the right edges of the list items are `7em` to the right of their left edges. If we offset the positioned submenus by the same amount, they'll be placed exactly where we want them, as shown in Figure 6.3.

```
div#nav ul ul {position: absolute; top: 0; left: 7em;}
```

FIGURE 6.3

The submenu lists are positioned with respect to their containing list items.

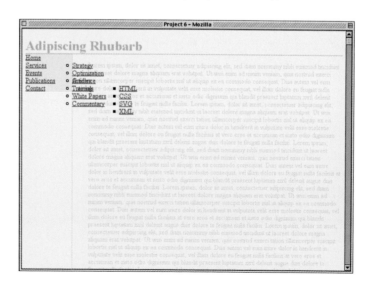

There are four things to note in Figure 6.3:

◆ The navigation `div` remains just as tall as its content. Now that we've absolutely positioned the submenus, though, they're no longer really a part of its content—not from a layout perspective, at any rate.

◆ The last two items in the first submenu overlap the first two items in the second. This makes them hard to read at the moment, but overlaps are actually no big deal because, by the time we're done, only one of those submenus will appear at any one time.

◆ The first level of submenus is exactly lined up along the right edge of the main-level links (Home, Services, and so on). The bullets, being in some sense attached to the list items, are actually hanging out of the unordered lists. We can't see them on the main links because the bullets are actually to the left of the browser window's left edge.

◆ There are still list bullets, at least in most browsers. We need to get rid of them pronto.

Before we move on then:

```
div#nav li {position: relative; list-style: none; margin: 0;}
```

Thus, the bullets are removed, as we'll see in the next figure.

Prettier Menu Styles

Now that the submenus are placed where we want them, it's time to start fleshing out their appearance. Let's give them a white background and, for the moment, a one-pixel solid border whose color is taken from the `color` value of the `ul` elements.

```
div#nav ul {margin: 0; padding: 0; width: 7em;
  background: white; border: 1px solid;}
```

That will "box in" each unordered list, from the main level to the deepest submenu. Because some browsers (like Opera) apply margins to list items by default, we'll zero out their margins as well.

```
div#nav li {position: relative; list-style: none; margin: 0;}
```

Now, about those submenus. To make some later styling easier, we'll need to add some structural hooks to the markup. For each of the three list items that contains a submenu, we're adding a `class` attribute with a value of `submenu`, as shown here:

```
<li class="submenu"><a href="/services/">Services</a>

<li class="submenu"><a href="/pubs/">Publications</a>

  <li class="submenu"><a href="/pubs/tuts/">Tutorials</a>
```

Class Naming

Just about any name could be used instead of submenu. We might have used sm, subm, or even reginald. The value submenu was picked because it's unambiguous. When you're doing your own designs, feel free to use a name that appeals to you more.

In effect, we're marking the submenu-containing list items with the label submenu. To make sure that we've classed the proper items, we'll add a highlighting rule, with the result shown in Figure 6.4.

```
div#nav li {position: relative; list-style: none; margin: 0;}
div#nav li.submenu {background: yellow;}
div#nav ul ul {position: absolute; top: 0; left: 7em;}
```

FIGURE 6.4

The submenus' appearance is improved, and list items that contain submenus are highlighted.

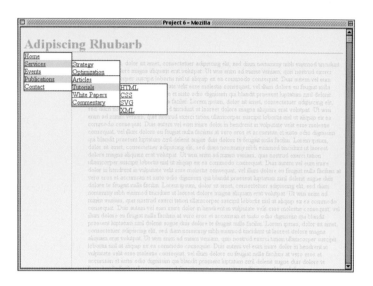

Now that the menus all have backgrounds, the overlap between the two first-level submenus is a little easier to understand. They still overlap, but the background of the second submenu obscures the first one entirely. As for the sub-submenu, we can now see that its left edge lines up quite nicely with the right edge of its parent list item.

Blocking Out Links

If you're following along with the project in your own file, you may have noticed something in the recent changes. The clickable area of the links in the menus aren't filling up the whole of each list item. This is because the links are inline elements. If we were to set a border on the links, for example, the border would wrap around just the text.

For the menus to work correctly, and to act like users expect, we really need the links to fill up all of the list items. To do that, we'll change the kind of boxes the links create when they're laid out.

```
div#nav li.submenu {background: yellow;}
div#nav li a {display: block;}
div#nav ul ul {position: absolute; top: 0; left: 7em;}
```

Doubled Heights

In IE/Win, the lists get spread apart by the `display: block;` we just added. This is due to a bug with IE/Win's handling of whitespace and block-box links in lists. But don't worry: We're going to overcome the bug by the time we reach the next figure.

Now each link will generate a block-level box, much like a `div` or paragraph would. Note that we have *not* changed the nature of the links themselves. The `a` elements are still inline elements. All that's happened is that the CSS is getting them to generate block boxes. This is a subtle distinction but a good one to keep in mind.

Now we not only can click anywhere within a menu entry and have it work (except in IE/Win, but we'll fix that in a moment), but we can style the links the same as we might a block-level element. To push the link text over to the right a bit, for example, we'd set a left padding for the links. We can also push the links apart a bit with some top and bottom padding.

```
div#nav li a {display: block; padding: 0.25em 0 0.25em 0.5em;}
```

We should also turn off the link underlining since users don't expect menu links to be underlined.

```
div#nav li a {display: block; padding: 0.25em 0 0.25em 0.5em;
   text-decoration: none;}
```

Now for IE/Win's problems. For whatever reason, block-box links like ours don't fill out the whole list item in IE/Win. This is a bug, but fortunately it's one we can work around. If we give the links an explicit width, we'll get the behavior we want. However, in other browsers, we just want them to set an automatic width, like they were doing before.

To pull this off, we'll first set an explicit width for the links, and then we'll use a rule IE/Win doesn't understand to unset that width.

```
div#nav li a {display: block; padding: 0.25em 0 0.25em 0.5em;
   text-decoration: none; width: 6.5em;}
div#nav>ul a {width: auto;}
div#nav ul ul {position: absolute; top: 0; left: 7em;}
```

With a content width of `6.5em` and a left padding of `0.5em`, the link's element box will be 7em wide, just like its parent element. Now we can just add a light gray border to the bottom of each list item, visually separating them.

```
div#nav li {position: relative; list-style: none; margin: 0;
   border-bottom: 1px solid #CCC;}
```

We could have added the border to the bottom of the links, too. Given the way we've styled the menus, that would have worked as well as styling the list items does. The cumulative effect of these changes is shown in Figure 6.5.

What's That Again?

The selector `div#nav>ul a` means "any `a` element that is descended from a `ul` element that is itself the child of a `div` with an `id` of nav." That will select all the links in our menu system. IE/Win doesn't understand the "child of a `div`" part of the selector, so it skips the whole rule.

FIGURE 6.5

Padding the links spreads out the list items a bit, and the links fill out their list items.

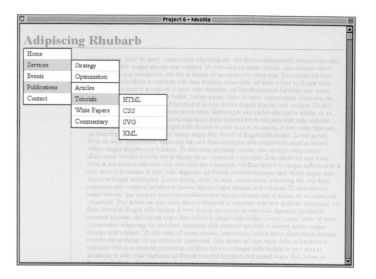

▶▶ BOX MODEL BLUES

Declaring a width of 6.5em for the links will work fine in IE6, which gets the CSS box model correct. In older versions of IE/Win, however, it won't because they got the model wrong. It's possible to construct a set of rules that takes all of these into account. This would involve using the "box model hack" as well as the child-selector hack we just saw. For example:

```
div#nav li a {display: block; padding: 0.25em 0 0.25em 0.5em;
  text-decoration: none; width: 100%;
  voice-family: "\"}\"";  voice-family:inherit;
  width: 6.5em;}
div#nav>ul a {width: auto;}
div#nav ul ul {position: absolute; top: 0; left: 7em;}
```

The first change sets the link width to 100%, which is what older versions of IE/Win require. That's the last width value those older versions will see because the next line (with the voice-family declarations) will make them skip the rest of the rule. IE6 will keep going, though, and see the width: 6.5em; declaration. The same is true of Opera, Mozilla, Safari, and other modern browsers. Then the child-selector line, which sets the width back to auto, is ignored by IE6 and older IE/Win versions but is handled by modern browsers.

Whether or not it's worth going to all this effort depends heavily on your audience demographic. If you have a lot of users on older machines, you'll probably want to go to this extent. For the rest of the project, we're going to assume that our audience members are using the latest version of whatever browsers they use, and we'll leave out the more complicated series of hacks just shown.

Hovering Entries

It's time to add a hover style to the menu entries so that when the user mouses over "Home," its background changes color. We can do this with the following rule:

```
div#nav li {position: relative; list-style: none; margin: 0;
  border-bottom: 1px solid #CCC;}
div#nav li:hover {background: #EBB;}
div#nav li.submenu {background: yellow;}
```

No, that isn't a mistake, so hold off on your errata reports. We are very intentionally applying a hover effect to the list items themselves and not the links. This is perfectly acceptable in CSS, which doesn't restrict hover effects to hyperlinks: Any element at all can be given hover styles. So, in this case, the background of any `li` element that's being hovered and that is descended from a `div` with an `id` of `nav` will change to `#EBB`.

Why don't more authors do this kind of thing? Because IE/Win actually does restrict hover effects to hyperlinks and doesn't apply them to other kinds of elements. At least, that's how it acts by default. Remember the `csshover.htc` file we associated with the `body` element back at the outset? The sole purpose of that file is to add arbitrary-element hover capabilities to IE/Win. In other words, thanks to that behavior file, IE/Win will now allow hover styles on any element, the same as what we see in Figure 6.6.

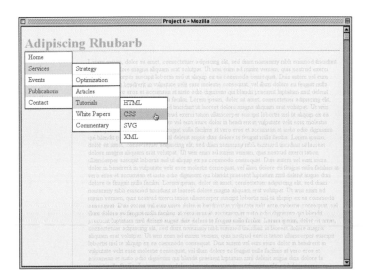

FIGURE 6.6

Adding hover effects to list items.

Again, the background is changing on the *list item*, not the link inside the list item. Those links all have transparent backgrounds so that we can see the list item backgrounds changing behind them.

It's difficult to understate the importance of this capability. In addition to allowing for nested pop-up menus based on simple markup and CSS, it's possible to use this capability to change information on one part of a page by hovering over other parts—and a whole lot more. Being able to add arbitrary-element hovering to IE/Win seems more than worth the price of a small amount of nonvalid CSS.

Special Submenu Styles

Take a moment to catch your breath, and then we'll move on. The yellow highlighting of the submenu links served its purpose, but now it's starting to look distinctly icky. We still want a visual indication of which menu entries will open a new menu, so let's replace the yellow with a background image of a small arrow called `submenu.gif`.

```
div#nav li.submenu {background: url(submenu.gif) 95% 50% no-repeat;}
```

This will place a single instance of the image 95% of the way to the right of the submenu list items and vertically centered, as shown in Figure 6.7.

FIGURE 6.7

Placing an arrow to show which entries will spawn submenus.

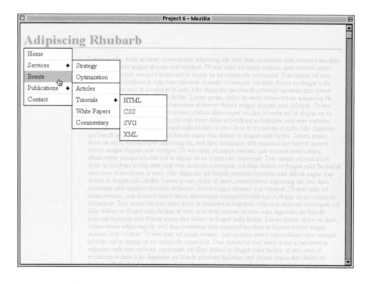

Explorer Weirdness

If you're using IE/Win, you may notice some oddities with the hover effects; for example, the arrow image disappearing. This is likely due to glitches in the behavior script, or in Explorer's handling of it. These are minor enough to ignore, but bear in mind the script's imperfections if you intend to use it for a public design.

That's quite a bit nicer. However, it means now that the same exact hover effect will be applied to all list items: They'll all get the same background color whether or not a submenu is present. Let's lighten up the hover color for submenu entries. Again, instead of the links, we'll apply the hover styles directly to the list items.

```
div#nav li.submenu {background: url(submenu.gif) 95% 50% no-repeat;}
div#nav li.submenu:hover {background-color: #EDD;}
div#nav li a {display: block; padding: 0.25em 0 0.25em 0.5em;
  text-decoration: none; width: 6.5em;}
```

We could style the links themselves, of course, but if we did that for the sub-menu entries, the link's background would obscure the arrow graphic in the background of the list item. If that's what we wanted, it would be a great solution, but it isn't. By changing the background color of the list item, the color and image can exist together, as shown in Figure 6.8.

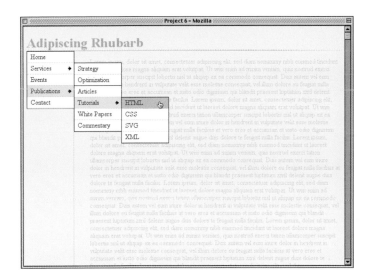

FIGURE 6.8

Defining a different hover style for submenu entries.

Preparing for Pop-Ups

At this point, we've really written all the styles we need for the presentation and placement of the menus, submenus, and individual entries. All that remains is to start the showing and hiding process.

Before we add more CSS, let's look at a few changes that need to be made to the HTML itself. We're adding classes to the various lists so that we can actually control the appearance and disappearance of submenus via the style sheet. These changes are highlighted in Listing 6.3.

Listing 6.3   Adding Level Information

```
<div id="nav">
<ul class="level1">
 <li><a href="/">Home</a></li>
 <li class="submenu"><a href="/services/">Services</a>
  <ul class="level2">
   <li><a href="/services/strategy/">Strategy</a></li>
   <li><a href="/services/optimize/">Optimization</a></li>
   <li><a href="/services/guidance/">Guidance</a></li>
   <li><a href="/services/training/">Training</a></li>
  </ul>
 </li>
 <li><a href="/events/">Events</a></li>
 <li class="submenu"><a href="/pubs/">Publications</a>
```

continues

Listing 6.3 Continued

```
<ul class="level2">
 <li><a href="/pubs/articles/">Articles</a></li>
 <li class="submenu"><a href="/pubs/tuts/">Tutorials</a>
  <ul class="level3">
   <li><a href="/pubs/tuts/html/">HTML</a></li>
   <li><a href="/pubs/tuts/css/">CSS</a>
   <li><a href="/pubs/tuts/svg/">SVG</a>
   <li><a href="/pubs/tuts/xml/">XML</a>
  </ul>
 </li>
 <li><a href="/pubs/wpapers/">White Papers</a></li>
 <li><a href="/pubs/comment/">Commentary</a></li>
 </ul>
</li>
<li><a href="/contact/">Contact</a></li>
</ul>
</div>
```

Here's why we need these changes: If we simply wrote in our CSS "Show any ul that's descended from a hovered submenu list item," then hovering over "Publications" would cause both the Publications submenu and the Tutorials submenu to appear at once. Instead, what we need to say is "Show any ul that's a child of a hovered submenu list item." The way to do that would be a child selector, which IE/Win doesn't understand. To work around this, we need to class the menus according to their nesting level.

Because our submenus are already visible, we need to hide them. Since we're hiding any ul that's descended from a ul, we can modify an already-existing rule, with the result shown in Figure 6.9.

```
div#nav ul ul {position: absolute; top: 0; left: 7em;
   display: none;}
```

FIGURE 6.9

Hiding the submenus.

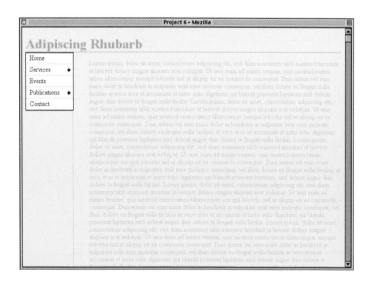

So, by default, all we can see is the top-level menu. That's good! It's exactly what we want.

Now to control the appearance of submenus. We want a second-level menu to appear when its parent list item is hovered, and we make it reappear by changing its `display` to `block`.

```
div#nav ul ul {position: absolute; top: 0; left: 7em;
  display: none;}
div#nav ul.level1 li.submenu:hover ul.level2 {display:block;}
</style>
```

So now any `level2` list that's descended from a hovered list item that is itself descended from a `level1` list (which is in turn descended from a `div` with an `id` of `nav`) will change its `display` from `none` to `block`. That's fine for second-level menus, but how about third level? We only need to modify the selector.

```
div#nav ul.level1 li.submenu:hover ul.level2,
div#nav ul.level2 li.submenu:hover ul.level3 {display:block;}
```

Now the rule will apply to third-level menus just as it does to second-level menus, with the result shown in Figure 6.10.

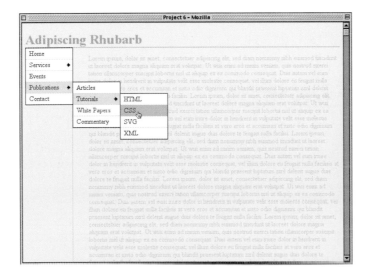

FIGURE 6.10

Showing the submenus in response to user actions.

And that's really all it takes to create nested pop-up menus with CSS and a little bit of behavior scripting.

▶▶ **DISPLAY OR VISIBILITY?**

Rather than use display: none *and* display: block *to hide and show the menus, we might have used* visibility *instead. In that case, the relevant rules in the style sheet would have read:*

```
div#nav ul ul {position: absolute; top: 0; left: 7em;
  visibility: hidden;}
div#nav ul.level1 li.submenu:hover ul.level2,
div#nav ul.level2 li.submenu:hover ul.level3 {visibility: visible;}
```

The difference is that an element with display: none *generates no element box at all; it is as though the element did not exist. An element set to* visibility: hidden *still generates an element box of the same size it would have if it were visible, but the element box is completely transparent.*

In normal-flow layout, this makes a difference since a transparent (hidden) element box will affect the layout of other elements. Because the menus are absolutely positioned, however, they don't affect other elements' layout anyway. Thus, visibility *and* display *would work equally well in this situation. We're sticking with* display *because that's what Peter used in his original demo, and it works just fine.*

Finishing Touches

With our menu system working, let's add a couple of extra touches to the presentation. As we can see from the preceding figure, the menus stand out kind of starkly with their black borders, and the main-level menu's top and right borders double up with the borders on the main content and page title.

We'll fix the first issue by pulling the menu up one pixel and to the left by the same amount, by way of negative margins.

```
div#nav {float: left; width: 7em; margin: -1px 0 0 -1px;
  background: #FDD;}
```

The list's borders can be toned down by making them match the border color already in use for the title. This is illustrated in Figure 6.11.

```
div#nav ul {margin: 0; padding: 0; width: 7em; background: white;
  border: 1px solid #AAA;}
```

Negative Margin Clip

During testing, it was observed that in some copies of IE/Win, the negative top and left margins would pull the menu up and to the left, but also cut off the borders on those sides. If you don't see this, bear in mind that it does happen and should be considered before publicly deploying any layout.

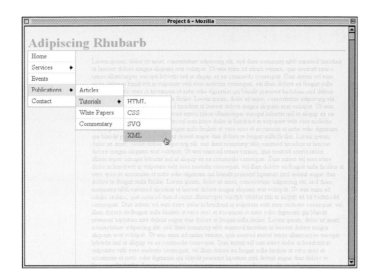

FIGURE 6.11

Merging the menu's appearance more closely with the rest of the layout.

Now everything fits together very neatly, and it's all thanks to the style sheet given in Listing 6.4 (plus the behavior file, which is not listed).

Listing 6.4   The Menu Styles

```
body {background: #EEE; color: #000;
  behavior: url(csshover.htc);} /* WinIE behavior call */
h1 {color: #AAA; border-bottom: 1px solid; margin-bottom: 0;}
#main {color: #CCC; margin-left: 7em; padding: 1px 0 1px 5%;
  border-left: 1px solid;}
div#nav {float: left; width: 7em; margin: -1px 0 0 -1px;
  background: #FDD;}
div#nav ul {margin: 0; padding: 0; width: 7em; background: white;
  border: 1px solid #AAA;}
div#nav li {position: relative; list-style: none; margin: 0;
  border-bottom: 1px solid #CCC;}
div#nav li:hover {background: #EBB;}
div#nav li.submenu {background: url(submenu.gif) 95% 50% no-repeat;}
div#nav li.submenu:hover {background-color: #EDD;}
div#nav li a {display: block; padding: 0.25em 0 0.25em 0.5em;
  text-decoration: none; width: 6.5em;}
div#nav>ul a {width: auto;}
div#nav ul ul {position: absolute; top: 0; left: 7em;
  display: none;}
div#nav ul.level1 li.submenu:hover ul.level2,
div#nav ul.level2 li.submenu:hover ul.level3 {display:block;}
```

REORIENTING THE MENUS

So far, we've managed to create a good multilevel menu system in which each submenu opens up to the right of its parent. That's great if the navigation is going to be in the sidebar, but what if it isn't? What if we want the main-level navigation to be a horizontal toolbar across the top of the page? Good news: With some small style adjustments and a few extra rules, we can do exactly that with the same markup we're already using.

Reorientation

Before anything else, let's rework the styles so that the main-level links are shown as a horizontal toolbar. This will require very few changes, as it happens. The first thing to do is strip out the width declarations from the div#nav and div#nav ul rules.

```
div#nav {float: left; margin: -1px 0 0 -1px;
   background: #FDD;}
div#nav ul {margin: 0; padding: 0; background: white;
   border: 1px solid #AAA;}
```

Removals

We don't see any code changes here because we've just removed stuff. Compare this code block to the same rule in Listing 6.4 if the changes aren't clear.

This will let the div and the lists within the div autosize themselves. Don't worry—we'll fix that for the menus themselves in a moment. Right now, though, we can't have a horizontal toolbar unless we let the toolbar set its own width.

To place the toolbar across the top of the main content, we'll change its left margin.

```
div#nav {float: left; margin: -1px 0 0 7em;
   background: #FDD;}
```

This will push the left edge of the toolbar over a distance equal to the width of the main content's left margin.

Because the navigation div is floated and has no explicit width, it "autosizes" itself to wrap around its content. (This is also known as "shrink-wrapping.") If we float them—and we are going to float them—the same will be true of the list items within the menus, including those at the top level. For some applications, this might be acceptable, but here we're going to want them all to be the same width. Why not 7em? It's worked well enough so far.

```
div#nav li {position: relative; list-style: none; margin: 0;
   float: left; width: 7em;
   border-bottom: 1px solid #CCC;}
```

Why did we float the list items? So they'd line up horizontally. If we didn't float them, we'd end up with a vertical list of links like we had before.

Now here's why we want those list items all to be the same width: The menus that drop down from the main level will need to be consistent widths. If not, the menu might be wider or narrower than the top-level link that made it appear. So we'll add a width to the lists that are second level or lower by way of the `div#nav ul ul` rule, and at the same time take out the `top` and `left` declarations.

```
div#nav ul ul {position: absolute; width: 7em;
  display: none;}
```

These few small changes, taken together, give us the result shown in Figure 6.12.

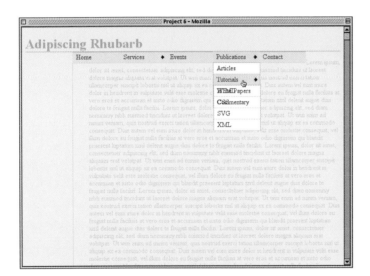

FIGURE 6.12

Reorienting the menu system to be a horizontal toolbar.

There are six things to note in Figure 6.12:

◆ The main content is wrapping around the floated `div`. We'll want to make sure it's pushed below the toolbar.

◆ The light red background of the navigation `div` is back. That's because we have an unordered list that has no normal-flow content; all its list items are floated, and all its descendant lists are positioned. Therefore, the `ul` has collapsed to have zero height, and the `div`'s background becomes visible.

◆ For the same reasons, the top-level `ul` element has no height, and the thick gray bar along the top is actually the top and bottom borders of the `ul` smashed up next to each other. The `div` stretches around the list items because it's floated, and floats stretch to contain floats that they contain.

◆ The bottom border of the list items is what creates the border along the bottom edge of the toolbar.

The Seventh

In IE/Win, there's a seventh thing to note: The left margin of the navigation bar has been doubled. This is due to a bug in IE/Win that causes it to double margins on floats for no discernable reason. Since the only difference between the figures and IE/Win should be in its placement of the navigation links, we're going to ignore this error for the rest of the project.

◆ The second-level menus appear exactly where we want them. This happens because they're still being positioned with respect to their containing list items. The reason they appear at the bottom edge of the list items is that they have a top of auto. (Remember, we took out the top declaration, and the default value of top is auto.). In this case, the top of the positioned element is placed where it would have been if the element weren't positioned. So the submenus show up right where they would have if there were no positioning in effect.

◆ The autoplacement discussed in the preceding point is happening for the sub-submenus as well, so they end up overlapping their parent submenus. We'll need to fix that.

Let's address these points in order.

Starting the Fixes

The easiest thing to fix is the main content wrapping around the toolbar. Rather than use clear, which would push down the entire content div (including the left border), we'll just bump up the top padding. The list items are about 1.5em tall, so we'll go slightly larger than that.

```
#main {color: #CCC; margin-left: 7em; padding: 2em 0 1px 5%;
    border-left: 1px solid;}
```

This will push the top of the first paragraph's content down by 3em because there's 2em of top padding on the div and 1em of top margin on the paragraph.

Now to erase the red background. We want a border to stretch around the links in the toolbar and give the whole thing a white background. Since the div itself is already stretching around the top-level links, we'll change its background and add a border (see Figure 6.13).

```
div#nav {float: left; margin: -1px 0 0 7em;
    background: #FFF; border: 1px solid #AAA;}
```

Notice the thick gray border still appearing along the top of the toolbar? That's the ul border still hanging around. We could just remove the border from ul elements entirely, but that would cause a problem: The submenus would have no borders.

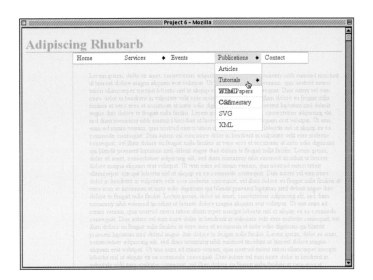

FIGURE 6.13

Pushing the main content past the toolbar and adding a background and border to the navigation div.

Instead, we'll lighten up the border just a bit and remove the top and bottom borders by setting their widths to zero.

```
div#nav ul {margin: 0; padding: 0; background: white;
  border: 1px solid #CCC; border-width: 0 1px;}
```

This will still give the submenus right and left borders, and for the top-level ul, no border will appear because the borders that have width have no height (since the element itself has no height).

Now, what about the bottom borders of the submenus? Those are handled by the bottom border of the list items. Visually speaking, there is no difference. Where the bottom border of list items might be considered a problem is along the bottom edge of the toolbar where the list item borders sit up against the bottom border of the navigation div. We can get rid of that by removing the border declaration from the div#nav li rule.

```
div#nav li {position: relative; list-style: none; margin: 0;
  float: left; width: 7em;}
```

But this will also remove the bottom borders from the submenu list items, and we've already established that we need those. So we'll add the borders back in for submenus with this rule.

```
div#nav ul ul {position: absolute; width: 7em;
  display: none;}
div#nav ul ul li {border-bottom: 1px solid #CCC;}
div#nav ul.level1 li.submenu:hover ul.level2,
div#nav ul.level2 li.submenu:hover ul.level3 {display:block;}
```

There's one more thing to fix at the top level: the arrow image. Having a right-pointing arrow doesn't really make sense anymore because the menus drop down, not pop out to the right. As long as we have an image of a downward pointing arrow (called, let's say, `dropmenu.gif`), we only need to change a single rule (see Figure 6.14).

```
div#nav li.submenu {background: url(dropmenu.gif) 95% 50% no-repeat;}
```

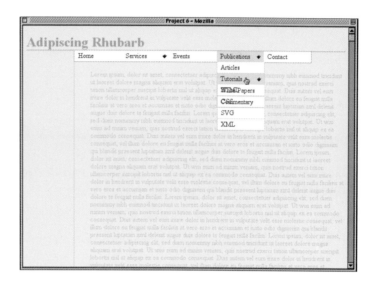

FIGURE 6.14

Corrections to the borders and a new arrow image.

Submenu Corrections

As you probably noticed in Figure 6.14, things are great at the top level but are not so great in the submenus. For one, the "Tutorials" entry has a downward-pointing arrow thanks to the last change we made. For another, the "Tutorials" submenu is still overlapping with the end of the "Publications" menu. Both need to be fixed.

The arrow is simple to fix. Well, really, both fixes are simple, but the arrow fix is simpler. All we have to do is drop the original background image (`submenu.gif`) into the background of any submenu list item that's descended from another submenu list item. This won't apply to the top-level links that contain submenus because they aren't descended from other submenu list items.

```
div#nav ul ul li {border-bottom: 1px solid #CCC;}
div#nav li.submenu li.submenu {background-image: url(submenu.gif);}
div#nav ul.level1 li.submenu:hover ul.level2,
div#nav ul.level2 li.submenu:hover ul.level3 {display:block;}
```

At least, that would be all we'd have to do if it weren't for a bug in the script we're using for IE/Win. It apparently resets all the background styles to their defaults when an element is hovered, so sticking with that last change means that the arrow will tile throughout the whole background of the submenu. So, we'll make sure it gets the right message by declaring all the values again.

```
div#nav li.submenu li.submenu {background: url(submenu.gif) 95% 50% no-repeat;}
div#nav li.submenu li.submenu:hover {background-color: #EDD;}
div#nav ul.level1 li.submenu:hover ul.level2,
div#nav ul.level2 li.submenu:hover ul.level3 {display:block;}
```

That fixes up the problem rather nicely.

Now for the placement of the sub-submenus. Actually, let's place the submenus first. We want their top to line up with the bottom of the top-level list items, like they do now, except we want to explicitly express that behavior. Also, we want the left side of the submenu's content to line up with the left edge of the list item's content. Because the submenu has a left border and the top-level list items don't, the content of the submenu is actually one pixel to the right. So we'll use a negative `left` value to compensate.

```
div#nav ul.level1 li.submenu:hover ul.level2,
div#nav ul.level2 li.submenu:hover ul.level3 {display:block;}
div#nav ul.level2 {top: 1.5em; left: -1px;}
</style>
```

The `top` value is set to match the sum of the top-level list item's `font-size` and top and bottom padding, but only if the height of each list item's line is exactly 1em tall. We haven't said that explicitly, and we need to do so. Therefore,

```
div#nav li {position: relative; list-style: none; margin: 0;
  float: left; width: 7em; line-height: 1em;}
```

Now we just need to position the sub-submenus correctly. For these, we want the top edges to line up and the sub-submenu to appear just to the left of its parent entry. So we'll bring back the `left: 7em;` that we used in the first half of the project and use a negative `top` value to pull the menu up to where we want it.

```
div#nav ul.level2 {top: 1.5em; left: -1px;}
div#nav ul.level3 {top: -1px; left: 7em;}
</style>
```

One more thing and we're done. Remember the change to borders that caused the top border to be taken away from submenus? That applies to sub-submenus as well, so we have to apply one to get the result shown in Figure 6.15.

```
div#nav ul.level3 {top: -1px; left: 7em;
  border-top: 1px solid #CCC;}
```

FIGURE 6.15

Polishing up the submenus and sub-submenus.

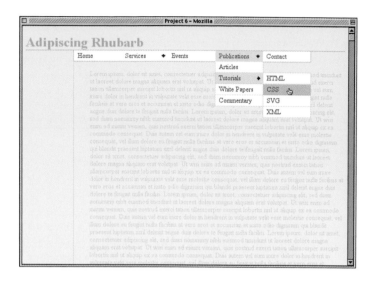

With that, we arrive at the style sheet shown in Listing 6.5.

Listing 6.5   Toolbar-Oriented Menu System Style Sheet

```
body {background: #EEE; color: #000;
  behavior: url(csshover.htc);} /* WinIE behavior call */
h1 {color: #AAA; border-bottom: 1px solid; margin-bottom: 0;}
#main {color: #CCC; margin-left: 7em; padding: 2em 0 1px 5%;
  border-left: 1px solid;}
div#nav {float: left; margin: -1px 0 0 7em;
  background: #FFF; border: 1px solid #AAA;}
div#nav ul {margin: 0; padding: 0; background: white;
  border: 1px solid #CCC; border-width: 0 1px;}
div#nav li {position: relative; list-style: none; margin: 0;
  float: left; width: 7em; line-height: 1em;}
div#nav li:hover {background: #EBB;}
div#nav li.submenu {background: url(dropmenu.gif) 95% 50% no-repeat;}
div#nav li.submenu:hover {background-color: #EDD;}
div#nav li a {display: block; padding: 0.25em 0 0.25em 0.5em;
  text-decoration: none; width: 6.5em;}
div#nav>ul a {width: auto;}
div#nav ul ul {position: absolute; width: 7em;
  display: none;}
div#nav ul ul li {border-bottom: 1px solid #CCC;}
div#nav li.submenu li.submenu {background-image: url(submenu.gif);}
div#nav ul.level1 li.submenu:hover ul.level2,
div#nav ul.level2 li.submenu:hover ul.level3 {display:block;}
div#nav ul.level2 {top: 1.5em; left: -1px;}
div#nav ul.level3 {top: -1px; left: 7em;
  border-top: 1px solid #CCC;}
```

FOR YOUR CONSIDERATION

There are some things to bear in mind if you're going to implement CSS-driven menus like those explored in this project. Leaving aside wider questions like whether or not drop-down menus are a good user interface (some say yes, others no), the actual behavior of these menus should be considered.

Because the appearance of submenus depends on list items being in a hover state, it's fairly easy for users to accidentally let the menus snap closed. The instant the mouse pointer moves outside any of the menus, all of the currently visible submenus will disappear. The same is often true of JavaScript-driven menus, but in JavaScript you can build in delay timers that give the user a small interval of time to move the mouse back inside the menus before they go away. CSS offers no capability to define such delay timers and is not likely to do so any time soon (if ever).

For this reason, it is imperative that submenus at least sit adjacent to their parent list items, if not actually overlap them by a small amount. If a gap even a pixel wide appears between a menu entry and its submenu, there is a high probability that the mouse pointer will exit the hover state while moving through that gap and cause any open submenus to disappear. Such a situation would basically make it impossible to use some (or all) of the submenus.

Of course, it is possible to use the techniques presented here to define the appearance of menus and then use JavaScript to drive the dynamic behaviors—that is, the showing and hiding of menus, any delay timers to make the menus more usable, and the event handling that glues it all together. Such a technique is beyond the scope of this book, but in essence it would involve leaving out the `display: block;` rule and `behavior` declaration, relying on JavaScript to take the place of those styles.

As to which is better, again, there is controversy that we do not presume to resolve here. Some say that behavior should not be driven by CSS, which is a presentation language, and should instead be handled by a scripting language like JavaScript. Others feel that this sort of behavior falls within the realm of what CSS covers, and so there's nothing wrong with such techniques. It is expected that the debate will continue for a long time to come, so authors need to make up their own minds about which they prefer and act accordingly.

BRANCHING OUT

Now that you know how to create drop-down menus using CSS, try sprucing them up in the following ways:

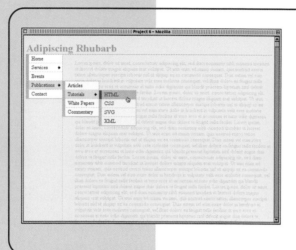

1. Take the style sheet from the first half of the project and expand it so that the entries have a gray stripe along their left edges, and do so without using a background image. The stripe should change to red for the menu entry currently being hovered. While you're at it, make the background of each level of submenu slightly darker.

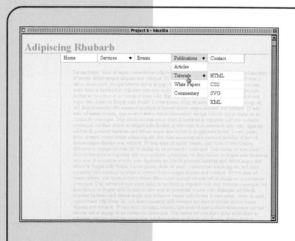

2. Extend the styles from the second half of the project so that gray borders separate the top-level links. Here's the challenge: Do it without changing the visual appearance of the submenus in any way.

3. Rework the styles from the second half of the project to make sub-submenus pop out to the left of their triggering menu entry instead of to the right. To look as good as possible, right-align the text in the submenus, but make sure it does run up against the right edge of the submenus. Also, you'll need a new arrow graphic. (Try flipping `submenu.gif` horizontally in a graphic editor like Photoshop.)

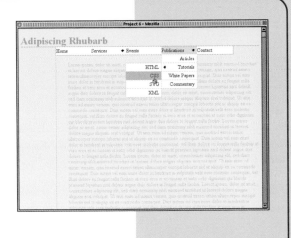

7

OPENING THE DOORS TO ATTRACTIVE TABS

Welcome evermore to gods and men is the self-helping man. For him all doors are flung wide: him all tongues greet, all honors crown, all eyes follow with desire.

—RALPH WALDO EMERSON

WITH THE TREND TOWARD using lists to represent "menus" (collections of links), there has been a good deal of interest in setting up not only link sidebars, but also horizontal rows of links. A good example of such links would be the ones across the top of Amazon.com or the Apple web site. In fact, such collections often are made to look like small tabs, although this isn't always the case.

For some time, translating an unordered list into a row of tabs meant that they were, well, kind of boxy. Not to mention a bit boring. This was the case because the tabs were usually created by setting borders on the list items or the links themselves. That's good for a basic design, but if you want a professional look, the result is rather lacking.

So, in late 2003, Douglas Bowman (`http://www.stopdesign.com/`), perhaps best known for his table-free redesign of Wired News, pioneered a new approach that allowed authors to create tabs just about as visually stunning as their imaginations would allow. He first described this technique in the article "Sliding Doors of CSS" (`http://alistapart.com/articles/slidingdoors/`) and followed it up with another article that dug more deeply into the technique. In this project, we'll be exploring some variants on Doug's original idea, but the core idea is all his.

Project Goals

Thanks to some outstanding efforts from the sales team, we've landed a contract to design a site for a new publishing house called "New Writers." Shaking off an inexplicable feeling of *dèjá vu*, we consider the goals for this phase of the project.

◆ We need a template showing how the persistent navigation elements will look. This template will use some basic styles that have already been worked out, particularly for the page title.

◆ The navigation will be contained in an unordered list, but it needs to be presented as a horizontal row of buttons or tabs situated between the page title and the main content.

◆ The buttons/tabs need to be visually attractive. The client has seen plenty of CSS-driven buttons that end up as plain rectangles with a background color, and he wants something better for this site.

◆ Whatever look we devise for the buttons/tabs, they need to be easy to update or change in case the site's design changes.

So we need to concentrate on turning the navigation elements into something pretty. This isn't the entire contract, of course; a full site design takes a lot more work than that. For the purposes of this project, though, it's enough to concentrate on creating a basic template for styling the navigation elements.

Preparation

See the Introduction for instructions on how to download files from the Web site.

Download the files for Project 7 from this book's Web site. If you're planning to play along at home, load the file `ch07proj.html` into the editing program of your choice. This is the file you'll be editing, saving, and reloading as the project progresses.

LAYING THE GROUNDWORK

The template page for our project is pretty bare, as Figure 7.1 reveals.

![New Writers - Mozilla]

New Writers

- Web Development
- Design
- Photo Editing
- New Media
- 3-D Rendering
- Server Tech

Lorem ipsum, dolor sit amet, consectetuer adipiscing elit, sed diam nonummy nibh euismod tincidunt ut laoreet dolore magna aliquam erat volutpat. Ut wisi enim ad minim veniam, quis nostrud exerci tation ullamcorper suscipit lobortis nisl ut aliquip ex ea commodo consequat. Duis autem vel eum iriure dolor in hendrerit in vulputate velit esse molestie consequat, vel illum dolore eu feugiat nulla facilisis at vero eros et accumsan et iusto odio dignissim qui blandit praesent luptatum zzril delenit augue duis dolore te feugait nulla facilisi. Lorem ipsum, dolor sit amet, consectetuer adipiscing elit, sed diam nonummy nibh euismod tincidunt ut laoreet dolore magna aliquam erat volutpat. Ut wisi enim ad minim veniam, quis nostrud exerci tation ullamcorper suscipit lobortis nisl ut aliquip ex ea commodo consequat. Duis autem vel eum iriure dolor in hendrerit in vulputate velit esse molestie consequat, vel illum dolore eu feugiat nulla facilisis at vero eros et accumsan et iusto odio dignissim qui blandit praesent luptatum zzril delenit augue duis dolore te feugait nulla facilisi. Lorem ipsum, dolor sit amet, consectetuer adipiscing elit, sed diam nonummy nibh euismod tincidunt ut laoreet dolore magna aliquam erat volutpat. Ut wisi enim ad minim veniam, quis nostrud exerci tation ullamcorper suscipit lobortis nisl ut aliquip ex ea commodo consequat. Duis autem vel eum iriure dolor in hendrerit in vulputate velit esse molestie consequat, vel illum dolore eu feugiat nulla facilisis at vero eros et accumsan et iusto odio dignissim qui blandit praesent luptatum zzril delenit augue duis dolore te feugait nulla facilisi.

FIGURE 7.1

The unstyled template document.

Before we get to work on the navigation elements, let's style the rest of the template. That will give us a framework for our button styles.

The first step is to style the overall document itself, in effect writing "global" styles that will apply to the document and all its constituent elements. We'll do this by removing any "gutter space" around the edges of the document, setting foreground and background colors, and defining a list of possible fonts for the `html` and `body` elements.

```
<style type="text/css">
html, body {margin: 0; padding: 0;
  color: #000; background: #EEF;
  font-family: Verdana, Arial, sans-serif;}
</style>
```

Why did we style both elements? For the same reason we set both padding and margins to zero—we're covering our bases. Although all known browsers enforce "gutter spacing" with either margins or padding on the body, it's possible that a browser might use padding on the `html` element instead. Since it only requires six more characters to make sure, we added `html` to the mix. As we can see in Figure 7.2, the result is just what we wanted.

Gutter Sniping

Most browsers enforce the "gutter" with margins on the body, but Opera does it with padding on the body. Opera's behavior is probably more correct, but the inconsistency is what led us to set both padding and margin to remove the gutter.

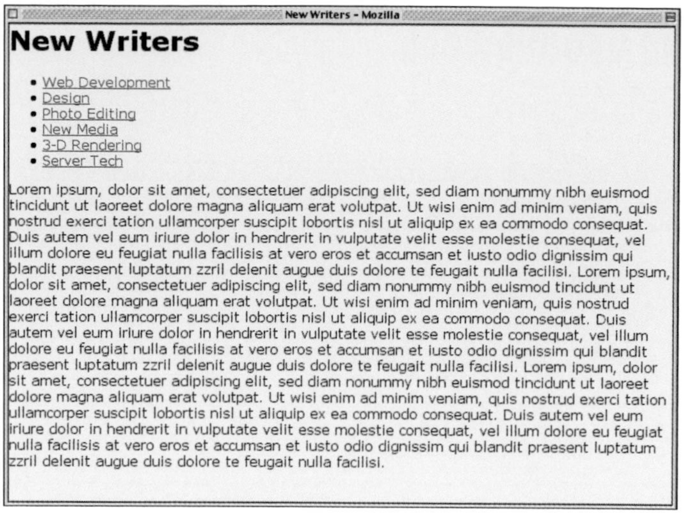

FIGURE 7.2

Setting the "global" styles for the document.

Let's next turn our attention to the main content. What we have is basically filler, meant to hold open space without being exactly representative of how a page will look. Nonetheless, we'll make the font size small because it will be in the final product. We'll also set a white background and a light gray foreground. This will visually de-emphasize the text without removing it entirely from sight.

```
html, body {margin: 0; padding: 0;
  color: #000; background: #EEF;
  font-family: Verdana, Arial, sans-serif;}
#main {font-size: small; color: #AAA; background: #FFF;}
</style>
```

The only real problem is that the text runs all the way out to the edges of the white background. Since this is just placeholder text, let's give it some distance from the edges of the main div. We can do this by adding some padding to the div itself, as shown in Figure 7.3.

```
#main {font-size: small; color: #AAA; background: #FFF;
  margin: 0; padding: 2.5% 12.5%;}
```

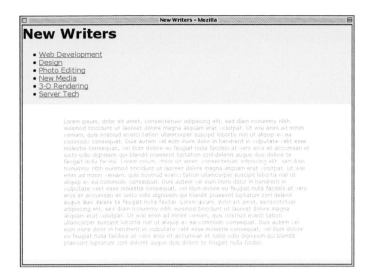

FIGURE 7.3

The main content gets a bit of style.

Now for the main title ("New Writers"). Marketing has told us we need to put white text over a particular blue, so we'll do that at the same time as we set the font size and family.

```
html, body {margin: 0; padding: 0;
  color: #000; background: #EEF;
  font-family: Verdana, Arial, sans-serif;}
h1 {color: #FFF; background: rgb(0%,56%,84%);
  font: bold 200%/1em Arial, Verdana, sans-serif;}
#main {font-size: small; color: #AAA; background: #FFF;
  margin: 0; padding: 2.5% 12.5%;}
```

Furthermore, we don't want the text crowding up against the edges of the blue background, and we want the heading to butt up against the edge of the page. We can accomplish both by adding some padding and removing the margins. While we're at it, let's drop a two-pixel border on the top and bottom of the h1. This will provide some subtle visual separation, as shown in Figure 7.4.

```
h1 {color: #FFF; background: rgb(0%,56%,84%);
  font: bold 200%/1em Arial, Verdana, sans-serif;
  padding: 1em 1em 0; margin: 0;
  border: 1px solid rgb(0%,31%,46%);
  border-width: 2px 0;}
```

The Height in Font

You may have noticed the 200%/1em portion of the declaration. That sets the font size to be 200% and the line-height to be 1em. Note that if you want to set the line-height from a font declaration, it *must* immediately follow the font-size value and be separated from it with a forward slash.

FIGURE 7.4

Setting the title apart from the page.

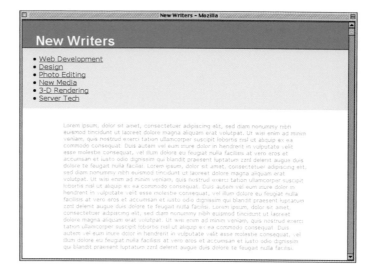

STYLING THE LINKS

Having set up the rest of the page, we're ready to tackle our navigation. We can see it in Figure 7.4, sitting there as an unordered list wedged between the title and main content. Frankly, it's rather ugly, and it's up to us to fix it.

Starting the Styles

There are two ways to take a list and make it into a horizontal set of links. One is to make the list items inline, and the other is to float them. The two approaches both have benefits and drawbacks, but one of the major benefits of the floating approach is that it lets us create graphically beautiful buttons that work in modern browsers—as well as Internet Explorer!

Let's consider the markup for the navigation elements, shown in Listing 7.1.

Listing 7.1   The Navigation Markup

```
<ul id="nav">
<li><a href="/webdev/">Web Development</a></li>
<li><a href="/design/">Design</a></li>
<li><a href="/photos/">Photo Editing</a></li>
<li id="current"><a href="/newmed/">New Media</a></li>
<li><a href="/render/">3-D Rendering</a></li>
<li><a href="/server/">Server Tech</a></li>
</ul>
```

That's it—nothing else is needed. We'll make use of the `id` value `current` later in the project, but for now we don't need it.

To make this technique work, we'll first make sure that the unordered list has no padding or margins. This will make it act, more or less, the same way a `div` would.

```
#main {font-size: small; color: #AAA; background: #FFF;
   margin: 0; padding: 2.5% 12.5%;}
#nav {margin: 0; padding: 0;}
</style>
```

Now we can get to work on the list items themselves. We're going to float all of them to the left so that they all line up horizontally, with the first link the furthest to the left. We'll also explicitly remove the bullets from the list items for Explorer's sake.

```
#nav {margin: 0; padding: 0;}
#nav li {list-style: none; float: left; margin: 0;}
</style>
```

There are 6 navigation links, so we could make them all the same size by dividing 100 by 6. That yields 16 2/3, which means they could all have a `width` of `16.6667%`. That would make things rather fragile, though—a single rounding error could upset the whole design, and it leaves no room to add margins or borders to the list items (which we'll want to do soon). Let's play things safe and make the list items `15%` wide. We'll add in dotted red borders so that we can see how they lay out, as illustrated by Figure 7.5.

```
#nav li {list-style: none; float: left; width: 15%;
   border: 1px dotted red;}
```

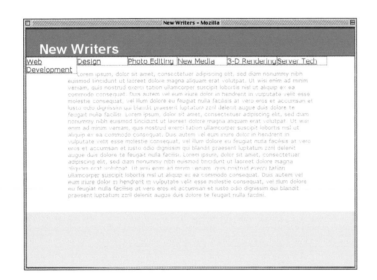

> **Biting the Bullets**
>
> In theory, a floated list item shouldn't generate a marker (bullet), but Explorer doesn't seem to agree. Therefore, always be sure to explicitly set `list-style` to none when using this technique.

FIGURE 7.5

The raw beginnings of the navigation tabs.

Text Wrapping

If you're working in a browser window that's much wider than 800 pixels, you may not see text wrapping in your project file. Try shrinking the window, at least temporarily.

The tabs are now lined up more or less how we want, but there's a problem there on the left. The "Web Development" tab not only is wrapping to two lines, but it's caused some of the main text to flow around it.

This is happening because we floated all the list items, of course. Normal-flow text (like that in the main content `div`) flows around floated elements (like the list items). What might not be so obvious is that the unordered list that contains those list items has zero height. If we were to give it a background color, it wouldn't appear on the screen. So the top of the main content `div` is actually lined up with the top of the navigation links, and the white background visible behind the links is actually the background of the content `div`.

This may seem a little odd, but it's definitely what's supposed to happen. Since we don't actually want it to happen, we'll have to push the content `div` below the floated list items. This is, as it happens, very easily accomplished: We'll just clear the `div` below the floats.

```
#main {font-size: small; color: #AAA; background: #FFF;
    margin: 0; padding: 2.5% 12.5%; clear: left;}
```

Now the top border edge of the `div` will be placed just below the bottom margin edge of any leftward floats that come before the `div` in the document—for example, the list items. This means that the body background will be visible between the `h1` and the content `div`, as we can see in Figure 7.6, but that's all right. We'll actually use that to our advantage later on.

FIGURE 7.6

Pushing the contents clear below the floated list items.

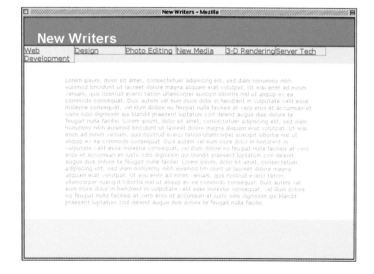

Refining the Tab Look

The preceding change solved the problem of the main content flowing around the links, but it didn't do anything to stop the "Web Development" text from wrapping to two lines. The fix for that is simple enough.

```
#nav li {list-style: none; float: left; width: 15%;
  white-space: nowrap;
  border: 1px dotted red;}
```

This is a lot like the old HTML nowrap attribute for table cells, except in CSS you can stop the wrapping of any element's content.

Before we go any further, we need to consider how this text is going to be used. Our intent is to place it over images that will make the tabs look lovely. Thus, it's important for the text to be of a size that's appropriate to the context in which it will appear (the tabs). Since images are sized in pixels, we'll do the same for the text. In fact, both the font's size and the height of the line can be set in pixels.

```
#nav li {list-style: none; float: left; margin: 0; width: 15%;
  font-size: 10px; line-height: 20px; white-space: nowrap;
  border: 1px dotted red;}
```

The next step to consider is the links themselves, which are sitting inside the floated list items. We'll strip off the underlines and add a solid border so that we can see how the links are laid out inside the list items (see Figure 7.7).

```
#nav li {list-style: none; float: left; margin: 0; width: 15%;
  font-size: 10px; line-height: 20px; white-space: nowrap;
  border: 1px dotted red;}
#nav a {text-decoration: none; border: 1px solid;}
</style>
```

Text Resizing

Remember that most modern browsers will let users resize any text—even text sized with pixels. IE/Win is the lone exception, albeit a rather popular one.

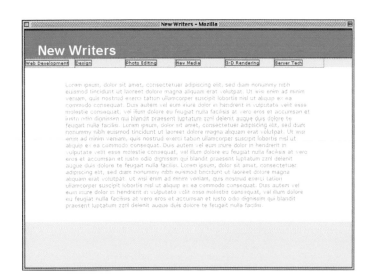

FIGURE 7.7

Examining the links in relation to the list items.

As Figure 7.7 shows us, the links are smaller boxes inside the floated list items. It would be better if we could get those links to fill out the list items or at least as much of them as possible.

Let's take a moment to consider the situation. Each list item is floated and thus generates a block-level box, much like that created by a `div`. In fact, to elements inside the list item, they see only that they're inside a block box. Only elements outside the float react to it by wrapping around the element. The link is just a link, generating an inline box. So to get an inline link to fill out a block-level list item, we can just make the links generate block boxes.

```
#nav a {display: block;
    text-decoration: none; border: 1px solid;}
```

Note that we have *not* changed the nature of the links themselves. The `a` elements are still inline elements. What's happened is that the CSS is getting them to generate block boxes. This is a subtle but crucial difference. If CSS changed the elements themselves to be block level, document validation could easily break down. This isn't what happens, however, as CSS is about affecting presentation, not altering document structure.

Speaking of presentation, the links in question look a little weak with normal-weight text. Let's boldface the links' text to make it stand out a little better.

```
#nav a {display: block;
    text-decoration: none; font-weight: bold;
    border: 1px solid;}
```

We can see the result of these two changes in Figure 7.8. Note how the borders of the links are right against the inside of the dotted red borders we set on the list items.

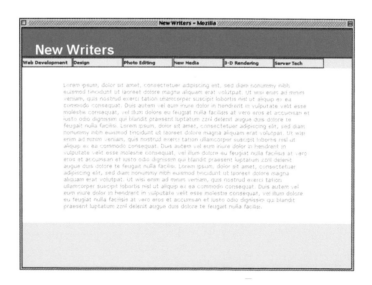

FIGURE 7.8

Boldfaced links generating block boxes.

This is how it will appear in most browsers, anyway. The major exception is IE5/Mac, which incorrectly makes the links as wide as the unordered list instead of as wide as the list items. We definitely don't want that, so a solution is needed, and it turns out that the solution is to float the links themselves inside the floated list items.

```
#nav a {display: block; float: left;
   text-decoration: none; font-weight: bold;
   border: 1px solid;
```

This fixes the layout problem for IE5/Mac, but we don't really want to float the links in other browsers. What we need is a way to turn the floating back off for any browser that isn't IE5/Mac. Fortunately, Doug Bowman gave us a way when he came up with the Sliding Doors technique: There's a parsing bug that affects IE5/Mac only, and it can be used to hide the unfloating rule from IE5/Mac.

```
#nav a {display: block; float: left;
   text-decoration: none; font-weight: bold;
   border: 1px solid;
/* Commented Backslash Hack hides rule from IE5-Mac \*/
#nav a {float: none;}          /* End IE5-Mac hack */
</style>
```

Thus, all browsers float the links (due to `float: left`), and then all browsers except for IE5/Mac defloat the links (thanks to `float: none`). This restores layout consistency in IE5/Mac, and we can move on.

Before we go on to use the full capabilities of the Sliding Doors technique, let's look at a more basic way to style the links by turning them into gray "raised" buttons. The first step is to color the foreground (text) and background of the links in varying shades of gray.

```
#nav a {display: block; float: left;
   text-decoration: none; font-weight: bold;
   border: 1px solid;
   background: #CCC; color: #333;}
```

Now we just need to create a raised effect. There's already a solid border in place, and we could change the `solid` to `outset`. The problem is that there's no control over how the border colors are modified to create the `outset` effect. One browser might just make the top and left borders white and the bottom and right borders black, while another could use more subtle shades. In fact, there is very little cross-browser consistency in outset shading (as well as `inset`, `ridge`, and `groove` shading). So instead we'll leave the border `solid` and declare our own shading by setting the color of each border side.

```
#nav a {display: block; float: left;
   text-decoration: none; font-weight: bold;
   border: 1px solid; border-color: #FFF #333 #333 #FFF;
   background: #CCC; color: #333;}
```

How It Works

The key to this hack is the backward slash (\) that comes right before the asterisk at the end of the first comment. This causes IE/Mac to think the comment hasn't ended yet, and so it thinks the next rule is part of a comment.

It's time to remove the dotted red border, so we'll do that as well, with the result shown in Figure 7.9.

```
#nav li {list-style: none; float: left; margin: 0; width: 15%;
    font-size: 10px; line-height: 20px; white-space: nowrap;}
```

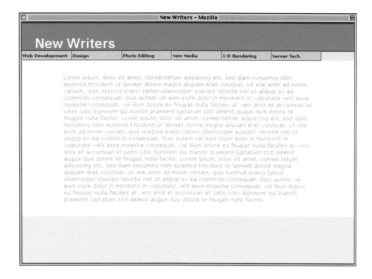

If we ever want to lower the contrast between the "highlight" and "shadow" edges, or introduce some subtle coloration, we need only alter the border-color values.

Adding Texture

We've made some pretty good progress so far, but there's more to be done. The biggest visual problem at the moment is that the text of the links is hard up against the left border, which doesn't look too attractive. We could add some left padding to the links to shove the text over, and in fact we'll do so in just a bit.

Since we're going to move the text over anyway, why don't we move it over enough to put an image into each link? That way, we could provide a little more visual texture to the links. Take, for example, the image in Figure 7.10, which is shown at 1600% magnification.

The large white and black pixels are visible, and the rest of the image is transparent (represented by the gray-and-white checkerboard pattern). Thus, placing this image into the links will allow the gray background color to "shine through" the transparent portions of the background image.

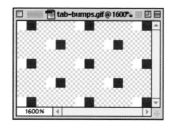

FIGURE 7.10

A small image to add some texture to the links' backgrounds.

We want this image to appear only once, inset just a bit from the left edge of the link and vertically centered, so we write the following:

```
#nav a {display: block; float: left;
  text-decoration: none; font-weight: bold;
  border: 1px solid; border-color: #FFF #333 #333 #FFF;
  background: #CCC url(tab-bumps.gif) 2px 50% no-repeat;
  color: #333;}
```

If we left things as they are now, the bumpy image would appear behind the text of the links. We'll fix that by adding some padding to the link; the image will appear within the padding, but the text will not. Since the image is 14 pixels wide and is inset a bit, we'll add 20 pixels of padding to the left sides of the links, with the result shown in Figure 7.11.

```
#nav a {display: block; float: left; padding: 0 0 0 20px;
  text-decoration: none; font-weight: bold;
  border: 1px solid; border-color: #FFF #333 #333 #FFF;
  background: #CCC url(tab-bumps.gif) 2px 50% no-repeat;
  color: #333;}
```

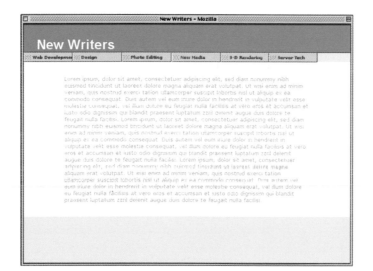

FIGURE 7.11

The links gain some texture via a background image.

Text Handling

If you're working in a browser window that's much wider than 800 pixels, you may not see the text get cut off in your project file. Try shrinking the window, at least temporarily. Also, IE/Win will not truncate the text but will stretch the list items to fit around the text. That sounds like a good idea until you realize that it makes it more likely the buttons will wrap to multiple lines.

It looks great except for one thing: The text of the "Web Development" link has been shoved over far enough that it's being cut off. For the moment, we're going to have to ignore this, although we will see a way around it later in the project.

Hovering and Finishing

Now that we have these nice buttons, let's add a hover effect to the links. Perhaps the simplest hover effect is to "invert" the colors of a link, and that's what we'll do here. We'll swap the foreground and background colors while we change the border colors to be the inverse of their unhovered state.

```
#nav a {float: none;}              /* End IE5-Mac hack */
#nav a:hover {background-color: #333; color: #CCC;
  border-color: #000 #CCC #CCC #000;}
</style>
```

The last touch to this phase of the project is to add a gray border to the top of the main content `div`. This will "box in" the links, visually placing them into a stripe that contains them alone, as we can see in Figure 7.12.

```
#main {font-size: small; color: #AAA; background: #FFF;
  margin: 0; padding: 2.5% 12.5%; clear: left;
  border-top: 1px solid gray;}
```

FIGURE 7.12

Hover styles and a border on the main content finish the look.

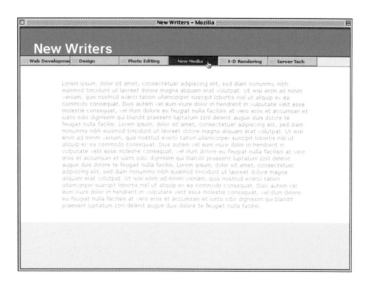

The style sheet we've created so far is shown in Listing 7.2.

Listing 7.2   The Styles So Far

```
html, body {margin: 0; padding: 0;
  color: #000; background: #EEF;
  font-family: Verdana, Arial, sans-serif;}
h1 {color: #FFF; background: rgb(0%,56%,84%);
  font: bold 200%/1em Arial, Verdana, sans-serif;
  padding: 1em 1em 0; margin: 0;
  border: 1px solid rgb(0%,31%,46%);
  border-width: 2px 0;}
#main {font-size: small; color: #AAA; background: #FFF;
  margin: 0; padding: 2.5% 12.5%; clear: left;
  border-top: 1px solid gray;}
#nav {margin: 0; padding: 0;}
#nav li {list-style: none; float: left; margin: 0; width: 15%;
font-size: 10px; line-height: 20px; white-space: nowrap;}
#nav a {display: block; float: left; padding: 0 0 0 20px;
  text-decoration: none; font-weight: bold;
  border: 1px solid; border-color: #FFF #333 #333 #FFF;
  background: #CCC url(tab-bumps.gif) 2px 50% no-repeat;
  color: #333;}
/* Commented Backslash Hack hides rule from IE5-Mac \*/
#nav a {float: none;}           /* End IE5-Mac hack */
#nav a:hover {background-color: #333; color: #CCC;
  border-color: #000 #CCC #CCC #000;}
```

Cut Off Text and Shrunken Hotspots

This is an appropriate point at which to address two potential problems with the styles we've written so far. These are:

◆ If a link's text is too long, it sticks out of the link box and can be cut off by other content. We first saw this in Figure 7.11.

◆ In IE/Win, the "hotspot" (clickable region) for each link is confined to the actual content and does not fill out the whole list item box.

Let's consider the first problem first. The text is cut off because we prevented the text from wrapping with `white-space: nowrap` and gave the list items an explicit `width` of `15%`. Thus, the list items have to each be 15% as wide as their parent element (the `ul` element), regardless of whether or not their content actually fits into that space. The same would be true of any explicit width, whether set in percentages, pixels, ems, or any other length measure.

We could allow the text to wrap by removing the `white-space` declaration, but then some links might have wrapped text whereas others would not, resulting in uneven heights for the links. This is definitely not the desired effect.

Excession

The text is actually flowing out of the list item and would be visible outside the list item if not for the other floats, which are overwriting the overflowing text. Thus, the text is not actually cut off, although it appears to be in our project files. To see what's really happening, try temporarily commenting out all but the first link in the navigation area.

Now let's consider the second problem, the resolution of which will also help us solve the first problem. In IE/Win, a bug prevents it from considering the entirety of a block-box link as "clickable." Unless some kind of explicit width is given, only the content area of the link is treated as clickable. We could set the links to have a `width` of `100%`, except then we couldn't add any padding to the links without making them stick out of the list items (because `width` defines the width of the content area plus any padding, borders, and margins that are added to it). In that case, we couldn't add images to the link backgrounds, which is too limiting.

In grappling with these issues, Doug Bowman came up with a solution that exploits a different bug in IE/Win to trick it into considering the whole link as clickable. It turns out that if you give the links a tiny `width` value, IE/Win will automatically (and incorrectly) expand the value to include all of the content, *plus* it will suddenly consider the padding clickable. This is fairly strange, but it works. Thus:

```
#nav a {display: block; float: left; padding: 0 0 0 20px;
   text-decoration: none; font-weight: bold;
   border: 1px solid; border-color: #FFF #333 #333 #FFF;
   background: #CCC url(tab-bumps.gif) 2px 50% no-repeat;
   color: #333;
   width: .1em;}
```

The problem is that more conformant browsers will take that value seriously and make the link content area exactly a tenth of an em wide, with the text over-flowing that thin sliver. So we need to undo the damage for these more advanced browsers by showing them a rule that IE/Win doesn't see. In this case, we rely on the fact that IE/Win doesn't understand child selectors, and we add a rule that sets the `width` back to `auto` for more advanced browsers.

```
#nav a {display: block; float: left; padding: 0 0 0 20px;
   text-decoration: none; font-weight: bold;
   border: 1px solid; border-color: #FFF #333 #333 #FFF;
   background: #CCC url(tab-bumps.gif) 2px 50% no-repeat;
   color: #333;
   width: .1em;}
html>body #nav a {width: auto;}    /* fixes IE6 hack */
/* Commented Backslash Hack hides rule from IE5-Mac \*/
```

So all browsers will see the width as `.1em`, and those that understand child selectors will also see `width: auto` and use it to override the `.1em`. Either way, the width of the link's content will equal the width of the text content, thanks to the way floats tend to shrink-wrap their contents, and the whole link will become clickable, as shown in Figure 7.13.

Uh-oh—what happened? Exactly what was described: The content area of the links became as wide as the contents. The list items, however, are still 15% wide, so the links are no longer filling out the list items.

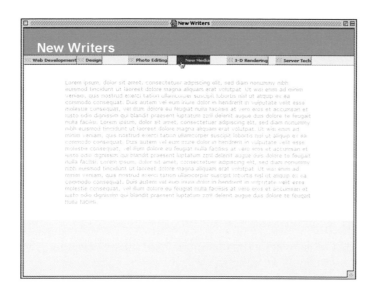

FIGURE 7.13

Shrink-wrapping the links to their contents.

At least, that's what happens in some browsers. (Figure 7.13 was taken in IE5/Mac, and IE/Win should look similar.) In others, the links will still fill out the list items. Clearly, this isn't much better than before, when our only problem was that one of the links had text sticking out of the button.

We can bring everything back to a kind of harmony by letting the list items also shrink themselves to fit their contents. To do this, we need the list items to have `auto` width, which we can accomplish by simply removing the `width: 15%` from the `#nav li` rule.

```
#nav li {list-style: none; float: left;
  font-size: 10px; line-height: 20px; white-space: nowrap;}
```

Now, for every button, the link will shrink around its content, and the list item will shrink around the link. This gives us the situation shown in Figure 7.14.

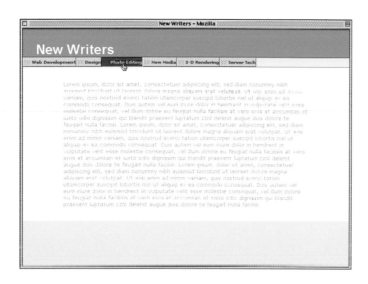

FIGURE 7.14

Shrink-wrapping both the list items and the links.

So what have we learned in this interlude?

- That it's difficult to get fully clickable links in IE/Win when their parents are set to an explicit width
- That links set to an explicit width risk having the contents of the links overflow
- That shrink-wrapping links and the list items that contain them solves both problems, once you work your way around some IE bugs

So the reasonable conclusion is that, in general, it's better to have autosized links than explicitly sized links. In fact, this is the approach used in the original Sliding Doors technique: tabs that autosize themselves to their contents.

There are other reasons why the technique uses shrink-wrapping, as we're about to find out.

CREATING ACTUAL TABS

Although the link styles we've created are nice in their own way, they share something in common with most links these days. They're boxy and somewhat boring. We need some more attractive link styles—some nice rounded-corner tabs, for example, with smooth highlighting and shading.

As you already guessed, we can do just that, and we won't even need to change the HTML markup to do it. All we need is some modified CSS and a large (yet compact) image.

Making Some Changes

Before we get to the really pretty stuff, let's make a few changes to the style sheet in Listing 7.2. The first change is to make the document background white instead of a pale gray-blue.

```
html, body {margin: 0; padding: 0;
  color: #000; background: #FFF;
  font-family: Verdana, Arial, sans-serif;}
```

Next we're going to remove the gray border from the top of the main content div so that the #main rule looks like this:

```
#main {font-size: small; color: #AAA; background: #FFF;
  margin: 0; padding: 2.5% 12.5%; clear: left;}
```

Finally, we're going to add a left margin and some left padding to the floated list items. This will separate them slightly and open up some space between the left edge of the list items and the left edge of the links they contain, as shown in Figure 7.15.

```
#nav li {list-style: none; float: left;
  margin-left: 1px; padding-left: 16px;
  font-size: 10px; line-height: 20px; white-space: nowrap;}
```

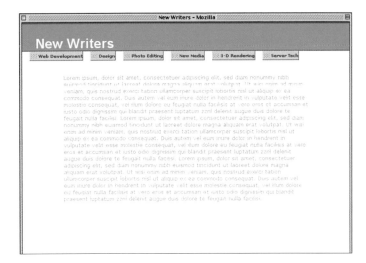

FIGURE 7.15

Pushing the links apart in preparation for more advanced styling.

Why have we done this? To open up room for some eye candy.

Putting in a Tab

Our general goal here is to place a visually sophisticated image into the backgrounds of both the list items and the links. We'll style these backgrounds in such a way that they blend seamlessly and look good on links of varying widths.

To make this effect work, we first need a background image suitable for the effect we want. In fact, we need a fairly big image... an image like the one in Figure 7.16, which is called `tabs2-big.gif`.

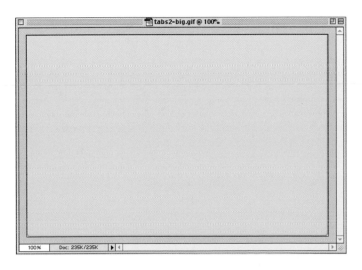

FIGURE 7.16

The über-tab image.

One Image or Two?

In the original technique, Doug actually split the image into two unequal pieces instead of leaving a single image. This was done because he set portions of the background to be transparent, which necessitates the split (see his original article for more). Since we aren't using transparency, we can stick with a single image.

Notice the rounded corners at the bottom of the image. Those represent the two sides of our tabs, which will appear to stick downward from the page title.

Let's take this a step at a time. First we'll add the tab image to the list items.

```
#nav li {list-style: none; float: left;
    margin-left: 1px; padding-left: 16px;
    font-size: 10px; line-height: 20px; white-space: nowrap;
    background: #BBB url(tabs2-big.gif);}
```

Remember that we gave the list items 16 pixels of left padding, so the image will appear in that space. The rest of each list item is filled up with the links, which have opaque backgrounds and so will obscure the image given to the list items' backgrounds.

What we can see, though, indicates that the top-left corner of tabs2-big.gif is aligned with the top-left corner of the list items. We want the lower-left corner of the image in the same corner of the list item, and for that matter we don't want the image to tile. Adding a few bits to the background declaration suffices to address these points and has the result shown in Figure 7.17.

```
#nav li {list-style: none; float: left;
    margin-left: 1px; padding-left: 16px;
    font-size: 10px; line-height: 20px; white-space: nowrap;
    background: #BBB url(tabs2-big.gif) 0 100% no-repeat;}
```

FIGURE 7.17

The über-tab image is placed into the list items' backgrounds.

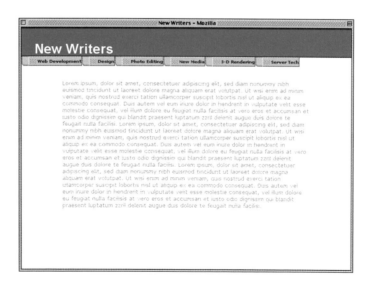

That by itself is, or could easily become, an interesting visual effect. We're going to take it to the next level, though. To have the tabs come together, we need to apply `tabs2-big.gif` to the links, only this time we'll have the bottom-right corner of the image align with the bottom-right corner of the links.

```
#nav a {display: block; float: left; padding: 0 0 0 20px;
   text-decoration: none; font-weight: bold;
   border: 1px solid; border-color: #FFF #333 #333 #FFF;
   background: #DDD url(tabs2-big.gif) 100% 100% no-repeat;
   color: #333;
   width: .1em;}
```

There's another change that is necessitated by changing the background image. Remember that, before, we had a background image on the left and added some padding to open up space for it to appear. Now we have the background image aligned to the right. Therefore, we need to adjust the padding of the links accordingly. We'll remove the left padding and add 16 pixels of right padding (to match the `padding-left: 16px` on the list items), with the result shown in Figure 7.18.

```
#nav a {display: block; float: left; padding: 0 16px 0 0;
   text-decoration: none; font-weight: bold;
   border: 1px solid; border-color: #FFF #333 #333 #FFF;
   background: #DDD url(tabs2-big.gif) 100% 100% no-repeat;
   color: #333;
   width: .1em;}
```

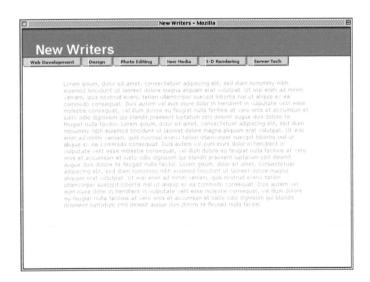

FIGURE 7.18

The über-tab image is placed into the links' backgrounds.

We're very close to being done, but there is the small matter of the link borders. They're no longer needed; in fact, they actively interfere with the effect we're trying to create. So we need to pull out the borders completely, leaving the `#nav a` rule looking like this:

```
#nav a {display: block; float: left; padding: 0 16px 0 0;
   text-decoration: none; font-weight: bold;
   background: #DDD url(tabs2-big.gif) 100% 100% no-repeat;
   color: #333;
   width: .1em;}
```

We also need to adjust the hover styles, which don't work nearly as well with the light blue tabs. Since we can only affect the links, we'll just change the text color.

```
#nav a:hover {color: rgb(62%,35%,22%);}
```

We could also change the background image, but that would leave us with just a changed link background. The background of the list item wouldn't change. Thus, it's quite difficult to apply hover effects to anything besides the link in these situations. Fortunately, it's usually enough, as we can see in Figure 7.19.

FIGURE 7.19

Adding a hover style to the links.

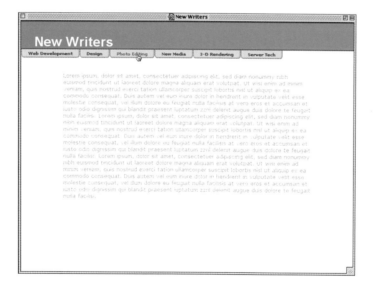

▶▶ BETTER HOVERS

It's actually possible to get hover effects on nonlink elements in most modern browsers. This could be used to create hover effects for the tabs we've created. For example, suppose we have a "highlight" image called `tabs2-big-hl.gif`*. Visually, this is the same file as* `tabs2-big.gif` *except the colors are brighter.*

We could create a highlight-hover effect with the following rules:

```
#nav li:hover, #nav li:hover a {
  background-image: url(tabs2-big-hl.gif);}
```

This would replace the background images of both the hovered list item and the link inside it with the highlight image.

The drawback to this approach is that Explorer will ignore the rule completely, meaning there will be no hover effect for users of that browser. Users of other browsers, such as Mozilla, Opera, and Safari, would see a highlight.

There are two ways to get even Explorer to use hover styles. One involves adding a span element inside the links and styling it and the link. See "Sliding Doors of CSS, Part II" (http://alistapart.com/articles/slidingdoors2/) for an example illustrating this technique. The other way is to make use of the IE/Win behavior file we used in Project 6.

Indicating the Current Tab

Remember the id="current" that we've been ignoring ever since the beginning of the chapter? Here's where it comes back with a vengeance. Using that hook, we can uniquely style the tab to be different from the others.

To do it, though, we'll need a new tab image, one that looks different from the normal tab image. Figure 7.20 shows us precisely that.

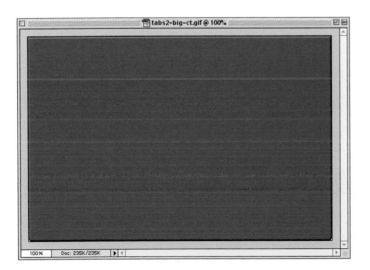

FIGURE 7.20

The current page über-tab image.

The file's name is `tabs2-big-ct.gif` (`ct` for "current tab"). The base color of the tab was taken from the borders running along the top and bottom of the page title, which is `rgb(0%,31%,46%)`, by the way, for reasons we'll see very shortly.

With that image ready to go, all we need to do is write a rule that will switch the basic tab image for this new one and modify the text color. That's right, all we need is one rule.

```
#nav a:hover {color: rgb(62%,35%,22%);}
#nav #current, #nav #current a {color: #FDB;
  background-image: url(tabs2-big-ct.gif);}
</style>
```

This will substitute the current-tab image for the default tab image while leaving the styles for its position, repetition, and so forth intact. The color will stay constant even when the tab is hovered because the selector `#nav #current a` has a higher specificity than `#nav a:hover` (that it comes after the hover rule is irrelevant in this case).

As we can see in Figure 7.21, the tab appears to grow out of the border above it while still maintaining visual consistency with the other tabs.

FIGURE 7.21

Altering the appearance of the current tab.

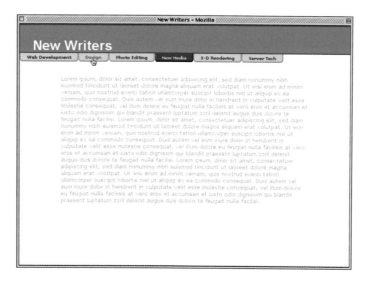

So, with two images, we can lay out some nice-looking tabs using nothing more than an unordered list and some links. Our new style sheet is shown in Listing 7.3.

Listing 7.3   The Tabbed Styles

```
html, body {margin: 0; padding: 0;
  color: #000; background: #FFF;
  font-family: Verdana, Arial, sans-serif;}
h1 {color: #FFF; background: rgb(0%,56%,84%);
  font: bold 200%/1em Arial, Verdana, sans-serif;
  padding: 1em 1em 0; margin: 0;
  border: 1px solid rgb(0%,31%,46%);
  border-width: 2px 0;}
#main {font-size: small; color: #AAA; background: #FFF;
  margin: 0; padding: 2.5% 12.5%; clear: left;}
#nav {margin: 0; padding: 0;}
#nav li {list-style: none; float: left;
  margin-left: 1px; padding-left: 16px;
  font-size: 10px; line-height: 20px; white-space: nowrap;
  background: #BBB url(tabs2-big.gif) 0 100% no-repeat;}
#nav a {display: block; float: left; padding: 0 16px 0 0;
  text-decoration: none; font-weight: bold;
  background: #DDD url(tabs2-big.gif) 100% 100% no-repeat;
  color: #333;
  width: .1em;}
html>body #nav a {width: auto;}     /* fixes IE6 hack */
/* Commented Backslash Hack hides rule from IE5-Mac \*/
#nav a {float: none;}               /* End IE5-Mac hack */
#nav a:hover {color: rgb(62%,35%,22%);}
#nav #current, #nav #current a {color: #FDB;
  background-image: url(tabs2-big-ct.gif);}
```

Odds and Ends

Just in case you're concerned about the additional page weight of having two large images used just to set up some tabs, take heart. The two images are less than 3KB each, with the normal tab being slightly smaller in file size (2,763 bytes). This means that use of this particular technique added less than 6KB to the page weight.

Of course, one doesn't have to use images that are 600 pixels wide by 400 pixels tall either, so the files could be smaller. Alternatively, in some cases it's possible to combine the current-tab and normal-tab appearances into a single image and make use of background-position to show the appropriate effect. We won't explore that technique here since Doug Bowman did it so well in his article "Sliding Doors of CSS, Part II," which you should definitely read (along with its prequel, which also shows how to make tabs visually merge with the main content area).

Another point is that it's really easy to change the appearance of your tabs—all you need to do is update the über-tab image, and you're done. (If you want to change the orientation of the tabs, you'll have to update the CSS, too.) Take, for example, the tabs shown in Figure 7.22, which were created using the über-tab image shown below them.

FIGURE 7.22

Radically altering the tabs by changing the über-tab.

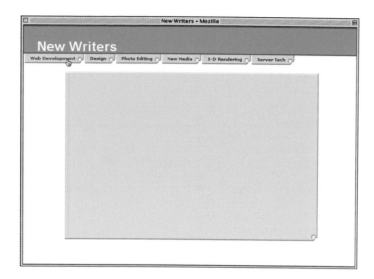

This brings us to the last point: the kinds of visual styles that can be created using the Sliding Doors technique. In general, any tab that uses a solid background color or that has horizontally oriented decorations will work just fine. For example, the tabs in Figure 7.22 have horizontal lines running through the background. The vertical lines on the left were carefully placed in the area that would appear in the list items' background; that is, the vertical lines stop before the left edge of the link.

Similarly, diagonal lines are difficult to pull off. The problem is that where the "doors" come together, diagonal lines might not meet up cleanly. This doesn't mean that diagonal lines can never be used in tabs. It just means you have to be more visually creative so that you can overcome the limitations just mentioned.

BRANCHING OUT

Now that we've seen how to create buttons and tabs with simple markup, here's your chance to take the concepts even further.

1. Try adapting the Sliding Doors technique to a vertical list of links that can be as tall or short as you prefer. Note that, in this case, it isn't as big a deal if links wrap to two or more lines.

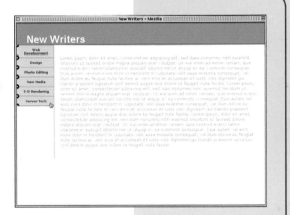

2. Create your own tab effect and implement it using the same markup and techniques explored in this project. The more creative, the better!

3. For an extra challenge, create diamond-tipped links that have a striped background behind them and carry the theme throughout the "navigation stripe." Hint: This will actually require two background images, one for the tabs and one for the element that contains them.

8

STYLING A WEBLOG

Quiet few days…well not really, but I'm not telling you lot.
Which is obviously the point of a weblog.

—DAVE WHYTE

FOR WHATEVER REASON, personal, Web-based journals have come to be called weblogs (at least by most people). Weblogs are kind of an interesting layout microcosm, when you think about it. Each entry in the weblog usually contains a title, the date the entry was posted, some content, and then some extra information such as the entry's category, a link to any comments, and so on.

From a layout point of view, each entry needs to be considered as if it were a mini-document within the larger page. Every entry should be styled the same as other entries while still relating visually to each other in an appealing way. It wouldn't be good if the entries overlapped each other, for example. In this project, we'll take a look at a weblog based on clean, structural markup and explore ways to style the entries.

Project Goals

This project is all about taking the entries in a weblog and making them look good. While we're at it, we need to make sure the entries relate to each other visually. This leads us to the following general goals:

◆ Visually speaking, make each entry seem distinct and self-contained. That doesn't mean drawing a box around each one—we just have to be sure it's obvious where one entry ends and another begins.

◆ Try to make the entry title and date come together in some sense so that they appear to be closely related.

◆ Take any extra information and reduce its visual emphasis so that it doesn't compete with the main entry text, but don't make the information completely disappear either.

Furthermore, we're going to use a natural theme for the design, all green and woodsy. That doesn't come from the preceding points; it's just a design decision we're making from the outset.

Preparation

See the Introduction for instructions on how to download files from the Web site.

Download the files for Project 8 from this book's Web site. If you're planning to play along at home, load the file `ch08proj.html` into the editing program of your choice. This is the file you'll be editing, saving, and reloading as the project progresses.

Laying the Groundwork

As usual, we'll need to dive into the markup of the project document—the better to understand what we have to work with—and get a peek at the document before we start adding CSS to it. Listing 8.1 gives us a detailed look at the markup for the weblog, and Figure 8.1 shows it in its raw, unstyled glory.

Listing 8.1 A Look at the Weblog's Markup

```
<div id="weblog">

<h3><span>Eric's Thoughts</span></h3>

<div class="entry">

<h4 class="title">
<a name="t20031125" href="/eric/thoughts/200311.html#t20031123"
  rel="bookmark">Hot Steaming Internet</a>
</h4>
```

```
<h5 class="date">
Tuesday, 23 November 2003
</h5>

[...entry content...]

<ul class="moreinfo">
<li class="categories"><a href="/eric/thoughts/wifi">WiFi</a></li>
<li class="comments">No comments</li>
<li class="pingbacks"><a href="/eric/thoughts/pingbacks/t20031123">3
 Pingbacks</a></li>
</ul>

</div>

[...more entries...]

</div>
```

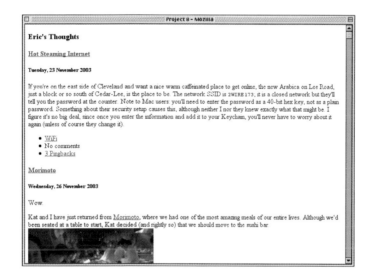

FIGURE 8.1

The unstyled weblog entries.

There are a few things to note in particular:

◆ The weblog's title ("Eric's Thoughts") is contained in an h3 element and a span element. This gives us two elements to work with when styling the title.

◆ Each entry is enclosed in a div with a class of entry. This effectively groups all of the information related to a single entry into one piece of the document structure.

◆ The title and date of a post, while given unique elements to contain the content (h4 and h5, respectively), have also been classed. This will allow us to style these aspects of an entry without worrying that an h4 or h5 might one day be used in the main text of an entry.

◆ In a like manner, the extra information, contained in an unordered list, has been classed in a manner that will make each piece easy to style independently of the others and without letting the styles leak into the main text of an entry.

We'll take advantage of each of these points, and a great many other things, as we make these entries look better than ever.

STYLING THE WEBLOG

A good first step would be to define baselines for the background color, text color, and font family and sizing for the overall document. We're going to be aiming for a natural kind of feel, so we'll go with some green shades for the colors. The font will be, as is so often the case for personal sites, a smaller-than-default sans-serif font.

```
<style type="text/css">
body {color: rgb(18%,19%,17%); background: rgb(85%,92%,81%);
  font: 0.85em Verdana, sans-serif;}
</style>
```

With that in place, we'll work our way down through the document source, styling pieces as we come to them. That puts the weblog's title at the head of the line.

Tackling the Title

Our first stop is the title of the weblog, "Eric's Thoughts." Perhaps the simplest things to do are to make the font bigger and center the text.

```
body {color: rgb(18%,19%,17%); background: rgb(85%,92%,81%);
  font: 0.85em Verdana, sans-serif;}
#weblog h3 {font-size: 150%; text-align: center;}
</style>
```

That, by itself, won't really set the title apart from the rest of the document, though. To give it more visual definition, we'll color the text, add top and bottom borders and also a bottom margin wider than usual. This will push the rest of the content downward a bit, as shown in Figure 8.2.

```
#weblog h3 {font-size: 150%; text-align: center;
  color: rgb(10%,30%,10%);
  border: 1px solid rgb(30%,50%,30%); border-width: 1px 0;
  margin-bottom: 1.5em;}
```

Ems or Percents?

When it comes to sizing fonts, there's no theoretical difference between em and percentage values. 150% and 1.5em should have the same result, as should 0.85em and 85%. However, it's often recommended that if you're setting the body element's font size to 1em, you should use that value instead of 100%, which triggers an odd rounding bug in Opera.

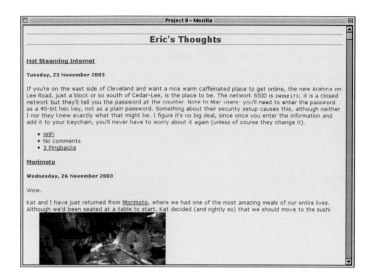

FIGURE 8.2

Some basic styles and title styles have been added.

Okay, the title certainly stands out...but is it attractive? No, not really. It would look nicer with a script font, actually. CSS offers cursive as a generic font family type, but browsers tend not to support it very well. If the user has configured his or her browser to recognize a particular script font, you'll be all set. Most don't. So if we were to say font-family: cursive;, most users would just get a serif or sans-serif font.

So, instead, we'll use an image in place of the text. This is what's known as an *image-replacement technique*. What we'll do is take an image (the one shown in Figure 8.3, in fact) and drop it into the background of the h3 while moving the text out of the way entirely.

FIGURE 8.3

An image-based version of the weblog's title.

First we add the image to the h3's background, positioning it at the bottom center of the h3's background area and making sure it appears only once.

```
#weblog h3 {font-size: 150%; text-align: center;
   color: rgb(10%,30%,10%);
   border: 1px solid rgb(30%,50%,30%); border-width: 1px 0;
   margin-bottom: 1.5em;
   background: url(title.gif) 50% 100% no-repeat;}
```

Now we have the background image sitting underneath the foreground text, which can be a nice visual effect in some situations but not this one. We need to move the text entirely out of the way. Easier done than said: We'll just take the span element and throw it a long way offscreen. Although the color of the h3 won't be important any more, since the text won't be visible, we'll leave it in place anyway.

```
#weblog h3 {font-size: 150%; text-align: center;
  color: rgb(10%,30%,10%);
  border: 1px solid rgb(30%,50%,30%); border-width: 1px 0;
  margin-bottom: 1.5em;
  background: url(title.gif) 50% 100% no-repeat;}
#weblog h3 span {position: absolute; left: -50em; width: 50em;}
</style>
```

Containing Root

In an HTML document, the root element is the html element (not too surprising).

Now the span, and the text within it, has been placed so that the left edge of the span is 50em to the left of its containing block. In this case, the containing block is the root element, which means the span is about 50em to the left of the left edge of the browser window. We've also made the width of the span the same as the offset distance, just in case the h3 ever gets changed to have a whole bunch of content for some reason. That takes care of the text.

There's a side effect we'll have to counteract, though. By absolutely positioning the span, we've removed it from the normal flow. That means the h3 has no normal-flow content and thus no height. If it has no height, the top and bottom borders will sit right next to each other, and we won't be able to see the background at all. To fix this, we need to force the h3 to have an explicit height, even though it has no content.

We can do this easily enough with a height declaration. The background image is 38 pixels tall, so that plus a little more (to keep the top border a few pixels away from the background image) should be about right. Let's call it 45 pixels, which will give us the result shown in Figure 8.4.

```
#weblog h3 {font-size: 150%; text-align: center;
  color: rgb(10%,30%,10%);
  border: 1px solid rgb(30%,50%,30%); border-width: 1px 0;
  margin-bottom: 1.5em; height: 45px;
  background: url(title.gif) 50% 100% no-repeat;}
```

Effectively, we've visually replaced the text with a background image, which is where the term "image-replacement technique" arises. Obviously, the background image could be fancier than the one we're using, employing faded photos, blur lines, and anything else you can imagine.

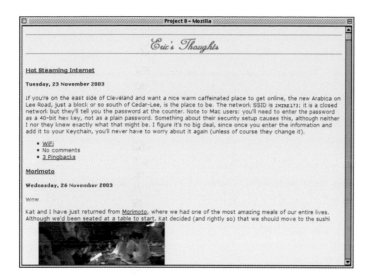

FIGURE 8.4

The title's appearance is improved with an image-replacement approach.

Note that there are a number of image-replacement techniques, many of which rely on removing the text by setting the span element to display: none; or visibility: hidden;. Others use a large negative text indentation or negative left margin. The positioning approach we've used here is another technique.

▶▶ IMAGES VERSUS IMAGE REPLACEMENT

Does it make sense to use a background to simulate what an image could do as well? Consider the markup we're using in this project:

```
<h3><span>Eric's Thoughts</span></h3>
```

Now compare that, plus the CSS we've written to get the image to appear, to the more prosaic approach:

```
<h3><img src="title.gif" alt="Eric's Thoughts"
  width="167" height="38"></h3>
```

It might appear at first glance that the former is more efficient, but is it? Not necessarily. Consider the amount of extra CSS that was required to move the span offscreen and drop the image into the h3's background. For a one-off effect like this, using an img is likely to make more sense. It's just as accessible, thanks to the alt text, and contributes less to overall page weight.

continues

continued

So why would we bother with the image-replacement approach? For one, it's interesting and worth exploring. More importantly, though, the image-replacement technique makes sense if you're using it on multiple pages. Suppose, for example, you want to include the company's name on every page and replace it with a logo. Overall, you'll save more bandwidth with an image-replacement approach than with just embedding the img elements in every page.

So, although image replacement probably isn't the smartest choice for the particular project we're working on, it is a useful technique in many cases. Illustrating how it works is the primary reason it was used here.

Entry Title and Date

Now that the title is all nice and pretty, it's time to work on the entries. At the top of each entry is an entry title and the date the entry was posted. To make the two consistent, let's give them some common styles: We'll strip away the margins and padding and set them both to use Arial as the preferred font (followed by Verdana and then by any available sans-serif font).

```
#weblog h3 span {position: absolute; left: -50em; width: 50em;}
#weblog h4.title, #weblog h5.date {margin: 0; padding: 0;
  font-family: Arial, Verdana, sans-serif; line-height: 1em;}
</style>
```

Padding Questions

Another reason to use padding instead of margins is that if we ever add a background image to the title, the padding will increase the area in which it can be seen. The reason for using pixels will be revealed in just a bit.

We can make the titles stand out in three ways. The most obvious is to bump up the font size a bit. Less obvious, but also important, is to give them a bit of top padding so that there's some blank space above the text. Finally, we'll run a border along the bottom.

```
#weblog h4.title, #weblog h5.date {margin: 0; padding: 0;
  font-family: Arial, Verdana, sans-serif; line-height: 1em;}
#weblog h4.title {font-size: 1.25em; padding: 5px 0 0;
  border-bottom: 1px solid rgb(50%,66%,50%);}
</style>
```

At the moment, all we really need to do to the date is reduce the font size a bit and set a color, as shown in Figure 8.5.

```
#weblog h4.title { font-size: 1.25em; padding: 5px 0 0;
  border-bottom: 1px solid rgb(50%,66%,50%);}
#weblog h5.date {font-size: 0.9em; color: rgb(50%,66%,50%);}
</style>
```

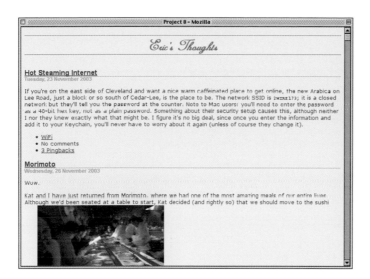

FIGURE 8.5

Entry titles and dates come closer together and change appearance.

Okay, it's progress, but so far it isn't very pretty progress. Don't worry—things will quickly get better. We're about to make the title and date look as if they're sitting next to a leafy stem.

Splitting and Rejoining

What these entries need is a really nice effect for the title and date. There are any number of things we could attempt, but what would be interesting is to have the title and date sort of meet in the middle, with a leaf image capping the end of each. For example, the title might sit just to the left of a leaf, while the date sits to the right.

To pull this off, we'll need a couple of leaf images. How about the ones shown in Figure 8.6? Lovely.

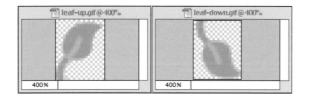

FIGURE 8.6

The leaf images we'll use to spruce up the entries.

Now for the CSS. Let's take the title first. If the upward-pointing leaf is going to sit to the right of the text, the text should also be right-aligned.

```
#weblog h4.title {font-size: 1.25em; text-align: right;
   padding: 5px 0 0;
   border-bottom: 1px solid rgb(50%,66%,50%);}
```

Now to add the leaf. We want it to the right, so we'll place it in the top-right corner of the title's background. Why the top right instead of the bottom right? Because this way, if the image is taller than the background, it will be "clipped" by the bottom border instead of disappearing along the top of the title.

```
#weblog h4.title {font-size: 1.25em; text-align: right;
  padding: 5px 0 0;
  background: url(leaf-up.gif) 100% 0 no-repeat;
  border-bottom: 1px solid rgb(50%,66%,50%);}
```

Having done this, however, the text of the title is more than likely to overlap the background image. We don't want that, so we'll add 25 pixels of right padding to the title. Also, to push the title's text near to the center of the layout, we'll add a large left margin. 45% is about right; we don't want to use 50% because we want both the title and the date to straddle the layout center. Our progress so far is shown in Figure 8.7.

```
#weblog h4.title {font-size: 1.25em; text-align: right;
  padding: 5px 25px 0 0; margin: 0 45% 0 0;
  background: url(leaf-up.gif) 100% 0 no-repeat;
  border-bottom: 1px solid rgb(50%,66%,50%);}
```

FIGURE 8.7

Adding an image and some margin to the entry titles.

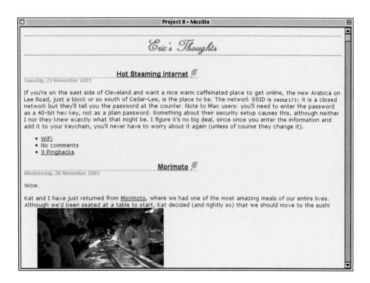

Okay, the blue link text is starting to get annoying, and we really don't need the underline either. Let's fix both.

```
#weblog h4.title {text-align: right; font-size: 1.25em;
padding: 5px 25px 0 0; margin: 0 45% 0 0;
  background: url(leaf-up.gif) 100% 0 no-repeat;
  border-bottom: 1px solid rgb(50%,66%,50%);}
#weblog h4.title a {text-decoration: none;
  color: rgb(15%,30%,15%);}
#weblog h5.date {font-size: 0.9em; color: rgb(50%,66%,50%);}
```

Now for the dates. Effectively, what we need to do is invert the styles we applied to the titles. That would mean a 45% left margin, some left padding, left-aligned text, and a background image of a downward-pointing leaf placed into the lower-left corner of the element's background. Oh, and a top border as well. Let's do it all at once. Ready?

```
#weblog h5.date {font-size: 0.9em; text-align: left;
   padding: 0 0 5px 25px; margin: 0 0 0 45%;
   background: url(leaf-down.gif) 0 100% no-repeat;
   border-top: 1px solid; color: rgb(50%,66%,50%);}
```

We're basically there except for one thing. The bottom border of the title and the top border of the date sort of stack on top of each other in the middle, which leads to a weird jag that doesn't look very nice. It would be better if the borders effectively merged into a single line.

How do we accomplish this? Simple: a one-pixel negative bottom margin on the title. This will pull the dates upward by a pixel and cause the borders to overlap each other. Visually, they'll create a single line, as shown in Figure 8.8.

```
#weblog h4.title {font-size: 1.25em; text-align: right;
   padding: 5px 25px 0 0; margin: 0 45% -1px 0;
   background: url(leaf-up.gif) 100% 0 no-repeat;
   border-bottom: 1px solid rgb(50%,66%,50%);}
```

Rounding Errors

For some reason, the Gecko line (Mozilla and so on) seems to suffer random rounding errors that can throw off the alignment we've created here. Setting padding and margins with ems seems to exacerbate the problem, while using pixels does not. That's why we used pixel-based padding for both the title and the date.

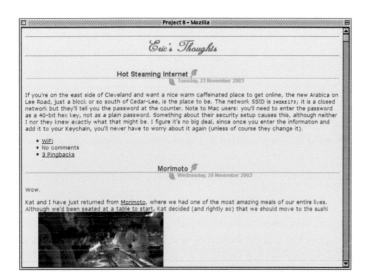

FIGURE 8.8

The title and date borders come together thanks to a negative margin.

There's one thing we need to do before moving on. For some reason, IE/Win will mess up the margin calculations for the title and date if we leave things as they are. This may be related to the somewhat-infamous margin-doubling bug that IE/Win suffers, although the margins aren't really doubled.

At any rate, this can be resolved by reducing the width of a containing element to less than 100%. Since the weblog `div` encloses all the entries, we'll just lower its width by one percent.

```
body {color: rgb(18%,19%,17%); background: rgb(85%,92%,81%);
 font: 0.85em Verdana, sans-serif;}
#weblog {width: 99%;}
#weblog h3 {font-size: 150%; text-align: center;
  color: rgb(10%,30%,10%);
  border: 1px solid rgb(30%,50%,30%); border-width: 1px 0;
  margin-bottom: 1.5em; height: 45px;
  background: url(title.gif) 50% 100% no-repeat;}
```

The solution is fairly inexplicable, but then so is the bug. Either way, this seems to solve the error in IE/Win, so we'll use it, shake our heads, and move on.

Text and Information

There really isn't a whole lot to do to the main text of the entries, but the entries themselves could stand to be spread out a bit. Because each entry is enclosed in a `div`, we can push them apart by adding some margins. Let's use bottom margins.

```
#weblog h3 span {position: absolute; left: -50em; width: 50em;}
#weblog .entry {margin: 0 0 2em;}
#weblog h4.title, #weblog h5.date {margin: 0; padding: 0;
  font-family: Arial, Verdana, sans-serif; line-height: 1em;}
```

Modifying Space

The value of `letter-spacing` is a modifier to the distance between characters, not the raw distance. This has to do with how character glyphs are formed in modern computer systems, and it's far too convoluted to get into here. Just remember that `-1px` reduces the spacing by a pixel, and `0` is the same as normal, unmodified letter spacing.

Actually, there is something we could do for the entry text. If you examine the text in Figure 8.8 closely, it seems sort of spread out, as if the letters are too far apart. It would improve the appearance if we could tighten up that spacing. In typography, we'd set an autokerning feature or else mess with the kerning value ourselves. CSS isn't quite so advanced, but it will let you alter the distance between characters.

```
#weblog .entry {margin: 0 0 2em; letter-spacing: -1px;}
```

With that rule, we're also tightening up the text of the title and date, and it doesn't look so good. So we'll override the value using a rule we already have hanging around.

```
#weblog h4.title, #weblog h5.date {margin: 0; padding: 0;
  font-family: Arial, Verdana, sans-serif; line-height: 1em;
  letter-spacing: 0;}
```

One more thing: Let's spread the lines apart just a touch, but only for paragraphs of text. This will not touch other elements, like lists or preformatted text, but that's probably for the best anyway. We can see the results illustrated in Figure 8.9.

```
#weblog h5.date {font-size: 0.9em; text-align: left;
  padding: 0 0 5px 25px; margin: 0 0 0 45%;
  background: url(leaf-down.gif) 0 100% no-repeat;
  border-top: 1px solid; color: rgb(50%,66%,50%);}
#weblog p {line-height: 1.4;}
</style>
```

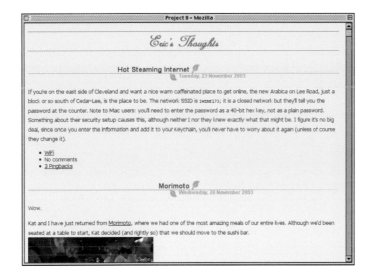

FIGURE 8.9

Tightening up letter spacing while spreading out line spacing.

Now for the information that comes at the end of each entry. We could use the Sliding Doors approach from Project 7, "Opening the Doors to Attractive Tabs," to makes these guys look really fancy, but that would actually be counter-productive. The information there should really fade into the background, so to speak, not call more attention to itself than the main entry text.

So, even though we won't be trying something as complex as creating tabs, let's have the three pieces of information appear in a single line, each separated visually from the others. We can separate them using vertical bars, for example, or something similar.

We'll start by lining up the three list items into a single line.

```
#weblog h5.date {font-size: 0.9em; text-align: left;
  padding: 0 0 5px 25px; margin: 0 0 0 45%;
  background: url(leaf-down.gif) 0 100% no-repeat;
  border-top: 1px solid; color: rgb(50%,66%,50%);}
#weblog .moreinfo li {display: inline;}
#weblog p {line-height: 1.4;}
```

This will make the list items generate inline boxes, just like the links inside them do. That by itself should be enough to make the list items' markers (the bullets) disappear, but not every browser agrees, so let's make sure they go away.

```
#weblog .moreinfo li {display: inline; list-style: none;}
```

Playing with Markers

It might be tempting to try to force the markers to remain since they would make good separators between the list items. The problem is that inline boxes don't generate markers even if you explicitly say they should. Markers only appear on list item boxes, at least in a CSS-conformant browser.

Now for some visual separation. In many cases, authors will use the vertical-bar character (|) to separate a line of links. We don't have any characters available, but we do have the edges of the list items' inline boxes. So if we add a left border to each list item, along with a little left padding, we'll get the result shown in Figure 8.10.

```
#weblog .moreinfo li {display: inline; list-style: none;
  border-left: 1px solid rgb(65%,75%,65%);
  padding-left: 0.5em;}
```

FIGURE 8.10

Stringing the list items into a
single line of text.

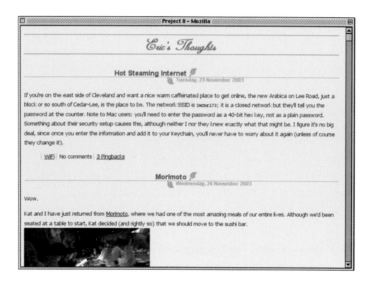

Spacing

In IE5/Win, the spacing may appear a bit off. This is related to the handling of whitespace between the list items and can be reduced by altering the padding we've just added.

Looking at this change closely, the borders are too close to adjacent text. For example, the space between "WiFi" and the border to its right (which is the left border on the "No comments" list item) is too narrow. So let's alter the last declaration to apply half an em of padding to both the left and right—but none to the top and bottom—of the list item.

```
#weblog .moreinfo li {display: inline; list-style: none;
  border-left: 1px solid rgb(65%,75%,65%);
  padding: 0 0.5em;}
```

More important, at least for the moment, is the indentation of the list items. That's caused by the ul element that contains them, which still has a left margin (or, in Gecko-based browsers, left padding). Let's remove that completely.

```
#weblog h5.date {font-size: 0.9em; text-align: left;
  padding: 0 0 5px 25px; margin: 0 0 0 45%;
  background: url(leaf-down.gif) 0 100% no-repeat;
  border-top: 1px solid; color: rgb(50%,66%,50%);}
#weblog .moreinfo {margin: 0; padding: 0;}
#weblog .moreinfo li {display: inline; list-style: none;
  border-left: 1px solid rgb(65%,75%,65%);
  padding: 0 0.5em;}
```

Now the big question: Do we even want the links over to the left? It's certainly a defensible design decision, but let's shift them over to the right. That will let them stand apart from the main text and will set us up to "cap off" the set of links. Because the list items are now generating inline boxes, they are subject to values of `text-align`, just like any other inline text.

```
#weblog .moreinfo {margin: 0; padding: 0;
  text-align: right;}
```

Now to cap the links. Remember that we gave each list item a left border. Since they're all over to the right, we can use the right edge of the `ul` element to add a trailing separator, as it were. This is illustrated in Figure 8.11.

```
#weblog .moreinfo {margin: 0; padding: 0;
text-align: right;
  border-right: 1px solid rgb(50%,66%,50%);}
```

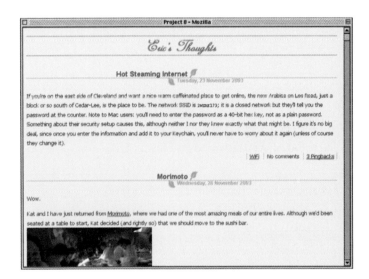

FIGURE 8.11

The links are shifted over to the right and "capped" with a border.

Okay, that's good, but the colors are bad. That blue really has to go. Changing it to a shade of green is easy enough.

```
#weblog .moreinfo li {display: inline; list-style: none;
  border-left: 1px solid rgb(65%,75%,65%);
  padding: 0 0.5em;}
#weblog .moreinfo a {color: rgb(50%,66%,50%);}
#weblog p {line-height: 1.4;}
```

Great, the blue is gone, but the "No comments" text, which isn't contained in a link, is still black. Fortunately, this is also easy to fix. All we have to do is add the color we want to either the list items or the `ul` element itself. Because `color` is inherited, the value we declare will be applied to the nonlink text. Because the links have an explicitly assigned color, they won't change. It's more or less a toss–up, but let's add the color to the `ul` element.

```
#weblog .moreinfo {margin: 0; padding: 0;
  text-align: right;
  border-right: 1px solid rgb(50%,66%,50%);
  color: rgb(50%,66%,50%);}
```

Let's use a similar technique to italicize any nonlink text but leave the links with a normal font style. We can add a declaration to italicize all text in the list like so:

```
#weblog .moreinfo {margin: 0; padding: 0;
  text-align: right; font-style: italic;
  border-right: 1px solid rgb(50%,66%,50%);
  color: rgb(50%,66%,50%);}
```

At the moment, links will be italicized along with nonlink text. To restore them to their normal appearance, we explicitly set `font-style` to be `normal` for the links. (Remember that the separators are borders, so they aren't affected by italicization.)

```
#weblog .moreinfo a {color: rgb(50%,66%,50%); font-style: normal;}
```

Before we move on, let's do one more thing: boldface the category ("WiFi") link. This is as simple as applying a `font-weight` declaration to the list item with the class name `categories`, as illustrated in Figure 8.12.

```
#weblog .moreinfo a {color: rgb(50%,66%,50%); font-style: normal;}
#weblog .moreinfo .categories {font-weight: bold;}
#weblog p {line-height: 1.4;}
```

Borders and Color

Now that we've added a color value that's the same as the border color, we could remove the color value from the `border-right` declaration. That's because if an element's border has no explicitly defined color, the value is taken from the value of `color` for the same element. We're going to leave it, but it's a behavior worth remembering.

No Comments Link

In a real weblog, the "No comments" text would likely be a link to a comment form. We're leaving it as a nonlink here to illustrate the styling of the list and the links in order to make unlinked text look different.

FIGURE 8.12

Mixing italicized, boldfaced, and normal-style text.

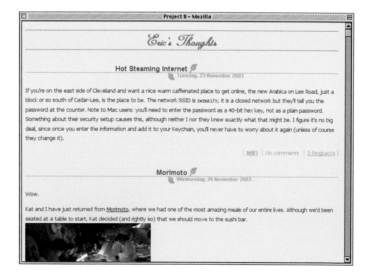

Finishing Touches

We're almost done, but there is one major thing we need to fix. If you look at the picture in the second entry, it's just sitting in the middle of a paragraph of text, completely messing up the layout. That needs to be fixed.

We could just float all images that appear in an entry, but there might be cases in which we don't want to float an image (say, for example, a small icon). We'll need to use another hook to float the picture, and fortunately we have one. Notice the `class` attribute just before the close bracket.

```
<img src="morimoto.jpg" alt="A view of the sushi bar from our seats,
  with Morimoto and his sushi staff slicing away"
  title="Morimoto's Sushi Bar" class="pic border">
```

So the image has a `class` value containing two names: `pic` and `border`. These aren't technically separate `class` values, but they are separate names, and we can address them individually. For any `pic` image, we'll float it to the right and add some margins so that text doesn't flow too closely to the floated image.

```
#weblog p {line-height: 1.4em;}
#weblog .pic {float: right; margin: 1em 0 1em 2em;}
</style>
```

The `class` name `border` indicates a desire to have a border applied to the image. Let's be extra fancy and give the picture a gray double border and also a light green background. This will have the effect shown in Figure 8.13.

```
#weblog .pic {float: right; margin: 1em 0 1em 2em;}
#weblog .border {border: 3px double #666; background: #ABA;}
</style>
```

Multiclassing

The `class` attribute can accept any number of space-separated class names, not just two. Any of them can be used in a selector. In theory, you can select elements based on their having two or more class names (for example, the selector `.pic.border` selects any element with a `class` that contains both `pic` *and* `border`), but IE/Win doesn't support this capability. It can only handle selecting one word at a time, like we did here.

FIGURE 8.13

Floating and bordering the image.

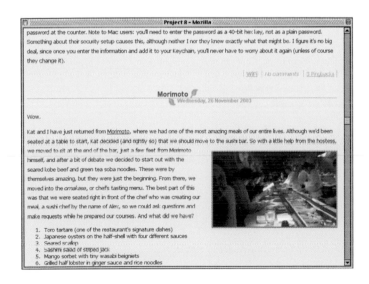

Yes, images can have backgrounds! Furthermore, since the background extends to the outer border edge of the element, the background is visible in the gap between the two lines in the double border. Subtle, yet slick.

To close out this project, let's add something advanced. Most browsers won't recognize this, but they won't be missing anything if they don't.

Let's look at the entry titles again, specifically at the links within them. These links are what are called "permalinks," or pointers to archived copies of the entry. This allows other people to link to the entry without fear that it will disappear in the future. A common way of denoting a permalink is with an octothorpe (#). It would be interesting if an octothorpe appeared when the user moved the mouse pointer over the permalink, wouldn't it? Let's have it appear before the link and also be a lighter color than the link text.

```
#weblog h4.title a {text-decoration: none;
  color: rgb(15%,30%,15%);}
#weblog h4.title a:hover:before {content: "# ";
  color: rgb(50%,61%,48%);}
#weblog h5.date {font-size: 0.9em; text-align: left;
  padding: 0 0 5px 25px; margin: 0 0 0 45%;
  background: url(leaf-down.gif) 0 100% no-repeat;
  border-top: 1px solid; color: rgb(50%,66%,50%);}
```

What this will do is actually insert the string we declared (an octothorpe followed by a blank space) as content at the beginning of the link. Content added in this manner is called *generated content*. The generated content is set to the declared shade of green without changing the color of the overall link.

As of this writing, you're only going to see the effect in recent versions of Mozilla (1.5+) and Opera (7+). Safari 1.1+ should show it, but we'll need a slight hack to make it work. If we add a border to the link itself, suddenly the generated content will appear.

```
#weblog h4.title a {text-decoration: none;
  color: rgb(15%,30%,15%);}
#weblog h4.title a:hover {border-top: 1px dotted rgb(50%,61%,48%);}
#weblog h4.title a:hover:before {content: "# ";
  color: rgb(50%,61%,48%);}
```

It's not clear why adding a border to the link gets Safari doing what it should, but it does. As a bonus, the border will appear in most browsers, including Internet Explorer, which won't show the generated content. So, in advanced browsers, you'll see the result shown in Figure 8.14, and it's all thanks to the style sheet given in Listing 8.2.

A Better Safari

The generated content support in Safari 1.2 was improved so that it's no longer necessary to add a border to make the generated content appear. The border is only needed for Safari 1.1 to show it.

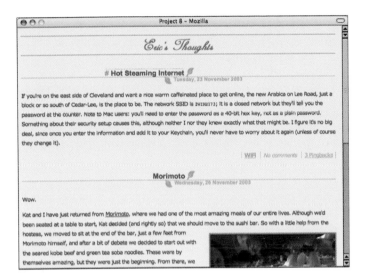

FIGURE 8.14

Applying some dynamic styles to the title links.

Listing 8.2   The Complete Style Sheet

```
body {color: rgb(18%,19%,17%); background: rgb(85%,92%,81%);
 font: 0.85em Verdana, sans-serif;}
#wcblog {width: 99%;}
#weblog h3 {font-size: 150%; text-align: center;
  color: rgb(10%,30%,10%);
  border: 1px solid rgb(30%,50%,30%); border-width: 1px 0;
  margin-bottom: 1.5em; height:45px;
  background: url(title.gif) 50% 100% no-repeat;}
#weblog h3 span {position: absolute; left: -50em; width: 50em;}
#weblog .entry {margin: 0 0 2em; letter-spacing: -1px;}
#weblog h4.title, #weblog h5.date {margin: 0; padding: 0;
  font-family: Arial, Verdana, sans-serif; line-height: 1em;
  letter-spacing: 0;}
#weblog h4.title {font-size: 1.25em; text-align: right;
  padding: 5px 25px 0 0; margin: 0 45% -1px 0;
  background: url(leaf-up.gif) 100% 0 no-repeat;
  border-bottom: 1px solid rgb(50%,66%,50%);}
#weblog h4.title a {text-decoration: none;
  color: rgb(15%,30%,15%);}
#weblog h4.title a:hover {border-top: 1px dotted rgb(50%,61%,48%);}
#weblog h4.title a:hover:before {content: "# ";
  color: rgb(50%,61%,48%);}
#weblog h5.date {font-size: 0.9em; text-align: left;
  padding: 0 0 5px 25px; margin: 0 0 0 45%;
  background: url(leaf-down.gif) 0 100% no-repeat;
  border-top: 1px solid; color: rgb(50%,66%,50%);}
#weblog .moreinfo {margin: 0; padding: 0;
  text-align: right; font-style: italic;
  border-right: 1px solid rgb(50%,66%,50%);
  color: rgb(50%,66%,50%);}
```

continues

Listing 8.2 Continued

```
#weblog .moreinfo li {display: inline; list-style: none;
  border-left: 1px solid rgb(65%,75%,65%);
  padding: 0 0.5em;}
#weblog .moreinfo a {color: rgb(50%,66%,50%); font-style: normal;}
#weblog .moreinfo .categories {font-weight: bold;}
#weblog p {line-height: 1.4;}
#weblog .pic {float: right; margin: 1em 0 1em 2em;}
#weblog .border {border: 3px double #666; background: #ABA;}
```

BRANCHING OUT

Here are some stylistic variations to try:

1. Change the extra information so that the category sits on its own line before the other two bits of information. Also try adding a top border to the comment and pingback items and making sure that the pingback border does not touch the border to its right.

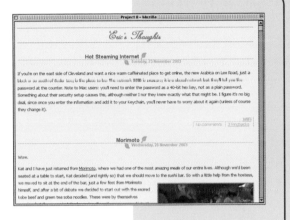

2. Get rid of the margins on the entry titles and instead use padding and background positioning to place the title text and background image as they were in the project. This will also necessitate the removal of another border.

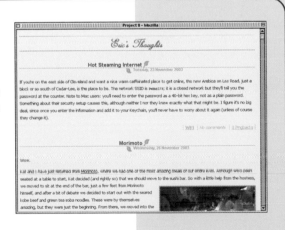

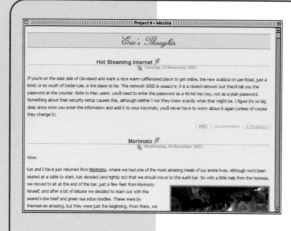

3. This is a double change. First, darken up the weblog's title with some background and border changes. Second, push the borders on the image outward by a pixel so that the background is visible between the image and the double border.

9

DESIGNING A HOME PAGE

Good design keeps the user happy, the manufacturer in the black, and the aesthete unoffended.

—RAYMOND LOEWY

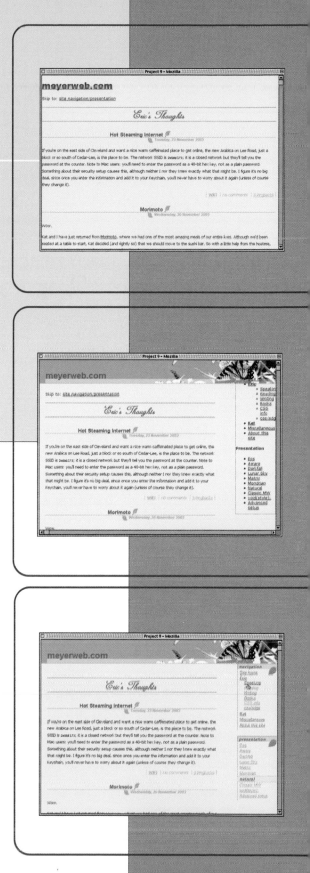

STYLING A WEBLOG, as in the preceding project, can be a challenge, but weblog style in itself isn't enough. Any weblog entries are likely to appear in the context of a site design, and the two need to go together. After all, it would look odd to have a leafy, natural theme for the weblog and a bunch of neon, J-pop decorations for the rest of the site's design. It would be even stranger to have both on the same page.

Since we already have a weblog design, let's actually work outward and create a site design that is consistent with the weblog styles, instead of going the other way around. This will let us build on the work we've already done while providing an example of how the various components of a page can fit together.

Project Goals

The nature (no pun intended) of this project doesn't lend itself to a lot of specific goals. In fact, the sum total of what we need to do can be expressed in three points:

◆ Take the weblog we styled in Project 8 and place it into a full page. This means styling the masthead, sidebar, and footer to be consistent with the visual theme we established when styling the weblog.

◆ Place the navigation and presentation links to the right of the main content and make this "sidebar" touch the masthead.

◆ Highlight the name of the current theme.

These are fairly open guidelines, it's true, but they'll be enough to guide us to a finished design.

Preparation

Download the files for Project 9 from this book's Web site. If you're planning to play along at home, load the file `ch09proj.html` into the editing program of your choice. This is the file you'll be editing, saving, and reloading as the project progresses.

Laying the Groundwork

Since we're going to be using the weblog styles, we already have a simple embedded style sheet, which is shown in Listing 9.1 as a part of the overall document structure.

Listing 9.1   The Basic Document Structure and Starting Style Sheet

```
<!DOCTYPE HTML PUBLIC "-//W3C//DTD HTML 4.01//EN"
         "http://www.w3.org/TR/html4/strict.dtd">
<html>
<head>
 <title>Project 9</title>
 <style type="text/css">
  @import url(project08.css);
 </style>
</head>
<body>
 <div id="sitemast">
 <h1>
  <a href="http://www.meyerweb.com/"><span>meyerweb</span>.com</a>
 </h1>
 </div>
```

See the Introduction for instructions on how to download files from the Web site.

Import Restrictions

As you'll see, the styles we add in this project will all come after the @import. This isn't by accident: The CSS specification requires that any @import statements come at the beginning of the style sheet, before any other rules.

```
<div id="main">
 <div class="skipper">
  Skip to: <a href="#navpres">site navigation/presentation</a>
 </div>
 <div id="weblog">
  [...weblog content...]
 </div>
</div>
<div class="panel" id="navpres">
 [...navigation and presentation links...]
</div>
<div id="footer">
 [...footer content...]
</div>
</body>
</html>
```

The embedded style sheet uses an @import to call in the Project 8 style sheet, which we've split off into a separate file called project08.css. (To see this style sheet, refer to Listing 8.2 in the preceding project.) We can see the result in Figure 9.1.

FIGURE 9.1

The design with the weblog styles applied but nothing else.

All we've really done is take the weblog content from the preceding project and drop it into a slightly larger document, one that has a masthead and navigation elements, plus presentation options and a footer.

The page also has a "skip-link" near the top of the document; that's the stuff in the div with the id of skipper. Clicking on (or otherwise activating) the skip-link will jump the browser display to the navigation and presentation links, which are found at the end of the document. This is illustrated in Figure 9.2.

FIGURE 9.2

The result of following the skip-link.

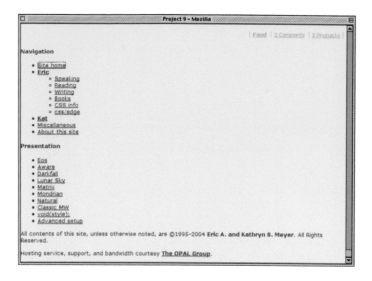

The placement of these links in the document source makes it pretty clear that we'll have to either float the main content to the left or else absolutely position the "sidebar" to get it placed to the right of the main content, as our project goals require.

I say "sidebar" with quotes because there's nothing about the document structure that requires it to be a sidebar. We could style it however we want—as a series of drop-down menus, perhaps, as we did in Project 6, "CSS-Driven Drop-Down Menus." It could also all stay at the bottom of the design. We're referring to the navigation and presentation links as a sidebar merely because it's a convenient way to refer to our intent to place those links to one side of the main content.

Creating the Design

As is usually the case, we'll start at the top of the document and work our way down. After getting the masthead put together, we'll move on to the main content and sidebar. This will let us effectively divide the layout into two zones: "masthead" and "the rest of the page." While it's true that the main content and sidebar will be placed in relation to each other, they'll both be placed in relation to the masthead, so in many ways it is the most important aspect of the design.

Two Images Behind the Masthead

Since the masthead is a key portion of the design, it stands to reason that it should look pretty. It's hard to create beautiful Web design without images, and in this case, we have two images to use in the masthead. They're shown in Figure 9.3.

FIGURE 9.3

The images available for use in the masthead.

All right, so it's really two variants of the same image, `masthead.jpg` and `mh-light.jpg`, the latter of which is a washed-out version of the former. We'll be able to use them together to create a translucency effect, as we did in Project 4, "Positioning in the Background."

First let's get the `h1` element styled. It will be getting `masthead.jpg` for its background, so we need to match its background color to the background of the image. We're also going to be placing the image to the right edge of the element.

```
@import url(project08.css);
#sitemast h1 {background: rgb(45%,65%,45%) url(masthead.jpg)
   100% 0 no-repeat;}
</style>
```

For reasons that will become clear later (and were explored in Project 4), we need to explicitly set the **font-size** of the `h1` and define any margins or padding. These will all be set using ems for the sake of consistency…and also to make life easier for us later on. Let's do the padding and margin first.

```
#sitemast h1 {margin: 0; padding: 1.5em 0.5em 0 0;
   background: rgb(45%,65%,45%) url(masthead.jpg) 100% 0 no-repeat;}
```

Now for the size of the `h1` font. Making it twice as big as that of its parent element (the sitemast `div`) seems like a good size. That's large enough to be easily noticeable but not so large as to completely overwhelm everything else. For consistency, let's also make the font family the same as the titles in our weblog. That leads us to make the following addition:

```
#sitemast h1 {margin: 0; padding: 1.5em 0.5em 0 0;
   font: 2em Arial, Verdana, sans-serif;
   background: rgb(45%,65%,45%) url(masthead.jpg) 100% 0 no-repeat;}
```

This will have exactly the result we declared *and no more*—which means the text won't be boldfaced. Our new declaration sets the `font-weight`, `font-style`, and `font-variant` all to `normal`. That's just how shorthand properties like `font` work. So let's just drop `bold` into the declaration, thus restoring the boldfacing, as shown in Figure 9.4.

```
#sitemast h1 {margin: 0; padding: 1.5em 0.5em 0 0;
   font: bold 2em Arial, Verdana, sans-serif;
   background: rgb(45%,65%,45%) url(masthead.jpg) 100% 0 no-repeat;}
```

FIGURE 9.4

Dramatic improvements to the masthead's appearance.

It's already looking pretty good, but there are some improvements yet to make. First, let's get the descender in the "y" to stick out of the background of the `h1`. We can accomplish this by reducing the `line-height` of the element to a sufficiently low number. Some experimentation reveals that `0.75em` is a good choice for Arial. We'll take advantage of `font`'s unique ability to accept a `line-height` value after the `font-size` value, so long as the two are separated by a forward slash.

```
#sitemast h1 {margin: 0; padding: 1.5em 0.5em 0 0;
   font: bold 2em/0.75em Arial, Verdana, sans-serif;
   background: rgb(45%,65%,45%) url(masthead.jpg) 100% 0 no-repeat;}
```

Now for the link itself. It's kind of weird having normal link styles in the masthead, so let's both set the color and remove the underline.

```
#sitemast h1 {margin: 0; padding: 1.5em 0.5em 0 0;
   font: bold 2em/0.75em Arial, Verdana, sans-serif;
   background: rgb(45%,65%,45%) url(masthead.jpg) 100% 0 no-repeat;}
#sitemast h1 a {color: rgb(20%,40%,20%); text-decoration: none;}
</style>
```

Okay, now for the masthead `div` itself. Since we gave the `h1` the normal-color image, we'll apply the washed-out version to the `div`. At the same time, let's remove any possible margins that might be applied.

```
@import url(project08.css);
#sitemast {margin: 0;
  background: rgb(73%,82%,73%) url(mh-light.jpg) 100% 0 no-repeat;}
#sitemast h1 {margin: 0; padding: 1.5em 0.5em 0 0;
  font: bold 2em/0.75em Arial, Verdana, sans-serif;
  background: rgb(45%,65%,45%) url(masthead.jpg) 100% 0 no-repeat;}
```

All right, so now we have a `div` that's wrapped around an `h1`. That means none of the `div` is actually visible at the moment; if we added borders they'd be visible, but that doesn't do much for the background. We need to get some of that background visible. Easy enough: We'll add some bottom padding to the `div`, and as Figure 9.5 shows, some of the background is thus revealed.

```
#sitemast {margin: 0; padding: 0 0 1em;
  background: rgb(73%,82%,73%) url(mh-light.jpg) 100% 0 no-repeat;}
```

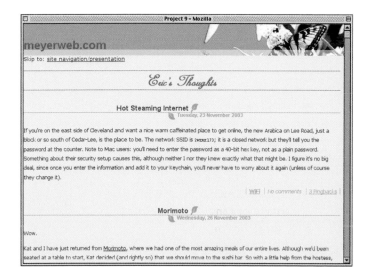

FIGURE 9.5

Adding the lighter image to the masthead `div` and making it visible.

Shifts and Borders

As it stands, the masthead is in pretty darned good shape, but let's take things a step further. Let's reveal more of the butterfly by shifting it upward. We can do this by changing the positions of the background images in both the `h1` and the `div`. Since they both line up along their top edges, we can just shift them upward by the same number of pixels.

```
#sitemast {margin: 0; padding: 0 0 1em;
  background: rgb(73%,82%,73%) url(mh-light.jpg) 100% -30px no-repeat;}
#sitemast h1 {margin: 0; padding: 1.5em 0.5em 0 0;
  font: bold 2em/0.75em Arial, Verdana, sans-serif;
  background: rgb(45%,65%,45%) url(masthead.jpg) 100% -30px no-repeat;}
```

Shifting Versus Image Editing

Once we decide that the masthead's appearance is how we want it, we ought to crop the images using an image editor like Photoshop so that their top edges are the same as what we see in the design. We could then reset the background positions to `100% 0` and save some bandwidth to boot. Until that time, though, using `background-position` to try out different image placements can be a real time-saver.

There's one last touch to apply to the masthead. By creatively using borders, we can actually shift over the h1 and the visible portion of the div. Consider the styles shown here and illustrated by Figure 9.6.

```
#sitemast {margin: 0; padding: 0 0 1em;
  border: 1px solid rgb(45%,65%,45%); border-width: 0 0 1px 1.5em;
  background: rgb(73%,82%,73%) url(mh-light.jpg) 100% -30px no-repeat;}
```

FIGURE 9.6

Putting the finishing touches on the masthead.

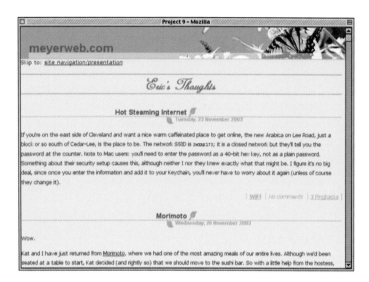

This works because we've added an em-and-a-half left border to the masthead div and also set the color of that border to match the background color of the h1. Visually, the two blend together with nary a seam. Changing the border color to anything else will clearly show how the effect works.

The one-pixel border along the bottom of the masthead also serves to subtly separate it from the rest of the design. In fact, it's about time we turned our attention to the rest of the design.

Content and Sidebar

As you'll recall, the main content of the page is contained in a div with an id of content, and the sidebar is contained in a div with an id of navpres and a class of panel. It's also the case that our project goals call for us to put the navigation and presentation links to the right of the main content.

To make that happen, we'll need to do one of two things:

◆ Float the main content to the left, leaving enough room for the sidebar to flow (or float) next to it.

◆ Absolutely position the sidebar to the right of the main content, which will be left in the normal flow.

Let's position the sidebar. Doing so will make it easy for us to move it around at will, and this is actually a little less prone to strange interactions (see "Positioning Rather Than Floating" at the end of this section for details). To do so, however, we'll need to open up space for it to appear; otherwise, it will overlap the main content. The content could use some padding anyway, to push its contents away from the edges of the browser window as well as from the masthead.

```
#sitemast h1 a {color: rgb(20%,40%,20%); text-decoration: none;}
#main {padding: 2em 25% 3em 1.5em;}
</style>
```

The `1.5em` left padding is taken from the width of the left border on the masthead. By setting them to be the same, the left visible edge of the content will line up with the left visible edge of the masthead's text. As for the `25%` right padding, that value was picked because it sounded like a good amount of space to leave for a sidebar.

We don't want the sidebar to fill that entire space, though—if it did, the main and sidebar content would practically touch each other. We'll absolutely position the sidebar into the top-right corner and supply a width of `17%`. Again, that's a number that was picked more or less on a whim. We'll also add a dotted red border so that we can see the edges of the sidebar, as seen in Figure 9.7.

```
#main {padding: 2em 25% 3em 1.5em;}
.panel {position: absolute; right: 0; top: 0; width: 17%;
  border: 1px dotted red;}
</style>
```

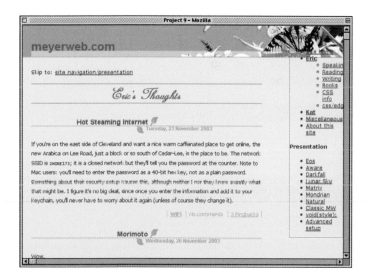

FIGURE 9.7

The sidebar is positioned in the top right corner.

Well, there's certainly enough room to the right of the main content for the sidebar! The real problem, of course, is that we positioned the sidebar over the masthead. We'll need to move it down so that it's just underneath the masthead's bottom border.

How far is that? Well, the `h1` has a `font-size` of `2em` (in comparison to normal-size text), which means everything about it is doubled. It has 1.5em of top padding but a 0.75em content height (thanks to the `line-height` value). That's a total of 2.25em, which doubled is 4.5em. The masthead `div` has another em of bottom padding, so that's a total of 5.5em.

```
.panel {position: absolute; right: 0; top: 5.5em; width: 17%;
   border: 1px dotted red;}
```

Using Margins When Positioning

If we didn't want the borders to overlap, we could shift the sidebar down a pixel (or more, if necessary) by setting a top margin.

This change will actually cause the top border of the sidebar to overlap the bottom border of the masthead. Why? Because that one pixel of bottom border is placed below the 5.5em we just added up. So the top edge of the masthead's bottom border is 5.5em below the top of the document, and the top edge of the top border of the sidebar is in exactly the same place. That's actually a good thing because, in this case, we want the two borders to overlap.

Now might be a good time to get rid of some of the list indentation, too. We don't want to remove all of it; some of the vertical separation created by top and bottom margins and padding is a good thing. In addition, the sublist under "Eric" should be indented with respect to the rest of the links. So we'll leave a bottom margin and some top and bottom padding on the top-level lists. For the nested lists, we'll remove everything except some left padding. This is shown in Figure 9.8.

```
.panel {position: absolute; right: 0; top: 5.5em; width: 17%;
   border: 1px dotted red;}
.panel ul {margin: 0 0 1.5em; padding: 0.25em 0 0.5em;}
.panel ul ul {margin: 0; padding: 0 0 0 0.5em;}
</style>
```

FIGURE 9.8

The repositioned sidebar and its slightly restyled lists.

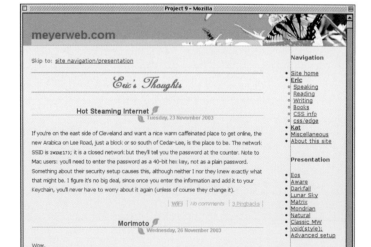

Some of you may have noticed that the bullets don't appear in IE6. So far as I could tell, this happens because IE clips anything sticking out of the positioned element. We could try to fix the problem by explicitly changing the value of `overflow` for the sidebar, except we're about to remove the bullets anyway, so that would be sort of silly.

►► POSITIONING RATHER THAN FLOATING

It's worth explaining why we positioned the sidebar instead of floating the main content and leaving the sidebar in the normal flow. To use floating, we might have written styles something like this:

```
#main {float: left; width: 75%;}
.panel {margin-left: 75%;}
```

Obviously, these are simplified versions of what we'd really write, but they capture the essence of the method. This would put the content to the left and the sidebar to the right.

The main reason not to do this is the bugs lurking in IE/Win's rendering engine, which doesn't take well to floating an element over the margin (or padding) of a following element in the normal flow. These bugs aren't totally reliable, but they do exist and can seriously mangle a page's layout.

The other floating method would involve floating both content and sidebar, something like this:

```
#main {float: left; width: 75%;}
.panel {float: right; width: 25%;}
```

Explorer is much happier with this kind of thing, and so are all other modern browsers. The drawback is the difficulty in setting padding or margins for these elements based on anything other than percentages. If we were to add that 1.5em of left padding back onto the main-content `div`, the two `div`s wouldn't fit next to each other because the left padding would be added to the width of the `div`, thus resulting in an element box (75% + 1.5em) wide.

We could fiddle with the numbers until we got something that worked for most people, but it would still be a fragile solution. The only reasonable alternative would be to use only percentages, like this:

```
#main {float: left; width: 70%; padding: 2em 0 3em 5%;}
.panel {float: right; width: 25%;}
```

If your layout needs are amenable to using percentages like this, great! Floats will work for you. If not, positioning makes life a lot easier.

Simple Sidebar Styling

The bullets really have to go. Doing so is easy.

```
.panel ul {margin: 0 0 1.5em; padding: 0.25em 0 0.5em;
  list-style: none;}
```

This will remove the bullets from all `ul` elements that descend from the sidebar `div` (because of its `panel` class), no matter how deeply they're nested inside other lists.

Let's back up for a moment and change the font used in the sidebar. The weblog titles are all in Arial and so is the site's masthead, so let's have the sidebar use Arial as well. We'll supply Verdana as a fallback in case Arial is not available for some reason.

```
.panel {position: absolute; right: 0; top: 5.5em; width: 17%;
  font-family: Arial, Verdana, sans-serif;
  border: 1px dotted red;}
```

Then there are the `h4` elements, the ones containing the words "Navigation" and "Presentation." We should take off their margins, add in a darker green background, and slide in a little padding for visual appeal, as shown in Figure 9.9. We'll also set the `font-size` to 1em to keep the text from getting bigger or smaller than the rest of the text.

```
.panel {position: absolute; right: 0; top: 5.5em; width: 17%;
  font-family: Arial, Verdana, sans-serif;
  border: 1px dotted red;}
.panel h4 {margin: 0; padding: 0.33em 0.5em 1px 0.25em;
  background: rgb(75%,85%,70%);
  font-size: 1em;}
.panel ul {margin: 0 0 1.5em; padding: 0.25em 0 0.5em;
  list-style: none;}
```

FIGURE 9.9

The seeds of a better-looking sidebar.

Let's keep going with the `h4` elements. Rather than black on green, let's have them be dark green on green.

```
.panel h4 {margin: 0; padding: 0.33em 0.5em 1px 0.25em;
  background: rgb(75%,85%,70%);
  font-size: 1em;}
  color: rgb(20%,40%,20%);}
```

The addition of some borders would make the headings stand out even more, but just adding solid borders is kind of dull. To increase their visual appeal, we'll make the left-edge borders a little thicker, the bottom border dotted, and set them all to the same color. This can be done in any number of ways, but we'll try adding in one rule for each aspect of the borders: style, width, and color.

```
.panel h4 {margin: 0; padding: 0.33em 0.5em 1px 0.25em;
  background: rgb(75%,85%,70%);
  font-size: 1em;
  border-style: solid solid dotted; border-width: 1px 0 1px 2px;
  border-color: rgb(40%,60%,40%); color: rgb(20%,40%,20%);}
```

Not bad, but there's so much more we could do! Italicizing them would add more interest while also making them visually distinct from the rest of the text in the sidebar, so we'll do that. We can also reduce the `line-height`, just like we did for the masthead, so that the descenders stick down past the bottom border of the element itself.

```
.panel h4 {margin: 0; padding: 0.33em 0.5em 1px 0.25em;
  background: rgb(75%,85%,70%);
  font-size: 1em; font-style: italic; line-height: 0.7em;
  border-style: solid solid dotted; border-width: 1px 0 1px 2px;
  border-color: rgb(40%,60%,40%); color: rgb(20%,40%,20%);}
```

This will have the desired effect for "Navigation," but "Presentation" doesn't have any letters that descend. Of course, it would if we changed all of the letters to be lowercase; the "P" would then become a "p." Let's make that change plus spread out the letters just a bit to give them more of an airy feel. We get the result shown in Figure 9.10.

```
.panel h4 {margin: 0; padding: 0.33em 0.5em 1px 0.25em;
  background: rgb(75%,85%,70%);
  font-size: 1em; font-style: italic; line-height: 0.7em;
  text-transform: lowercase; letter-spacing: 1px;
  border-style: solid solid dotted; border-width: 1px 0 1px 2px;
  border-color: rgb(40%,60%,40%); color: rgb(20%,40%,20%);}
```

Reduced Line Heights

When you decide to reduce the `line-height` of an element to put a border along the "baseline," as we've done here, the exact amount of `line-height` will depend on the font in use. Finding the right value is often a matter of experimentation.

FIGURE 9.10

Polishing the headings to a high sheen.

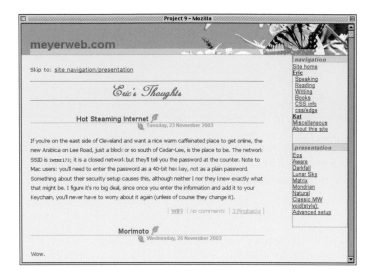

Adding Another Leaf

At this point, things have been almost too easy, so let's take on a small challenge. Notice the blank space to the right of the links in the sidebar? Let's put something there. It should have visual appeal without being overly distracting.

A good choice would be a small graphic. That part's easy. To make it more interesting, let's have the same image straddle the bottom border of the headings so that the image starts in the headings and stretches down below the bottom border. Visually speaking, anyway.

To do this, we'll use the image shown in Figure 9.11. (It appears there at 500% normal size.)

FIGURE 9.11

The leaf image we'll be using in the sidebar.

The first thing to do is add the leaf image to the background of the headings. We want it all the way to the right and partway down the element box, so that its top starts somewhere near the middle of the heading. The top padding plus content height is 1.03em, and there's another pixel of bottom padding. So we'll guess and say around 0.66em.

```
.panel h4 {margin: 0; padding: 0.33em 0.5em 1px 0.25em;
   background: rgb(75%,85%,70%) url(nav-bg.gif) 100% 0.66em no-repeat;
   font-size: 1em; font-style: italic; line-height: 0.7em;
   text-transform: lowercase; letter-spacing: 1px;
```

```
border-style: solid solid dotted; border-width: 1px 0 1px 2px;
border-color: rgb(40%,60%,40%); color: rgb(20%,40%,20%);}
```

That takes care of the top part of the leaf effect. Now we need to continue the leaves on past the bottom border. Fortunately, we have elements ready-made for this purpose. We'll just put the same image in the background of the unordered lists and shift it upward so that the two come together.

How far up should it be shifted? Well, we know that the top of the image is about 0.37em above the bottom of the heading content's bottom edge. Then there are the top and bottom borders, each of which adds a pixel, and the one-pixel bottom padding. So we'll take a guess and say it's in the rough vicinity of 0.5em.

```
.panel ul {margin: 0 0 1.5em; padding: 0.25em 0 0.5em;
  list-style: none;
  background: url(nav-bg.gif) 100% -0.5em no-repeat;}
```

The results are shown in Figure 9.12.

FIGURE 9.12

The leaves are added to the sidebar.

Pretty cool, except for one oddity: There's an extra leaf piece! That's because we applied the background image to all ul elements in the sidebar, and that includes the nested list. We need to get rid of it, and we'll do so by adding a declaration to the `.panel ul ul` rule.

```
.panel ul ul {margin: 0; padding: 0 0 0 0.5em;
  background: none;}
```

While we're here, let's italicize the text in that nested list.

```
.panel ul ul {margin: 0; padding: 0 0 0 0.5em;
  background: none; font-style: italic;}
```

Sliced Opera

Okay, there's another oddity: Opera doesn't paint the image underneath the border, so the leaf ends up with a slice through it. If we'd used a solid border, this wouldn't have been a problem. We'll stick to the dotted border for the rest of the project, but Opera users might want to make it solid.

Sidebar Links

Now we'll deal with the actual links. The link text has been far too cramped for far too long in this project, and a little padding on the list items is just the thing to give them some room. With top and bottom padding we can push them away from each other, and with left padding we can indent the text a bit from the edge of the sidebar.

```
.panel ul {margin: 0 0 1.5em; padding: 0.25em 0 0.5em;
  list-style: none;
  background: url(nav-bg.gif) 100% -0.5em no-repeat;}
.panel ul li {padding: 0.15em 0 0.1em 0.5em;}
.panel ul ul {margin: 0; padding: 0 0 0 0.5em;
  background: none; font-style: italic;}
```

We don't want the exact same spacing rules to apply to the nested list, though. To tighten those nested links up a bit, we'll take the top padding off of the list items.

```
.panel ul ul {margin: 0; padding: 0 0 0 0.5em;
  background: none; font-style: italic;}
.panel ul ul li {padding-top: 0;}
</style>
```

Now for the colors. Blue and purple, the default unvisited and visited colors, don't really go well with the green theme we have in place. Let's define some basic colors for these link styles, providing a dark green for unvisited links and a lighter green for the visited links. This is what's shown in Figure 9.13.

```
.panel ul ul li {padding-top: 0;}
.panel a:link {color: rgb(30%,50%,30%);}
.panel a:visited {color: rgb(50%,60%,50%);}
</style>
```

FIGURE 9.13

Improving the presentation of the links.

We can take things a step further by styling the presentation links differently than the navigation links. Since the presentation options aren't really navigation related, they probably shouldn't look like unvisited links. The simplest thing to do is make them look like visited links.

```
.panel a:visited, #presolinks a {color: rgb(50%,60%,50%);}
```

This will set the presentation link colors to be a consistent color no matter whether a browser thinks they've been visited or not.

Since we're talking about the colors of sidebar links, a hover effect might be nice. We want this to apply to any navigation link but not the presentation links. (Why? Just because.) So we'll add a new rule that makes any hovered navigation link a woodsy brown.

```
.panel a:visited, #presolinks a {color: rgb(50%,60%,50%);}
.panel a:hover {color: rgb(50%,30%,20%);}
</style>
```

This rule won't affect the presentation links because the specificity of `#presolinks a` is higher than that of `.panel a:hover`. Thus, the hover color will lose out to the color assigned by `#presolinks a`. The order the rules come in doesn't matter in this case, thanks to the differences in specificity.

Border Changes

At this stage, it's time to remove that dotted red border—probably well past time, really. So we'll take that declaration out of the `.panel` rule.

```
.panel {position: absolute; right: 0; top: 5.5em; width: 17%;
   font-family: Arial, Verdana, sans-serif;}
```

This change means that the top border of the "navigation" heading will now overlap the bottom border of the masthead, the same as the dotted red border did before we removed it.

Having removed the sidebar's border, we need to restore some form of visual separation between the sidebar links and the main content. Rather than add a left border back onto the panel, let's instead add left borders to the unordered lists that contain the links.

```
.panel ul {margin: 0 0 1.5em; padding: 0.25em 0 0.5em;
   list-style: none; border-left: 1px solid rgb(45%,65%,45%);
   background: url(nav-bg.gif) 100% -0.5em no-repeat;}
```

Remember what happened with the leaf, the way it showed up at the top of the nested list? We need to prevent a recurrence of that nested-list repetition here by removing the left border from any nested lists. This is shown in Figure 9.14.

```
.panel ul ul {margin: 0; padding: 0 0 0 0.5em;
   background: none; border-left: none; font-style: italic;}
```

Link Specificity

As it happens, specificity is exactly the reason behind the recommendation that link styles be in this order: link, visited, hover, active. You can read more at http://www.meyerweb.com /eric/css/ link-specificity.html.

FIGURE 9.14

Adding borders to the lists enforces visual separation.

Natural Highlighting

We're almost done, but there are a few minor things left to do. One is to fulfill the third of our project goals: to highlight the name of this theme in some fashion. The theme's name is, appropriately enough, "Natural." If we take a look at the markup for that link, we can see an easy way to highlight the theme's name.

```
<li id="natural"><a href="#"
  onclick="setActiveStyleSheet('Natural'); return false;"
  title="Wildlife and greenery">Natural</a></li>
```

This `id` gives us all we need to style the theme's name different from the others. For starters, let's make the link color a dark green.

```
.panel ul ul li {padding-top: 0;}
.panel #natural a {color: rgb(30%,40%,30%);}
.panel a:link {color: rgb(30%,50%,30%);}
```

With that done, let's boldface and italicize the text by styling the `#natural` list item directly. These new font styles will be inherited by the link, although the color will not because we just explicitly assigned it a color.

```
.panel ul ul li {padding-top: 0;}
.panel #natural {font-weight: bold; font-style: italic;}
.panel #natural a {color: rgb(30%,40%,30%);}
```

Come to think of it, this is starting to make the link look like the headings, so let's bring in a couple more of the styles we used for the headings: the increased letter spacing and the lowercase text.

```
.panel #natural {font-weight: bold; font-style: italic;
  letter-spacing: 1px; text-transform: lowercase;}
```

In that same vein, let's add a dotted border to this list item to set it apart from the others. We don't want it to appear on the right edge, so we'll just define an overall border and then turn off the right side. We'll also add a background color that's just a touch darker than the page background.

```
.panel #natural {font-weight: bold; font-style: italic;
  letter-spacing: 1px; text-transform: lowercase;
  border: 1px dotted rgb(45%,65%,45%); border-right: none;
  background: rgb(83%,90%,78%);}
```

If we consider the presentation of the "natural" link, it's definitely different from its neighbors. There's just one little detail—the left border. It's sitting just inside the list's border, which doesn't look all that great. We could remove it, but here's a better idea: Let's make it overlap the list's border, effectively punching a hole in that border and visually blurring the distinction between the theme name and the rest of the page. All that's required is a one-pixel negative left margin for the list item, as shown in Figure 9.15.

```
.panel #natural {font-weight: bold; font-style: italic;
  letter-spacing: 1px; text-transform: lowercase;
  border: 1px dotted rgb(45%,65%,45%); border-right: none;
  background: rgb(83%,90%,78%); margin-left: -1px;}
```

FIGURE 9.15

Highlighting the name of the current theme.

Finishing Touches

There are but a few things left to do. First, the skip-link doesn't really have to stay in place. We could use one of several methods to remove it from display, including just setting it to `display: none`. In fact, let's just do that, as it's the simplest course of action. We'll drop this style in at the top of the style sheet for no good reason other than to get it out of the way early.

Removing Accessibility

Although the skip-links are supplied for accessibility reasons, setting them to `display: none` means most screen readers won't see them. The same is true of just about every other method of removing skip-links from your Web design. Until these broken screen readers fix their behavior, nondisplayed skip-links are not likely to be accessible.

```
@import url(project08.css);
.skipper {display: none;}
#sitemast {margin: 0; padding: 0 0 1em;
   border: 1px solid rgb(45%,65%,45%); border-width: 0 0 1px 1.5em;
   background: rgb(73%,82%,73%) url(mh-light.jpg) 100% -30px no-repeat;}
```

We might also do something about the color of links in the overall page instead of just in the sidebar. We'll go with sort of a bright medium green for unvisited links and a more washed-out green for visited links. This will apply to any links that aren't already being styled by other means, which means the rule will not affect the sidebar links nor the weblog links that we styled in the preceding chapter.

We'll put the rules to drive the new link-color effects at the end of the style sheet for no good reason other than we can.

```
.panel a:hover {color: rgb(50%,30%,20%);}
a:link {color: rgb(0%,50%,40%); background: transparent;}
a:visited {color: rgb(30%,50%,30%); background: transparent;}
</style>
```

Background Warnings

We supplied explicit transparent backgrounds for the links to avoid triggering warnings in most CSS validators. Note that a warning does not prevent validation; only an error prevents that.

The result of removing the skip-link and coloring the document's links can be seen in Figure 9.16.

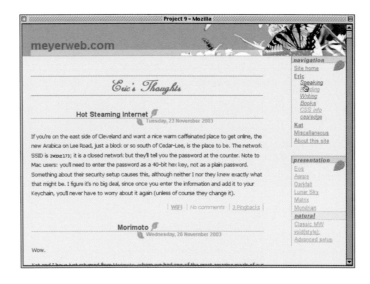

FIGURE 9.16

Removing the skip-link and changing link colors.

Now let's style the footer at the bottom of the page. We don't have to worry about its separation from the text in the main content because that's been handled by the bottom padding on the content div itself. All we need do is concentrate on styling the footer. We'll start with a double border across the top, a zeroed-out margin, and some padding on the top and bottom of the footer itself.

```
a:visited {color: rgb(30%,50%,30%); background: transparent;}
#footer {border-top: 3px double; margin: 0; padding: 0.75em 1em 1em;}
</style>
```

The padding ensures that the footer's content doesn't crowd up against the edges of the browser window. Now, footers are usually given over to boring stuff like copyright statements and other legalese, so we'll crank down the size of the text.

```
#footer {border-top: 3px double; margin: 0; padding: 0.75em 1em 1em;
  font-size: 75%;}
```

To finish off the visual separation of the footer, we'll alter its text and background colors. These colors are based on variations of the overall page background and the page theme. (If you don't like them, feel free to use different values.)

```
#footer {border-top: 3px double; margin: 0; padding: 0.75em 1em 1em;
  font-size: 75%;
  color: rgb(20%,40%,20%); background: rgb(73%,82%,73%);}
```

There's just one more thing to do, and that's close up the space between the two paragraphs in the footer. By stripping the margins and padding off of the paragraphs, we get them to look like two lines in the same paragraph, as illustrated in Figure 9.17.

```
#footer {border-top: 3px double; margin: 0; padding: 0.75em 1em 1em;
  font-size: 75%;
  color: rgb(20%,40%,20%); background: rgb(73%,82%,73%);}
#footer p {margin: 0; padding: 0;}
</style>
```

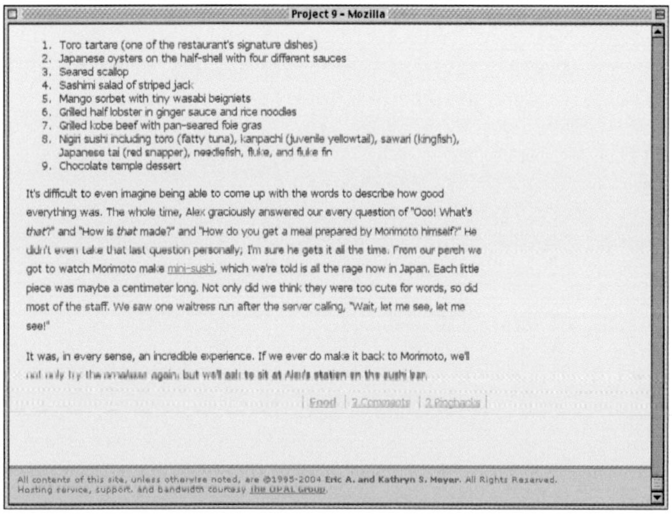

Text Reduction

We also could have used a value like `smaller` to reduce the text size. In such situations, the exact value used is often a matter of the designer's taste.

FIGURE 9.17

Giving the footer some style.

The end result of all our work is shown in Listing 9.2.

Listing 9.2   The Full Style Sheet

```
@import url(project08.css);
.skipper {display: none;}
#sitemast {margin: 0; padding: 0 0 1em;
  border: 1px solid rgb(45%,65%,45%); border-width: 0 0 1px 1.5em;
  background: rgb(73%,82%,73%) url(mh-light.jpg) 100% -30px no-repeat;}
#sitemast h1 {margin: 0; padding: 1.5em 0.5em 0 0;
  font: bold 2em/0.75em Arial, Verdana, sans-serif;
  background: rgb(45%,65%,45%) url(masthead.jpg) 100% -30px no-repeat;}
#sitemast h1 a {color: rgb(20%,40%,20%); text-decoration: none;}
#main {padding: 2em 25% 3em 1.5em;}
.panel {position: absolute; right: 0; top: 5.5em; width: 17%;
  font-family: Arial, Verdana, sans-serif;}
.panel h4 {margin: 0; padding: 0.33em 0.5em 1px 0.25em;
  background: rgb(75%,85%,70%) url(nav-bg.gif) 100% 0.66em no-repeat;
  font-size: 1em; font-style: italic; line-height: 0.7em;
  text-transform: lowercase; letter-spacing: 1px;
  border-style: solid solid dotted; border-width: 1px 0 1px 2px;
  border-color: rgb(40%,60%,40%); color: rgb(20%,40%,20%);}
.panel ul {margin: 0 0 1.5em; padding: 0.25em 0 0.5em;
  list-style: none; border-left: 1px solid rgb(45%,65%,45%);
  background: url(nav-bg.gif) 100% -0.5em no-repeat;}
.panel ul li {padding: 0.15em 0 0.1em 0.5em;}
.panel ul ul {margin: 0; padding: 0 0 0 0.5em;
  background: none; border-left: none; font-style: italic;}
.panel ul ul li {padding-top: 0;}
.panel #natural {font-weight: bold; font-style: italic;
  letter-spacing: 1px; text-transform: lowercase;
  border: 1px dotted rgb(45%,65%,45%); border-right: none;
  background: rgb(83%,90%,78%); margin-left: -1px;}
.panel #natural a {color: rgb(30%,40%,30%);}
.panel a:link {color: rgb(30%,50%,30%);}
.panel a:visited, #presolinks a {color: rgb(50%,60%,50%);}
.panel a:hover {color: rgb(50%,30%,20%);}
a:link {color: rgb(0%,50%,40%); background: transparent;}
a:visited {color: rgb(30%,50%,30%); background: transparent;}
#footer {border-top: 3px double; margin: 0; padding: 0.75em 1em 1em;
  font-size: 75%;
  color: rgb(20%,40%,20%); background: rgb(73%,82%,73%);}
#footer p {margin: 0; padding: 0;}
```

BRANCHING OUT

1. Convert the design to use floats for the two columns, as discussed in the aside "Positioning Rather Than Floating." Remember that the styles given in the aside will not be enough—you'll still need to deal with things like margins, padding, and the placement of the footer.

2. Reverse the layout so that the sidebar is on the left and the main content on the right. This will require changing the borders on the sidebar, and some text alignment should probably change as well. Also try altering the masthead to fit visually with the change in sidebar placement.

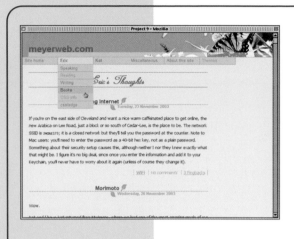

3. Here's an ambitious undertaking: Turn the sidebar into a horizontal toolbar, complete with drop-down menus, using the techniques explored in Project 6. If you want to really go all out, combine the drop-down styles with the Sliding Doors technique discussed in Project 7, "Opening the Doors to Attractive Tabs," to create a really outstanding toolbar.

10

DESIGNING IN THE GARDEN

I love you twisted
And I love you straight
I'd write it down but I can't concentrate
Words won't me obey they do as they please
And all I am left with is these

—ELVIS COSTELLO

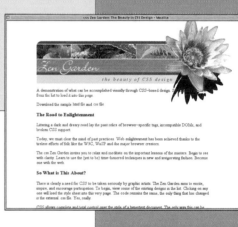

IN MAY 2003, the CSS world was introduced to an amazing new resource: the CSS Zen Garden. The goal of this site was to provide designers with an HTML document that they could not change in any way and to challenge them to write a style sheet that would present the file with flair, visual appeal, and originality.

As of this writing, there were close to 100 different official Zen Garden designs, every one striking and every one different, some radically so. The site's goal had been to show that CSS design could be beautiful, that such beauty could be created on top of a relatively simple document structure, and that the same document could be presented in totally different ways. It has succeeded brilliantly on all counts.

Since *Eric Meyer on CSS* finished with a challenging project (in that case, re-creating the book's layout in CSS), it seemed to me that taking on a similar challenge would be fitting for this book. Creating a Zen Garden design seemed to fit the bill nicely.

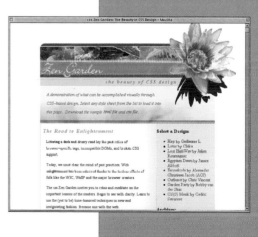

There was only one problem. I freely admit that I'm not a strong visual artist (and some would label that a gross understatement), and Zen Garden designs need to look really good. So I decided to go to someone who is a strong visual artist: Dave Shea, founder of the CSS Zen Garden and a technical reviewer for this very book. Dave produced a beautiful design, and I turned it into a CSS-driven layout. This project is a recounting of the steps I took to make that happen.

Project Goals

We really only have one project goal this time around: to take a visual design and convert it to a CSS-driven layout. This simple goal contains a trio of more specific goals, however, especially since we're creating this design for the CSS Zen Garden.

◆ Create the layout without changing a single character of the content and markup in the HTML document provided. Only the CSS is under our control.

◆ Make sure the layout looks good in IE5.5+/Win, IE5/Mac, Safari, and the latest Gecko-based browsers (as of this writing, Mozilla 1.6 and Firefox 0.8).

◆ Have the design tolerate changes in font size up to 150% of the size of the user's default text size.

What we'll be doing is combining two very common situations in the life of a Web designer. The first is an attempt to reproduce a layout that a visual artist has created; this often happens in large companies (or any other organization) where the look of a site is under the direction of artists, not programmers. The second situation is one in which you have unchangeable markup that you need to style. In this case, the markup is specifically set up to make CSS layout easier, which is a good thing.

Preparation

See the Introduction for instructions on how to download files from the Web site.

Download the files for Project 10 from this book's Web site. If you're planning to play along at home, load the file ch10proj.html into the editing program of your choice. This is the file you'll be editing, saving, and reloading as the project progresses.

Laying the Groundwork

As always, we need to understand the document skeleton before we try to clothe it in CSS. The basic document skeleton is given in Listing 10.1.

Listing 10.1   The Document Skeleton

```
<body id="css-zen-garden">
<div id="container">
  <div id="intro">
    <div id="pageHeader">
      <h1><span>css Zen Garden</span></h1>
      <h2><span>The Beauty of <acronym
       title="Cascading Style Sheets">CSS</acronym> Design</span></h2>
    </div>
    <div id="quickSummary">
      [...content...]
    </div>
    <div id="preamble">
      <h3><span>The Road to Enlightenment</span></h3>
      [...content...]
    </div>
  </div>
  <div id="supportingText">
    <div id="explanation">
      <h3><span>So What is This About?</span></h3>
      [...content...]
    </div>
    <div id="participation">
      <h3><span>Participation</span></h3>
      [...content...]
    </div>
    <div id="benefits">
      <h3><span>Benefits</span></h3>
      [...content...]
    </div>
    <div id="requirements">
      <h3><span>Requirements</span></h3>
      [...content...]
    </div>
    <div id="footer">
      [...content...]
    </div>
  </div>
  <div id="linkList">
    <div id="linkList2">
      <div id="lselect">
        <h3 class="select"><span>Select a Design:</span></h3>
        [...list of links...]
      </div>
      <div id="larchives">
```

continues

Extra divs?

The "[...extra divs...]" mentioned at the end of Listing 10.1 are content-free divs that were included to provide designers with extra elements to style if needed. We won't need them, so they won't be mentioned again.

Listing 10.1   Continued

```
      <h3 class="archives"><span>Archives:</span></h3>
      [...list of links...]
    </div>
    <div id="lresources">
      <h3 class="resources"><span>Resources:</span></h3>
      [...list of links...]
    </div>
   </div>
  </div>
 </div>
[...extra divs...]
</body>
```

There's a lot more to the document's structure, but Listing 10.1 covers the parts we'll actually need for this project. Listing 10.1 shows just the bare minimum needed to understand the rest of the project because a full listing of the document source would go on for pages and pages, and these fancy color books get more expensive the more pages you have.

Now let's take a look at the design we're going to re-create. It's the Photoshop file shown in Figure 10.1.

FIGURE 10.1

The visual design reference file (shown at 50% of normal size).

So that's what we're going to do with CSS. To make this work, we're going to need to pull out a number of images that will come in handy later. These are the backgrounds and design elements that we'll need to get the same visual appearance as that shown in Figure 10.1. These images are as follows:

◆ The page header containing the script-font "Zen Garden"

◆ The flower on the right side of the page header

◆ The blurry light green background of the "quick summary" portion

◆ The faded flowers at the bottom of the main content column

◆ The sidebar's background and the gradient fade along the right side of the main content column

◆ The footer's background

◆ The three sidebar headings ("Design List" and so on)

We'll take a closer look at each of these as we come to need them. Now, let's get styling!

Creating the Design

To start out, we'll set some "global" styles: rules that will apply throughout the document. This includes stripping off the page margins (or padding), setting basic background and foreground colors, and removing the borders and underlines from acronym and link elements, respectively.

```
<style type="text/css" title="currentStyle">
body {margin: 0; padding: 0; text-align: center;
  color: #000; background: #FFF;}
acronym {border: none;}
a {text-decoration: none;}
</style>
```

As you can see, we also centered all the text in the document. That was done because we want the design to be centered, and the best way to center elements in IE5.5/Win is to declare text-align: center;. The CSS specification is clear that text-align shouldn't center elements, but it does anyway in IE5.5/Win. We'll compensate for this very soon, but first let's define some link styles. We'll make unvisited links a pinkish red color, visited links a dull red, and any hovered link will get an underline, as shown in Figure 10.2.

```
a {text-decoration: none;}
a:link {color: rgb(179,63,96);}
a:visited {color: rgb(90,32,48);}
a:hover {text-decoration: underline;}
</style>
```

FIGURE 10.2

The first styles are applied.

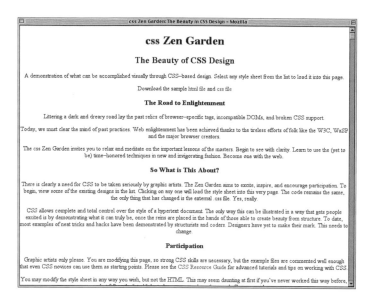

Remember, the text centering is a temporary effect, undertaken solely to work around the bug in IE5.5/Win. In the next section, in fact, we're going to override it and get the text back on the left where it belongs.

Planting the Seeds

If you refer back to Listing 10.1, you'll find that the entire page content is enclosed in a div with an id of container. Therefore, our first step in actually styling the content is to set some basic parameters for this container.

Let's refer back to Figure 10.1. The width of the main column (not counting the large flower in the upper-right corner) is 647 pixels. We don't know why that's the width—it just is. So we'll make the container that wide. At the same time, we'll strip off any padding and set a specific top margin as well as auto side margins.

```
a:hover {text-decoration: underline;}
#container {width: 647px; margin: 75px auto 0; padding: 0;}
</style>
```

The 75-pixel top margin is just a working figure, something we can change later if necessary. The idea is to create enough space above the masthead for the big flower to fit.

As for the auto margins, they will center the container, but only because it has an explicit width. In CSS, a block-level element that is given an explicit width and auto right and left margins is centered inside its containing block. IE5.5/Win doesn't do that, but it does center elements if their parent is set to text-align: center;. Thus, we centered text in the body element in order to center the container in IE5.5/Win, and we set the auto margins to center the container in more recent browsers.

Fixed Versus Liquid Design

There is a good deal of contention regarding fixed-width versus "liquid" design (which is based on the width of the browser window) and we do not seek to resolve it here. Given the task before us and the image files we have available, a fixed-width design makes more sense. A similar design can be created that is not fixed-width, however.

Because `text-align` is an inherited property, text within the container will still be centered. So let's override that centering within the container by giving it a different `text-align` value.

```
#container {width: 647px; margin: 75px auto 0; padding: 0;
  text-align: left;}
```

This will restore text to be left-aligned within the container without breaking the centering in IE5.5/Win.

The Page Header

Once we get inside the container, the first thing we find is the page header, whose markup is given in Listing 10.2.

Listing 10.2   The Page Header Markup

```
<div id="pageHeader">
  <h1><span>css Zen Garden</span></h1>
  <h2><span>The Beauty of <acronym
    title="Cascading Style Sheets">CSS</acronym> Design</span></h2>
</div>
```

As it happens, that's far more than we need to re-create the page header design. Figure 10.3 shows one of the two images we'll be using in the page header. Its dimensions are 477 pixels wide by 157 pixels tall.

FIGURE 10.3

The page header image we'll be using.

All we need to do is add this image to the background of the `pageHeader` and make sure that the `div` will be tall enough to show the whole image. We'll also want the image to appear just once, so we'll make sure it doesn't repeat.

```
#container {width: 647px; margin: 75px auto 0; padding: 0;
  text-align: left;}
#pageHeader {background: url(pageHeader.jpg) 0 0 no-repeat;
  height: 157px; width: auto;}
</style>
```

Case-Sensitive

HTML defines `class` and `id` values to be case-sensitive, so we have to write `pageHeader` instead of, for example, `pageheader`. Older browsers were sloppy about enforcing this, but newer browsers are not, so be sure you keep capitalization consistent.

Although we made the height exactly as tall as the image itself, we've left the width to be automatically calculated. This means it will be as wide as possible while still fitting inside its parent element, which is the `container`. So we know that the `pageHeader` will be 647 pixels wide, the same as the `container`. That's why, in Figure 10.4, the image isn't as wide as the text that follows.

FIGURE 10.4

The image added to the background of the page header.

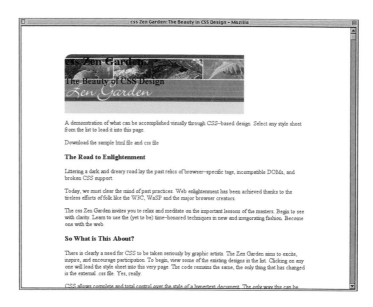

This is not a problem at all because we need space to drop in our big decorative flower. You may also note that the text of the `h1` and `h2` elements is still visible over the background. That, too, is to be expected. Not to worry, we're about to use them both to good effect.

Before we move on, we need to back up a step and do something we overlooked. Because we can only use CSS to create this layout, we'll need to position various elements. To have them all positioned with respect to the container, it needs to be relatively positioned with no offset.

```
#container {width: 647px; margin: 75px auto 0; padding: 0;
   text-align: left; position: relative;}
```

This establishes a containing block for any relatively positioned elements inside the container without actually moving the `container` from its position in the document's normal flow.

Adding a Floral Touch

Now we're ready to place the flower image shown in Figure 10.5. Its dimensions are 250 pixels wide by 333 pixels tall, and it has transparent areas (represented in Figure 10.5 by the gray-and-white checkerboard pattern) through which other backgrounds or even content will be visible.

FIGURE 10.5

The image that will decorate the right side of the page header.

GIF Versus PNG

The image in Figure 10.5 is a GIF (more precisely, a GIF89a) with transparent areas. A much more visually attractive choice would have been to use a PNG with a full 8-bit alpha channel, but IE/Win doesn't correctly support PNG alpha channels. We'll talk about the hows and whys of overcoming this limitation at the end of the project.

So now we just have to figure out how to get it in place. We can't use the `pageHeader` background because it already has an image. Instead, we'll use the `h1` itself, sizing its content to be the exact size of the background image.

```
#pageHeader {background: url(pageHeader.jpg) 0 0 no-repeat;
  height: 157px; width: auto;}
#pageHeader h1 {background: url(ph-flower.gif) 0 0 no-repeat;
  height: 330px; width: 250px;}
</style>
```

Great! Except that makes it taller than its parent (`div#pageHeader`), and it's on the left, nowhere near where it needs to be. So we'll absolutely position the `h1` to sit in the top right of its containing block.

```
#pageHeader h1 {background: url(ph-flower.gif) 0 0 no-repeat;
  height: 330px; width: 250px; position: absolute; z-index: 101;
  top: 0; right: 0; margin: 0;}
```

This places the `h1` in the top-right corner of the `container`, which we turned into a containing block at the end of the last section. As an added bonus, absolutely positioning it takes it completely out of the normal flow, so its height no longer affects the height of the `pageHeader div`.

There's just one problem: Putting it in the top-right corner of the container isn't enough. It's nowhere close to lining up with the rest of the masthead. By referring to the original design, we discover that the top of the flower is 95 pixels above the top of the masthead, and its right edge is 80 pixels to the right of the right edge of the main content column. So we pull it up and over by those distances.

```
#pageHeader h1 {background: url(ph-flower.gif) 0 0 no-repeat;
  height: 330px; width: 250px; position: absolute; z-index: 101;
  top: -95px; right: -80px; margin: 0;}
```

The Big Z

The `z-index` value `101` was picked more or less at random. Any integer can be used as a z-index value. The only restriction is that higher numbers go "in front" of lower numbers, so any positioned elements we want to make sure are placed on top of the `h1` will need to have z-index values of `102` or higher. Remember, `z-index` only works with positioned elements.

Now it lines up perfectly. All we need to do is suppress display of the text within the h1, and we'll have the result shown in Figure 10.6.

```
#pageHeader h1 {background: url(ph-flower.gif) 0 0 no-repeat;
  height: 330px; width: 250px; position: absolute; z-index: 101;
    top: -95px; right: -80px; margin: 0;}
#pageHeader h1 span {visibility: hidden;}
</style>
```

FIGURE 10.6

The flower is placed where we want it by way of the h1.

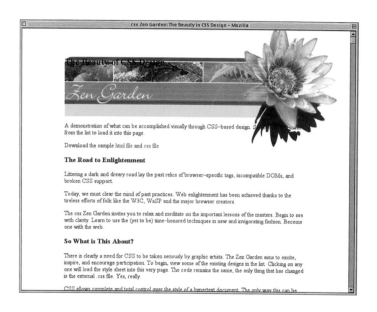

Although the original design didn't have the top of the flower being cut off by the top of the browser window, it's a nice effect so we'll keep it. If we change our minds later, all we have to do is change the top margin of the container to 100px or thereabouts.

Now for the h2, which is currently appearing as plain black text in the upper-left corner of the masthead. We want to place it in that light green stripe, so the obvious solution is to position it. Some quick measurements reveal that its top edge should be 134 pixels below the top of the masthead and its right edge 140 pixels to the left. Thus:

```
#pageHeader h1 span {visibility: hidden;}
#pageHeader h2 {position: absolute; z-index: 102;
  top: 134px; right: 140px; margin: 0; padding: 0;}
</style>
```

Of course, the text looks nothing like that in the design shown in Figure 10.1, so we'll start by making the serif text slightly larger than normal, bold, and italicized. We'll also right-align it.

```
#pageHeader h2 {position: absolute; z-index: 102;
   top: 134px; right: 140px; margin: 0; padding: 0;
   font: bold italic 1.1em/1em Times, serif; text-align: right;}
```

To get the color needed, we'll sample the pixels in the original design. While there, notice that everything but the acronym "CSS" is lowercase, and the letters are spread out a bit more than usual.

```
#pageHeader h2 {position: absolute; z-index: 102;
   top: 134px; right: 140px; margin: 0; padding: 0;
   color: rgb(91,131,104);
   text-transform: lowercase; letter-spacing: 0.2em;
   font: bold italic 1.1em/1em Times, serif; text-align: right;}
```

Of course, this will also lowercase "CSS," so we'll have to make sure it's upper-cased. We can do this by overriding the text-transform value that the acronym element inherits, just as we overrode the inherited text-align on the container. The result is illustrated in Figure 10.7.

```
#pageHeader h2 {position: absolute; z-index: 102;
   top: 134px; right: 140px; margin: 0; padding: 0;
   color: rgb(91,131,104);
   text-transform: lowercase; letter-spacing: 0.2em;
   font: bold italic 1.1em/1em Times, serif; text-align: right;}
#pageHeader h2 acronym {text-transform: uppercase;}
</style>
```

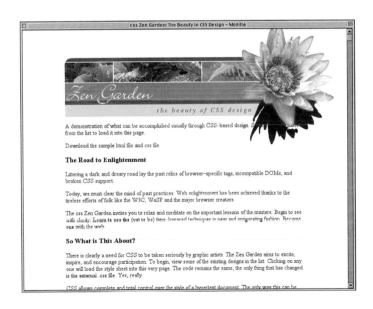

Clipped Fonts

During testing, it was discovered that some copies of IE/Win "clip off" the tops and bottoms of letters in the h2 when it is positioned. Other copies do not. If you're seeing this problem, try something like line-height: 1.2em; margin-top: -0.2em; That should put the text in the correct place and avoid the clipping, since the line-height of 1em appears to be what causes it.

FIGURE 10.7

The beauty of CSS design is demonstrated.

▶▶ REAL TEXT VERSUS IMAGE TEXT

The use of the actual text in the h2 element raises an interesting question: When is it a good idea to use styled text, and when is it a good idea to replace it with an image? This is, as you might expect, a controversial topic. Some feel you should never replace text with an image; others believe the more image-based text, the better.

The usual reason to replace text with an image is that the image text typically will look much better for nearly everyone who visits the site. Image-based text can be smoothed, kerned, adjusted, and otherwise made to look absolutely fabulous. It offers a great deal more visual flexibility than actual text, but at the expense of more page weight and some accessibility concerns.

Actual text, on the other hand, may or may not look good, depending on the user's operating system. Modern systems, such as Windows XP and Mac OS X, have built-in text smoothing that goes a long way toward making actual text look as good as image-based text. Older operating systems (and browsers) generally do not. Actual text has the distinct advantage of contributing a lot less to the overall page weight and of being highly accessible.

We've chosen to leave the h2 as actual text in this project, but of course, replacing it with a background image would be as easy as it was for the h1. It means greater page weight, but that may be a fair price to pay for knowing that the text will look pretty. In the end, this is (like so many other things) a case where you must use your best judgment to make a choice.

Styling the Summary

As you probably guessed, this is another area of the design that needs a background image. We can see this image in Figure 10.8; its dimensions are 647 pixels wide by 100 pixels tall.

As we did with the page header, we're going to drop this into the background of the quick summary area, but we are not going to set an explicit height. Let's drop in the font styles and the background all at once.

```
#pageHeader h2 acronym {text-transform: uppercase;}
#quickSummary {font: italic 1em/2 Times, "Times New Roman", serif;
  background: url(quickSummary.jpg) 0 100% no-repeat;}
</style>
```

In addition to double-spacing the text (with the `line-height` value of 2), we've placed the background image in the bottom-left corner of the element's background. To cover whatever portion of the background the image doesn't cover, we'll add the same color as that along the top edge of the image. While we're at it, let's change the text color to be a dark green.

```
#quickSummary {font: italic 1em/2 Times, "Times New Roman", serif;
   background: rgb(94%,98%,96%) url(quickSummary.jpg) 0 100% no-repeat;
   color: rgb(42,92,42);}
```

It's time to add the margins and padding. What margins? Well, refer to Figure 10.1 and notice the thin white lines along the top and bottom of the quick summary area. We're going to re-create those by giving the quick summary area a one-pixel top and bottom margin. This will let the page's white background "show through" and will separate the quick summary from the masthead before it and the main content that follows it.

```
#quickSummary {font: italic 1em/2 Times, "Times New Roman", serif;
   background: rgb(94%,98%,96%) url(quickSummary.jpg) 0 100% no-repeat;
   color: rgb(42,92,42);
   margin: 1px 0;}
```

As for the padding, that's an interesting mix. To keep the text within the quick summary away from the edges of its element box, we'll add top, bottom, and left padding in the one- to one-and-a-half-em range. On the right side, though, we need to provide enough padding so that the text and flower don't overlap. Since the flower is an image and thus has a width based in pixels, the quick summary area's padding on that side will be measured in pixels.

```
#quickSummary {font: italic 1em/2 Times, "Times New Roman", serif;
   background: rgb(94%,98%,96%) url(quickSummary.jpg) 0 100% no-repeat;
   color: rgb(42,92,42);
   margin: 1px 0; padding: 1em 180px 1.5em 1.5em;}
```

"Wait a minute," you might be thinking. "The paragraph margins would have kept the text away from the edges of the quick summary area." In the first place, that's not true because the paragraph margins would have stuck out of the quick summary, visually pushing it away from the masthead and main content. Second, the paragraphs aren't going to have margins that affect layout.

Notice in the original design that the quick summary appears to be a single paragraph of text, even though it contains two p elements. To reproduce this effect, we'll have those paragraphs generate inline boxes, with the result shown in Figure 10.9.

Backgrounds and Borders

Your first instinct might be to use a border to create the separators between the quick summary area and the surrounding content, and that's not a bad idea. If we have a patterned background instead of a plain white background, then it might be essential. In this case, it was easier to just spread pieces of the layout apart and then let the background do the visual work. It's more elegant in many ways than assigning borders to do the job.

```
#quickSummary {font: italic 1em/2 Times, "Times New Roman", serif;
  background: rgb(94%,98%,96%) url(quickSummary.jpg) 0 100% no-repeat;
  color: rgb(42,92,42);
  margin: 1px 0; padding: 1em 180px 1.5em 1.5em;}
#quickSummary p {display: inline;}
</style>
```

FIGURE 10.9

The quick summary area in its fully styled glory.

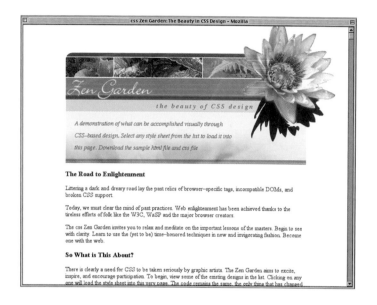

Those of you using IE/Win might notice that the two paragraphs are now jammed close together, as if there were no space between them. Of course, there is space, but never mind that now; let's push them apart a bit by adding a left margin to the second paragraph. We can do that because it has a `class` of `p2`.

```
#quickSummary p {display: inline;}
#quickSummary p.p2 {margin-left: 0.25em;}
</style>
```

This will add a quarter-em margin to the left side of the first line in the element; in other words, at the very beginning of the second paragraph. This will mean a little more separation than normal in non-IE browsers, but not so much that it will look bad.

We're already writing styles specific to the second paragraph, so let's tack a period onto the end of the sentence. We aren't allowed to change the HTML, but we can insert some generated content.

```
#quickSummary p.p2 {margin-left: 0.25em;}
#quickSummary p.p2:after {content: ".";}
</style>
```

No, Explorer won't render the generated content, but that's okay. It's a minor effect, and IE users won't be missing anything if they don't see it.

Main Content Styling

With the top of the design complete, let's turn our attention to the main content of the document. This is where it really gets interesting because, to reproduce the visual design we've been given, we'll have to get creative. A comparison of the partial document structure in Listing 10.3 with the design shown in Figure 10.1 illustrates why.

Listing 10.3   A Partial Document Skeleton

```
<div id="intro">
    [...page header and quick summary...]
    <div id="preamble">
      <h3><span>The Road to Enlightenment</span></h3>
      [...content...]
    </div>
</div>
<div id="supportingText">
  <div id="explanation">
    <h3><span>So What is This About?</span></h3>
    [...content...]
  </div>
  <div id="participation">
    <h3><span>Participation</span></h3>
    [...content...]
  </div>
  <div id="benefits">
    <h3><span>Benefits</span></h3>
    [...content...]
  </div>
  <div id="requirements">
    <h3><span>Requirements</span></h3>
    [...content...]
  </div>
  <div id="footer">
    [...content...]
  </div>
</div>
```

Seeing Double?

Listing 10.3 is an excerpt of Listing 10.1, included here to highlight the "content" parts of the document without the rest of the document skeleton to confuse things.

For example, there's a thin green border down the left side of the main content, stretching from the quick summary to the footer. (Refer to Figure 10.1 if you don't remember it.) Ordinarily, we might just add a left border to a div that contains all that text. This document, though, has only one div that qualifies—the one with an id of supportingText. The footer is also inside that div, so any border we add to its side will stretch down to the bottom of the footer. Furthermore, the preamble (the first paragraph in the main content column) is outside of supportingText, so the border wouldn't appear next to it. Both are unacceptable.

As another example, the list of links that goes in the right-hand sidebar has a background that stretches the entire height of the content. Because the links come after the footer, we're going to have to position them into place.

Positioned elements, though, are only as tall as their content. If we want that sidebar to visually stretch from quick summary to footer, we'll have to do it in some other way than just adding a background to the link list.

Let's address this last problem first. We know that we're going to position the link list, so we need to get the main column content out of its way. We could do so with a right margin, but instead we're going to apply consistent right padding to the preamble and supporting text. The exact amount of padding was determined by measuring the width of the sidebar background and the border that divides it from the content column.

```
#quickSummary p.p2:after {content: ".";}
#preamble, #supportingText {padding-right: 217px;}
</style>
```

The padding leaves us room to start on the sidebar's background, and at the same time introduce the gradient fade along the right edge of the content, as shown in Figure 10.10.

```
#preamble, #supportingText {padding-right: 217px;}
#preamble {background: url(side.jpg) 100% 100% repeat-y;}
</style>
```

FIGURE 10.10

Adding the first part of the sidebar and main content background.

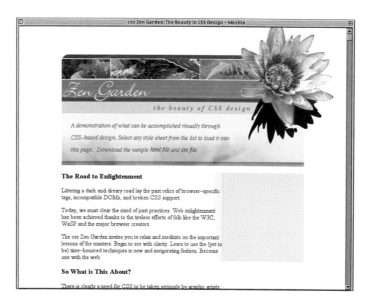

What you see in Figure 10.10 is a background image 302 pixels wide by 4 pixels tall that starts in the lower-right corner of the preamble and then repeats vertically—up as well as down, although we don't see any downward repetition because the image started at the bottom of the element.

This image contains not only the sidebar's background pattern but also the vertical line that runs between the sidebar and main content, and also the right-to-left gradient that appears now behind the main content. It's all one image repeated vertically. Because the right padding of the preamble is equal to the sidebar-plus-separator portion of the background image, the content can be placed over the gradient portion of the background.

Now, to make the pattern continue, we need only add the same image to the background of the supporting text `div`, starting it in the upper-right corner and repeating it vertically.

```
#preamble {background: url(side.jpg) 100% 100% repeat-y;}
#supportingText {background: url(side.jpg) 100% 0 repeat-y;}
</style>
```

Remember that border along the left side of the design? Now's the time to add it. As was discussed, we can't use `div#supportingText` since it doesn't contain the preamble and does contain the footer. On the other hand, we can add a border to each of the preamble, explanation, participation criteria, benefits, and requirements `div`s. Good thing they all have `id`s we can use! The result of adding borders to each of these `div`s is shown in Figure 10.11.

```
#supportingText {background: url(side.jpg) 100% 0 repeat-y;}
#preamble, #explanation, #participation, #benefits, #requirements {
  border-left: 1px solid rgb(184,214,194);}
</style>
```

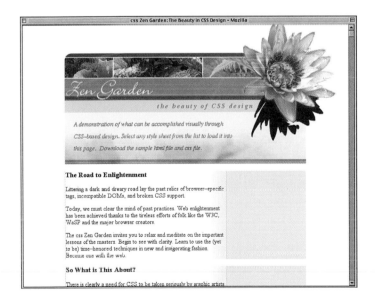

FIGURE 10.11

Borders are added to various `div`s.

Understanding Collapsing

It might seem ludicrous to allow an element's margins to stick out of its parent element, but it's necessary to deliver ordinary layout. Consider a case in which an unordered list is the first element in a `div`. Suppose that all `div`s have a 1em top margin, all unordered lists a 1.5em top margin, and list items a half-em top margin. Thanks to margin collapsing, the total margin before the first list item will be 1.5em. If margins didn't collapse, there would be 3em of space before that first list item.

Wait a minute! The border is broken up into pieces, and there's a big gap in the sidebar. How did that happen?

It happened because the margins of the `h3` and `p` elements collapsed with—in this case, *through*—the margins on the `div`s. That's part of how margin collapsing works. It allows the margins of an element to stick out of the element box of its parent element.

Fortunately, there's a way around this. If the `divs` have any top and bottom padding, they will expand to contain their descendant elements and all of their margins. So we'll just add one pixel of top and bottom padding to each of those `divs`.

```
#preamble, #explanation, #participation, #benefits, #requirements {
   border-left: 1px solid rgb(184,214,194);
   padding-top: 1px; padding-bottom: 1px;}
```

Creeping Text Bug

IE/Win users may have noticed that the main content text is suddenly drifting to the left, and even being cut off near the end of the document. This will be mostly resolved by the time the project is done, but you can read more about the bug and how to avoid it at `http://www.positioniseverything.net/explorer/creep.html`.

This will bring the borders together, as we'll see in the next figure. Before we do, though, let's start styling the actual content of these `divs`. We don't want the paragraphs running up against the edges of the column, for example, so some padding is in order for them as well. We also should define the separation between paragraphs via margins, crank down the text size just a bit, and spread the lines of text apart with an increased `line-height`.

```
#preamble, #supportingText {padding-right: 217px;}
#preamble p, #supportingText p {font-size: 90%; line-height: 1.66em;
   margin: 0 1.5em; padding: 0.5em 0;}
#preamble {background: url(side.jpg) 100% 100% repeat-y;}
```

In a similar manner, we can give appropriate margins, color, and text styling to the `h3` elements in these `divs`.

```
#preamble p, #supportingText p {font-size: 90%; line-height: 1.66em;
   margin: 0 1.5em; padding: 0.5em 0;}
#preamble h3, #supportingText h3 {letter-spacing: 0.1em;
   font: italic 1.2em Times, "Times New Roman", serif;
   color: rgb(107,153,139); margin: 1em 0 0.5em 0.5em;}
#preamble {background: url(side.jpg) 100% 100% repeat-y;}
```

There's one more touch to be added to the top of the main content. If you look closely at the original design, there's a green border running across the top of the main content and sidebar, the same color as the left borders we've added. We can drop that into place by adding a top border to the preamble—remember that it actually does stretch from one side of the container to the other, as we can see in Figure 10.12.

```
#preamble {border-top: 1px solid rgb(184,214,194);
   background: url(side.jpg) 100% 100% repeat-y;}
```

At this point, the main content is basically styled as desired except for one thing, and that's the flowery background at the bottom of the column.

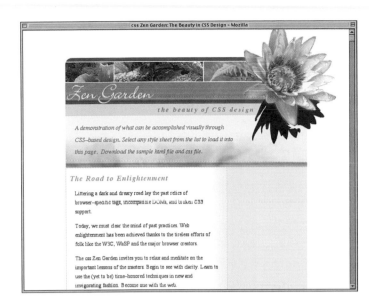

FIGURE 10.12

The borders come together, and the main column content becomes more stylish.

Fancy Footer Work

In the original visual design file, there was a faded background at the bottom of the main content column, so we need to have one in our styles. The trick is to pick the right element, and in this case it's the div with an id of requirements. It can't be the supportingText div because that already has a background and goes past the footer anyway. So we'll have to use the requirements div.

The image we'll use is shown in Figure 10.13; its dimensions are 429 pixels wide by 159 pixels tall.

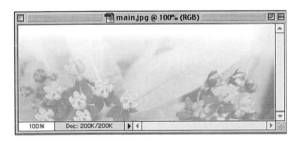

FIGURE 10.13

The image to be placed at the bottom of the main content column.

Notice the right-to-left gradient in the top-right corner of the image. If we get our styles right, this will line up with the gradient already in place, providing a seamless transition between the two.

Also notice the white stripe around the sides and bottom of the image. This will provide visual separation between the background and the borders that surround it. The obvious first step is to place the image in the background; a related step will be to add a bottom border to the element.

```
#preamble, #explanation, #participation, #benefits, #requirements {
  border-left: 1px solid rgb(184,214,194);
  padding-top: 1px; padding-bottom: 1px;}
#requirements {border-bottom: 1px solid rgb(184,214,194);
  background: url(main.jpg) 100% 100% no-repeat;}
</style>
```

A Slight Difference

There is still a visible difference between IE5/Mac and other browsers. The white stripe along the bottom slides under the bottom border of the `div`. Working around this would require removing the bottom border from the element and simulating it with a stripe at the bottom of the background image. Rather than do so, we'll just accept this slight difference in IE5/Mac and move on.

Why place the image in the bottom-right corner? To avoid a subtle problem in IE5/Mac, which calculates background placement with respect to the outer border edge of the element instead of the outer padding edge (otherwise known as the inner border edge). If we put it in the bottom-left corner, the white stripe along the left side of the background image would slide underneath the left border. However, since the right side of the element has no border, the border edge and padding edge are in the same place, and the layout is more consistent.

A quick check of the design reveals that the text intrudes a little too far into the background we just added, making the last few lines difficult to read. Correcting this is simple: We'll just add a bottom padding to the `div`, with the result shown in Figure 10.14.

```
#requirements {border-bottom: 1px solid rgb(184,214,194);
  background: url(main.jpg) 100% 100% no-repeat;
  padding-bottom: 100px;}
```

FIGURE 10.14

The main content column is finished off with a background.

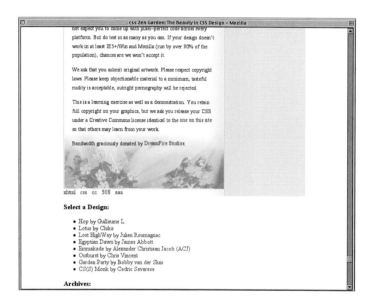

Now we can turn our attention to the actual footer—that is to say, the `div` with an `id` of `footer`. It doesn't have a lot of content: five hyperlinks. That's all. We have to somehow get it to look like the footer in the design with a `div` and five links.

The first challenge is getting it to be the right width at all. If you'll recall, the footer is contained inside the supporting text `div`, and that `div` has a right padding of `217px`. As we can see in Figure 10.15, the image we have to place in the background of the footer is wider than that. It is, in fact, 647 pixels wide by 123 pixels tall.

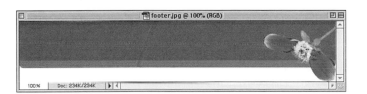

FIGURE 10.15

The image to be placed behind the content of the footer.

Thanks to the padding, the content area of the supporting text `div` is just 430 pixels wide (647–217). So we have a 647-pixel-wide footer and only 430 pixels of width to work with. We'll just have to bust out of that content area and set the footer's height at the same time.

```
#requirements {border-bottom: 1px solid rgb(184,214,194);
   background: url(main.jpg) 100% 100% no-repeat;
   padding-bottom: 100px;}
#footer {margin: 0 -217px 0 0; height: 123px;}
</style>
```

By giving the footer a negative right margin that exactly equals the right padding of its parent element, we've basically counteracted the padding, visually speaking. The content area of the footer itself is now 647 pixels wide, leaving us exactly the amount of room we need to display the image. So let's add it!

```
#footer {margin: 0 -217px 0 0; height: 123px;
   background: #FFF url(footer.jpg) 100% 1px no-repeat;}
```

Why did we put it on the right again? Not due to IE5/Mac, as it happens. Instead, we're doing this to avoid a bug in IE6/Win.

The bug is an odd one in that it seems to add a few-pixel negative margin to the left side of the footer. There's no reason on earth why it should do this, but it does. The effect is that the footer's background is pulled to the left and is also cut off. This throws off the alignment of the design and looks pretty dumb to boot. By putting the footer background over to the right, we can sidestep the bug. It doesn't matter how much negative margin IE/Win incorrectly applies if the background image never goes over there.

Now we just need to use the footer's padding to get the links into place. A little experimentation shows that we need about 60 pixels of top padding to push the text down where we want it. We'll add in a one-em right padding for the heck of it and a half-em left padding to keep the first link from getting too close to the left edge of the footer.

```
#footer {margin: 0 -217px 0 0; height: 123px;
  background: #FFF url(footer.jpg) 100% 1px no-repeat;
  padding: 60px 1em 0 0.5em;}
```

Now all we have to do is style the actual links to match (as closely as possible) their appearance in the visual design. The primary points of interest are their color and size, although setting a line-height and font-weight will help them be as close as possible to what was designed, as we can see in Figure 10.16.

```
#footer {margin: 0 -217px 0 0; height: 123px;
  background: #FFF url(footer.jpg) 100% 1px no-repeat;
  padding: 60px 1em 0 0.5em;}
#footer a {color: rgb(207,216,214); line-height: 1em;
  font-size: 1.25em; font-weight: 100;}
</style>
```

FIGURE 10.16

The fully styled footer.

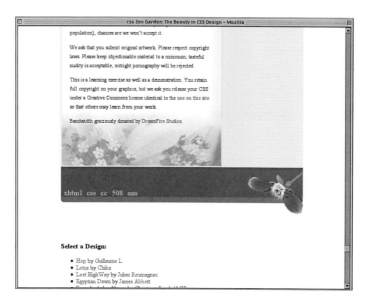

So that finishes the main column! All we have to do now is place and style the sidebar, and we'll be all done.

Sidebar Style

This is actually one of the easiest parts of the project because all we have to do is put the list of links where we want it and style its contents. Thanks to the work we've already put in, we don't have to worry about the background or any of that other stuff. It's already been done for us.

So let's position the link list. To start with, we'll position it in the top-right corner of its containing block and define its width to be 216 pixels (the same width as the sidebar pattern).

```
#footer a {color: rgb(207,216,214); line-height: 1em;
   font-size: 1.25em; font-weight: 100;}
#linkList {position: absolute; z-index: 11;
   width: 216px; top: 0; right: 0;}
</style>
```

As always, an absolutely positioned element's containing block is the closest ancestor element that's been absolutely or relatively positioned. For the link list, that's the container itself, so at the moment the link list is overlapping the flower in a pretty serious way. We need to get it down into the sidebar where it belongs.

Here's where it gets a little challenging, but not much. A quick measurement shows that the distance from the top of the container to the top of the quick summary is 157 pixels. No problem there. But what about the height of the quick summary? It wasn't set in pixels, so instead it's dependent on the height of its content. If we add up the top and bottom padding and line heights inside the quick summary, we get a result of 8.5em. We'll add just a bit to that and get 8.6em. To add the two together, we'll set the link list's top to be 157px and its margin-top to be 8.6em, with the result shown in Figure 10.17.

```
#linkList {position: absolute; z-index: 11;
   width: 216px; top: 157px; right: 0;
   margin-top: 8.6em;}
```

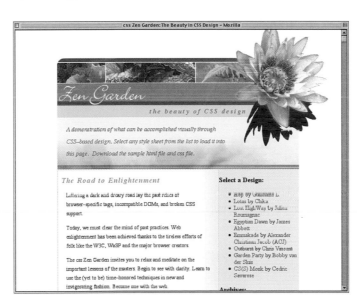

FIGURE 10.17

The link list is positioned and is ready for styling.

Okay, the links are where we want them, but they don't look much like what was in the original design. As an example, these lists have bullets, which the design does not. So we'll just remove them from the list items.

```
#linkList {position: absolute; z-index: 11;
   width: 216px; top: 157px; right: 0;
   margin-top: 8.6em;}
#linkList li {list-style: none;}
</style>
```

We don't want to lose the indentation of the lists since that was a feature of the design, but we don't really want to leave the indentation up to chance, either. So we'll explicitly set some margins for the unordered lists within the link list div and make sure they have no padding.

```
#linkList {position: absolute; z-index: 11;
   width: 216px; top: 157px; right: 0;
   margin-top: 8.6em;}
#linkList ul {margin: 0.5em 1em 0 2em; padding: 0;}
#linkList li {list-style: none;}
```

The links themselves could use a little help since they need to be italicized, green, and slightly larger than normal text. They are also, in the design, all low-ercase. A quick set of declarations gives us all that, as Figure 10.18 shows.

```
#linkList li {list-style: none;}
#linkList a {color: rgb(99,131,101);
   font: italic 1.15em Times, serif;
   text-transform: lowercase;}
</style>
```

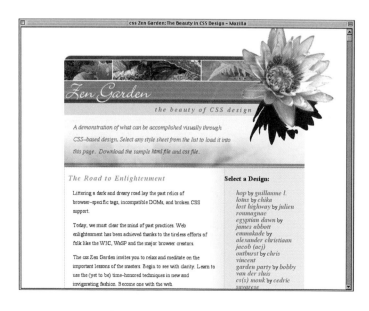

It's progress, but it's also a little crowded in the sidebar all of a sudden. We need to spread the entries apart, and so we shall, but first let's consider the three h3s ("Design List" and so on).

In Figure 10.1, they're each in a lovely script font and have some unique underlining effects. That's obviously well beyond the capabilities of regular text, so we'll have to use the three images shown in Figure 10.19.

FIGURE 10.19

The three images used to replace the heading text in the sidebar.

As you can see, the images are all GIFs with transparent parts, which will enable them to blend nicely with the sidebar background.

To place them, we'll actually style all three h3 elements in the sidebar at once. This will let us set not only common margins but also the same width and height for each one. We'll also give them all the "Resources" image for a background, prevent it from repeating, and place it 10 pixels to the right of the element's left edge and centered vertically.

```
#linkList a {color: rgb(99,131,101);
  font: italic 1.15em Times, serif;
  text-transform: lowercase;}
#linkList h3 {margin: 1em 0 0; width: 216px; height: 35px;
  background: url(resources.gif) 10px 50% no-repeat;}
</style>
```

Having done this, we can now leave it in place and just change the images used in the background of the "Design List" and "Archives" headings.

```
#linkList h3 {margin: 1em 0 0; width: 216px; height: 35px;
  background: url(resources.gif) 10px 50% no-repeat;}
#lselect h3 {background-image: url(design-list.gif);}
#larchives h3 {background-image: url(archives.gif);}
</style>
```

By taking this approach, it becomes much easier to rework the heading styles as a group. If we ever decide to change the placement of the images within their headings, we just have to edit the `background-position` keywords in the `#linkList h3` rule.

The last thing we need to do to the headings is remove the text from the foregrounds, with the end result shown in Figure 10.20.

```
#larchives h3 {background-image: url(archives.gif);}
#linkList h3 span {display: none;}
</style>
```

FIGURE 10.20

The headings are replaced with images.

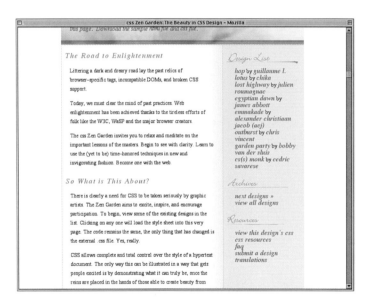

Now for those links—they've been scrunched together for far too long. Since the "Design List" links are styled differently than those in the other two sidebar sections, we'll take them each in turn.

If you look closely at the entries in the "Design List" in the visual design, you'll see that the second line of each entry (the author line) is a little smaller than normal. The name of each design, though, is about as big as regular text. If we just set the list items in this list to be about 85% of normal size, we'll be close to getting this exact effect. That's because we already wrote a rule (`#linkList a`) that sets the links in the sidebar to be 1.15 times the size of their parent's `font-size`. If we reduce the size of the list items to 0.85 times normal, the links will be 0.9775 times normal size—close enough to 1.0 to satisfy our needs.

So we'll do that and add a bottom margin to the list items at the same time.

```
#linkList h3 span {display: none;}
#lselect li {font-size: 85%; margin-bottom: 1.5em;}
</style>
```

Okay, now for the links themselves. Each design name needs to be on its own line and boldfaced. The name should also be all lowercase and the letters spread out a bit. We can easily make this the case for all links in the "Design List" section.

```
#lselect li {font-size: 85%; margin-bottom: 1.5em;}
#lselect li a {display: block; font-weight: bold;
  letter-spacing: 0.2em; text-transform: lowercase;}
</style>
```

Oops—we just applied these styles to all of the links in the "Design List," including the links containing the author names, which aren't supposed to look anything like that. In fact, they're just supposed to be boldfaced text—the same size and appearance as the word "by" that sits next to each name. And, for that matter, the author names have to sit next to the word "by," which means that they can't be block-level. In other words, we need to undo all the styles we just applied to them.

Fortunately, the author-name links share one thing in common: a `class` of `c`. With that `class` to guide our selector, we can fix the link appearance in just four declarations, with the result shown in Figure 10.21.

```
#lselect li a {display: block; font-weight: bold;
  letter-spacing: 0.2em; text-transform: lowercase;}
#lselect li a.c {display: inline;
  font: bold 1em Times, serif;
  letter-spacing: 0; text-transform: none;}
</style>
```

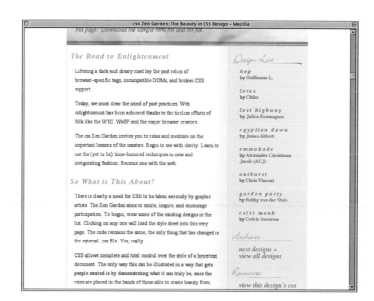

FIGURE 10.21

Spreading out the "Design List" links and formatting them as desired.

We are very, very close to being done. Really, all we have to do now is get the links in the "Archives" and "Resources" sections to look like they do in the original design. Although they are spread out a bit, it isn't as much as the links in the "Design List" section. So we'll go with a half em.

```
#lselect li a.c {display: inline;
   font: bold 1em Times, serif;
   letter-spacing: 0; text-transform: none;}
#larchives li, #lresources li {margin-bottom: 0.5em;}
</style>
```

The other difference is that the links in this section are a much lighter weight than those in the "Design List" section. Ideally, we'd set them to be incredibly light using something like `font-weight: 100;`, but that isn't really very well supported. Instead, we'll blend the color of the links into the background a little more than the dark green of the "Design List" links, using a lighter green to lessen the visual weight.

```
#larchives li, #lresources li {margin-bottom: 0.5em;}
#larchives li a, #lresources li a {color: rgb(126,164,139);}
</style>
```

With that small little color change, which has the result shown in Figure 10.22, we've reached the end of our style sheet, which is given in Listing 10.4.

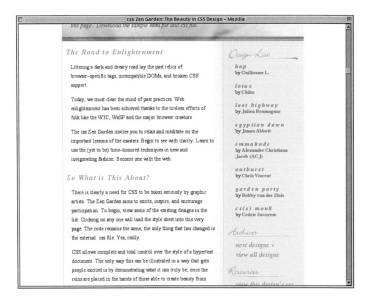

FIGURE 10.22

The "Archive" and "Resources" links are styled to have a little less visual weight.

Listing 10.4   The Complete Style Sheet

```
body {margin: 0; padding: 0; text-align: center;
  color: #000; background: #FFF;}
acronym {border: none;}
a {text-decoration: none;}
a:link {color: rgb(179,63,96);}
a:visited {color: rgb(90,32,48);}
a:hover {text-decoration: underline;}
#container {width: 647px; margin: 75px auto 0; padding: 0;
  text-align: left; position: relative;}
#pageHeader {background: url(pageHeader.jpg) 0 0 no-repeat;
  height: 157px; width: auto;}
#pageHeader h1 {background: url(ph-flower.gif) 0 0 no-repeat;
  height: 330px; width: 250px; position: absolute; z-index: 101;
  top: -95px; right: -80px; margin: 0;}
#pageHeader h1 span {visibility: hidden;}
#pageHeader h2 {position: absolute; z-index: 102;
  top: 134px; right: 140px; margin: 0; padding: 0;
  color: rgb(91,131,104);
  text-transform: lowercase; letter-spacing: 0.2em;
  font: bold italic 1.1em/1em Times, serif; text-align: right;}
#pageHeader h2 acronym {text-transform: uppercase;}
#quickSummary {font: italic 1em/2 Times, "Times New Roman", serif;
  background: rgb(94%,98%,96%) url(quickSummary.jpg) 0 100% no-repeat;
  color: rgb(42,92,42);
  margin: 1px 0; padding: 1em 180px 1.5em 1.5em;}
#quickSummary p {display: inline;}
#quickSummary p.p2 {margin-left: 0.25em;}
#quickSummary p.p2:after {content: ".";}
#preamble, #supportingText {padding-right: 217px;}
#preamble p, #supportingText p {font-size: 90%; line-height: 1.66em;
   margin: 0 1.5em; padding: 0.5em 0;}
#preamble h3, #supportingText h3 {letter-spacing: 0.1em;
  font: italic 1.2em Times, "Times New Roman", serif;
  color: rgb(107,153,139); margin: 1em 0 0.5em 0.5em;}
#preamble {border-top: 1px solid rgb(184,214,194);
  background: url(side.jpg) 100% 100% repeat-y;}
#supportingText {background: url(side.jpg) 100% 0 repeat-y;}
#preamble, #explanation, #participation, #benefits, #requirements {
  border-left: 1px solid rgb(184,214,194);
  padding-top: 1px; padding-bottom: 1px;}
#requirements {border-bottom: 1px solid rgb(184,214,194);
  background: url(main.jpg) 100% 100% no-repeat;
  padding-bottom: 100px;}
#footer {margin: 0 -217px 0 0; height: 123px;
  background: #FFF url(footer.jpg) 100% 1px no-repeat;
  padding: 60px 1em 0 0.5em;}
#footer a {color: rgb(207,216,214); line-height: 1em;
  font-size: 1.25em; font-weight: 100;}
```

continues

Listing 10.4 Continued

```
#linkList {position: absolute; z-index: 11;
  width: 216px; top: 157px; right: 0;
  margin-top: 8.6em;}
#linkList ul {margin: 0.5em 1em 0 2em; padding: 0;}
#linkList li {list-style: none;}
#linkList a {color: rgb(99,131,101);
  font: italic 1.15em Times, serif;
  text-transform: lowercase;}
#linkList h3 {margin: 1em 0 0; width: 216px; height: 35px;
  background: url(resources.gif) 10px 50% no-repeat;}
#lselect h3 {background-image: url(design-list.gif);}
#larchives h3 {background-image: url(archives.gif);}
#linkList h3 span {display: none;}
#lselect li {font-size: 85%; margin-bottom: 1.5em;}
#lselect li a {display: block; font-weight: bold;
  letter-spacing: 0.2em; text-transform: lowercase;}
#lselect li a.c {display: inline;
  font: bold 1em Times, serif;
  letter-spacing: 0; text-transform: none;}
#larchives li, #lresources li {margin-bottom: 0.5em;}
#larchives li a, #lresources li a {color: rgb(126,164,139);}
```

ADDING A PNG

You may recall that fairly early in the project, we added the image of the big flower to the design. That image file is a GIF89a with a transparent area (skip back to Figure 10.5 if you don't remember clearly how it looks). At the time, there was a brief mention that a PNG image would be a much prettier solution, and that we'd talk about it at the end of the project.

Well, here we are at the end of the project, so let's talk about using a PNG instead of a GIF.

From a visual design perspective, the primary advantage of PNG is that a PNG file can contain gamma-correction information (so you don't have to worry about your images becoming lighter or darker in different operating systems) and it can include up to a full 16-bit alpha channel. This allows for translucency and transparency that's far more sophisticated than the simple on/off transparency of GIF files. In a GIF, a pixel is either opaque or transparent; there's no in-between. In a PNG image, every pixel can be semi-opaque to whatever degree is desired. So, creating a PNG that fades smoothly from black at the top to totally transparent at the bottom of the image is a snap.

Let's take a look at Figure 10.23, which shows the PNG we'll be using as well as the channels in the file.

And PNG Means...?

PNG stands for Portable Network Graphics, and is usually pronounced "ping." It's an image format that was devised in the early 1990s and became a W3C Recommendation in 1996 (http://www.w3.org/TR/REC-png-multi.html). Its intent was to be a patent-free and technically superior replacement for the GIF format.

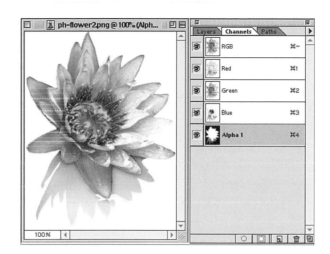

FIGURE 10.23

The PNG image and the RGBA channels it contains.

The red, green, and blue (RGB) channels are straightforward enough. The Alpha (A) channel, the one at the bottom, shows the transparency mask for the image. Any area of the channel that's fully black is fully transparent, and the fully white areas are opaque. Any shade of gray represents a semi-opaque area. The image itself is shown composited over a white background.

Given the alpha channel mask, the shadow will be translucent, and the area around the flower will be totally transparent. We can't just replace the GIF with this PNG, though, because the background of the page header stops right at the edge of the flower (refer to Figure 10.4). We'll need a new masthead background that stretches all the way across the top of the design, one like that shown in Figure 10.24.

FIGURE 10.24

The new, extended masthead background.

If we wanted to really be thorough, we'd fill in the rest of that white area with pictures, but since the flower will be placed over that section of the background, we can skip it. Let's replace the old images with the new background (pageHeader2.jpg) and PNG (ph-flower2.png) images.

```
#pageHeader {background: url(pageHeader2.jpg) 0 0 no-repeat;
  height: 157px; width: auto; }
#pageHeader h1 {background: url(ph-flower2.png) 0 0 no-repeat;
  height: 330px; width: 250px; position: absolute; z-index: 101;
  top: -95px; right: -80px; margin: 0;}
```

At this point, the PNG will work its magic in most current browsers. There is a glaring exception: Internet Explorer for Windows. (Even IE5/Mac will handle the PNG correctly.) It will display the PNG, but it won't do anything with the alpha channel. That sort of defeats the purpose. Fortunately, we can hack IE/Win to recognize and handle the alpha channel with an HTC file, otherwise known as a behavior file. By using a PNG-opacity behavior file (there are several available on the Web, although most concentrate on fixing inline PNGs instead of background PNGs) and hooking it into our style sheet, we can get the result shown in Figure 10.25 in IE/Win as well as Opera, Mozilla, Firefox, IE/Mac, Safari, and such.

```
#pageHeader h1 {background: url(ph-flower2.png) 0 0 no-repeat;
   height: 330px; width: 250px; position: absolute; z-index: 101;
   top: -95px; right: -80px; margin: 0;
   behavior: url(png-opacity.htc);}
```

FIGURE 10.25

The design with a PNG added for extra visual tastiness.

As we discussed in Project 6, `behavior` is not part of CSS, but is instead a CSS-like statement that's proprietary to Internet Explorer for Windows. Thus, using a `behavior` declaration will prevent your CSS from validating. There's really no way around that.

There is another potential drawback to using a PNG. Because the image contains not only color information but the alpha channel, it tends to be larger than other image file formats. If the PNG uses 32-bit color, which it's perfectly capable of doing, that will drive up the file size even further; the advantage is that the image can have a colorspace of millions of colors instead of just 256 colors or 32,768 colors. PNGs also use lossless compression, which can mean larger files. JPEG, by contrast, uses a lossy compression, which is why you get "wrinkles" in JPEGs that have been highly compressed.

What does that mean in real terms? Well, the GIF version of the flower is a 32KB file. The PNG saved out by Photoshop was a 152KB file. That's a whole lot of extra file size just to get a translucent shadow!

It is possible to lower the PNG's file size with utilities; Porter Glendinning, one of the book's technical reviewers, was able to get the flower PNG down to 60KB or so using various utilities. That's still twice the size of the GIF. Is it worth it? Perhaps, and perhaps not. But then Porter ran the image through the utility pngquant and got it down to 28KB—about 4KB *smaller* than the original GIF, and looking much, much better to boot.

So why aren't PNGs used all the time? There are two reasons. The first is the lack of convenient support by IE/Win; most authors wouldn't think that a behavior file called in via a style sheet would be able to fix an image format's support. (It certainly wouldn't have occurred to me.)

The second is that most commercial tools, such as Photoshop, do a very poor job of dealing with PNGs in an intelligent way. Typically, you get extreme choices like being able to save your PNG as an 8-bit color file with on/off transparency (basically, GIF in another format), which means a small file size; or else a full 24-bit color with an 8-bit alpha channel, which leads to really big files (the number 152KB comes to mind). This is very likely why PNGs have a reputation for being pretty but incredibly bloated. The fault, it would seem, lies not with the format but with the tools.

If authors were able to pick in-between possibilities, like an 8-bit color image with a full alpha channel, then we'd be getting somewhere. As it stands, authors could start using PNGs in their designs in three easy steps:

◆ Create PNGs with full alpha channels for use on the Web.

◆ Run the resulting PNGs through freely available optimization utilities like pngquant.

◆ Hook in an HTC file to get IE/Win to play nice.

It's one more step than usual, but in terms of better visual graphic design and reduced file sizes, the benefits are very much worth the small additional effort.

The lack of widespread support for PNGs in IE/Win and commonly used programs has undoubtedly hampered their adoption, and so there isn't the same breadth of knowledge that GIFs and JPEGs enjoy. It may be that all it will take to correct that situation is for authors to decide to use PNGs on a more frequent basis, and to share what they learn with one another.

Finding pngquant

You can obtain the pngquant utility at http://www.libpng.org/pub/png/apps/pngquant.html. It's available for just about any operating system you can think of, from Windows, Linux, and Mac OS to AmigaOS.

Indexed Success

In the late stages of editing, another way to get smaller-sized PNGs was found. Just before saving the PNG from Photoshop, convert the image to "Indexed" color, making sure to have the "Transparency" option checked. An initial test of saving an indexed-color version of ph-flower2.png yielded a file 43KB in size but with a full alpha channel intact. Details on how best to use PNGs for Web design are not available as we go to press, but hopefully this will change.

REFLECTIONS

In many ways, this was one of the most difficult projects I've created for the book. Why? Because I wasn't able to touch the markup and because I was working toward a very specific visual goal. The combination of these two constraints made the process very, very interesting.

The perfect example is the sidebar positioning. Sure, it's cool that we can use `top` and `margin-top` in combination to place the link list, but it turned out to be a fragile solution. Suppose the user bumps the text size up to 120% of normal. The quick summary text immediately flows to four lines, but there's no way for the `top` value to change as a result (short of using JavaScript, but that's outside the scope of the book). To keep everything aligned, it would need to change to `10.6em`. Instead, the sidebar content ends up overlapping the quick summary area.

As I say, this is the case because the document markup was off limits. If it had been changeable, I would have reworked things so that all of the main column content was in one `div` so that I could just give it a single border. I also would have moved the link list into that `div` and then used it as the containing block for the link list. That way, the user could change text size all he wanted, and the sidebar would still line up with the content column. There would be no more danger of overlap.

This illuminates an issue that is very important but often overlooked: *Presentation is dependent on structure*. You may have heard the phrase "complete separation of structure and presentation." That's impossible with current technology and may always be impossible, although I'm no prophet and can't guess what might be possible in 5, 10, or 30 years. I can say that, as of now, a document with no structure—that is to say, no elements, just an undifferentiated sea of text— cannot be styled in any meaningful way. Without paragraphs and headings and `div`s and anchor elements to mark your hyperlinks, there's no hope of making things look good.

Similarly, if the structure of a document doesn't relate very well to the visual result you want (as was the case in this project), you end up either getting very creative or else having to change something. Usually, designers will just change the structure to better meet their layout needs. That's okay; in fact, it's often a good idea. The other possibility is to change the visual layout from what you wanted to what the document's structure can support. That's fine too, although it's generally not as satisfying.

So always remember that your design will depend on the document's structure. Sometimes that means grafting in an occasional `div` or `span` for presentational purposes. As long as you're doing that only when necessary, don't worry about it. If you find yourself frequently nesting `spans` inside (or around) links, though, you might want to rethink how you're doing whatever you're doing. It's important to keep things as simple and structurally appropriate as possible while still meeting your design needs.

One last note: My respect for the designers who have created Zen Garden layouts increased substantially by undertaking this project. Adapting a known design to the markup was a challenge; to create a completely new and original design on top of that markup bespeaks incredible skill and talent. To each and every one of the Zen Garden designers, I bow in reverence and humility. Thank you, one and all.

Branching Out

This time around, I really only have one suggestion for taking the concepts in this chapter further.

1. Create your own Zen Garden design! It doesn't have to be the most beautiful design ever, nor does it have to be submitted, although you're certainly encouraged to do so if you like. All you need to do is create one or more style sheets that present the Zen Garden base file in a new and interesting way. Try different layouts with the markup, making them more and more complex as you learn. Remember: The markup is not to be touched. All you can do is write CSS. When you hit a limitation, see if you can find a creative way around it. Try things that don't seem like they have a chance in Hades of working. When you make a mistake, stop before you undo it. Was the result interesting in a way you didn't expect? If so, try following that path instead of the one you meant to follow. You never know what interesting technique or effect you might find just by working in the Zen Garden.

INDEX

Symbols

B

C

Q-R

Visit Peachpit on the Web at www.peachpit.com

- Read the latest articles and download timesaving tipsheets from best-selling authors such as Scott Kelby, Robin Williams, Lynda Weinman, Ted Landau, and more!

- Join the Peachpit Club and save 25% off all your online purchases at peachpit.com every time you shop—plus enjoy free UPS ground shipping within the United States.

- Search through our entire collection of new and upcoming titles by author, ISBN, title, or topic. There's no easier way to find just the book you need.

- Sign up for newsletters offering special Peachpit savings and new book announcements so you're always the first to know about our newest books and killer deals.

- Did you know that Peachpit also publishes books by Apple, New Riders, Adobe Press, Macromedia Press, palmOne Press, and TechTV press? Swing by the Peachpit family section of the site and learn about all our partners and series.

- Got a great idea for a book? Check out our About section to find out how to submit a proposal. You could write our next best-seller!

You'll find all this and more at www.peachpit.com. Stop by and take a look today!

VISIT OUR WEB SITE

WWW.NEWRIDERS.COM

On our Web site you'll find information about our other books, authors, tables of contents, indexes, and book errata. You will also find information about book registration and how to purchase our books.

EMAIL US

Contact us at this address: **nrfeedback@newriders.com**

- If you have comments or questions about this book
- To report errors that you have found in this book
- If you have a book proposal to submit or are interested in writing for New Riders
- If you would like to have an author kit sent to you
- If you are an expert in a computer topic or technology and are interested in being a technical editor who reviews manuscripts for technical accuracy

- To find a distributor in your area, please contact our international department at this address. **nrmedia@newriders.com**

- For instructors from educational institutions who want to preview New Riders books for classroom use. Email should include your name, title, school, department, address, phone number, office days/hours, text in use, and enrollment, along with your request for desk/examination copies and/or additional information.
- For members of the media who are interested in reviewing copies of New Riders books. Send your name, mailing address, and email address, along with the name of the publication or Web site you work for.

BULK PURCHASES/CORPORATE SALES

The publisher offers discounts on this book when ordered in quantity for bulk purchases and special sales. For sales within the U.S., please contact: Corporate and Government Sales (800) 382-3419 or **corpsales@pearsontechgroup.com**. Outside of the U.S., please contact: International Sales (317) 428-3341 or **international@pearsontechgroup.com**.

WRITE TO US

New Riders Publishing
1249 Eighth Street
Berkeley, CA 94710

CALL US

Toll-free (800) 571-5840. Ask for New Riders.
If outside U.S. (317) 428-3000. Ask for New Riders.

New Riders

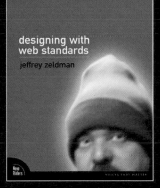

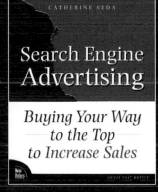

Eric Meyer
on CSS

Do you own Eric Meyer's first CSS project-based book?

"Eric Meyer is perhaps the most renowned expert on CSS. His understanding of the technology has pushed the boundaries for how we use CSS on the web and beyond. Through carefully planned projects, this book brings those ideas and solutions to the forefront so you can take advantage of them."

Nick Finck, Editor in Chief
Digital Web Magazine

Contents at a Glance

Eric Meyer on CSS
ISBN: 073571245X
$45.00 USA / $69.99 CAN / £34.99 Net UK

Tips

Starting with a Letter
We've started the rating **class** names with an "r" because CSS doesn't permit **class** or **id** values to begin with a number (unless you throw in an escape character), and thus some browsers won't recognize a **class** or **id** name that starts with a number.

Negative Effects
For some reason, IE5.x/Win treats negative right and left margins as if they were larger than they really are. In some cases, it practically doubles the distance specified. This makes negative margins on floats of limited value, although it's still possible in some designs to use them without major problems. Any design that requires the precise placement of an element shouldn't use floats with negative side margins.

Sizing Your Images
Once you've finished a good design, it's a good idea to add in the HTML attributes **height** and **width** for each image. You could try to set the image sizes with CSS, but it would be a lot more effort than it's worth because you'd have to give each image its own **id** and then write a rule for each image. Using the HTML attributes is a more direct method.

Combining States
The combination of link states was introduced in CSS2 and can be very handy. Unfortunately, very few browsers support this feature. As it happens, two browsers that do are Mozilla/Netscape 6.x (and their cousins) and IE5/Mac, which are the browsers that natively support fixed-attachment backgrounds. Although you can combine link states, it's a practice that's best avoided for most public designs.

Hidden Elements
The difference between **visibility: hidden** and **display: none** is that the former simply makes elements invisible while allowing them to affect the layout of the document. The latter completely removes an element from the layout, preventing it from having any layout effects.